Dust
Yourself
Off

Dust Yourself Off

THE GRAVEL ROAD TO A GOOD LIFE

BY TRICIA VELURE AND TOM SANDHEI

NDSU NORTH DAKOTA STATE UNIVERSITY PRESS

Fargo, North Dakota

NDSU NORTH DAKOTA STATE
UNIVERSITY PRESS

Dept. 2360, P.O. Box 6050, Fargo, ND, 58108-6050
www.ndsupress.org

Dust Yourself Off: The Gravel Road to a Good Life
By Tricia Velure and Tom Sandhei

LCCN: 2023930667
ISBN: 978-1-946163-50-9

Cover design by Jamie Trosen
Interior design by Deb Tanner

The publication of *Dust Yourself Off: The Gravel Road to a Good Life* is made possible by the generous support of the donors to the NDSU Press Fund, the NDSU Press Endowed Fund, and other generous contributors to NDSU Press.

Stephenson Beck, Interim Director
Suzzanne Kelley, Editor in Chief
Kyle Vanderburg, Assistant Acquisitions Editor
RoseE Hadden, Administrative Assistant
Mike Huynh, Graduate Research Assistant in Publishing
Connor McCormick, Editorial Intern
Tatum Hoff, Manuscript Production Intern

Printed in the United States of America

Publisher's Cataloging-in-Publication
(Provided by Cassidy Cataloguing Services, Inc.).

Names: Velure, Tricia Jill, author. | Sandhei, Tom, author.

Title: Dust yourself off : the gravel road to a good life / by Tricia Velure and Tom Sandhei.

Description: First edition. | Fargo, North Dakota : North Dakota State University Press, [2023] | Includes bibliographical references and index.

Identifiers: ISBN: 978-1-946163-50-9

Subjects: LCSH: Sandhei, Muriel L. | Norwegian American women--North Dakota--Biography. | Farmers' spouses--North Dakota--Biography. | Farm life--North Dakota--History--20th century. | LCGFT: Biographies. | BISAC: BIOGRAPHY & AUTOBIOGRAPHY / Cultural, Ethnic & Regional / General. | BIOGRAPHY & AUTOBIOGRAPHY / Women. | FAMILY & RELATIONSHIPS / Marriage & Long-Term Relationships. | HISTORY / United States / State & Local / Midwest (IA, IL, IN, KS, MI, MN, MO, ND, NE, OH, SD, WI) | HISTORY / Modern / 20th Century / General.

Classification: LCC F636 .S26 2023 | DDC: 978.4032092--dc23

CONTENTS

Introduction vii

Part One: The Henricksons

Muriel 3

John and Josephine 7

A Farm in the Valley 13

Mothering 20

Always Working 23

Politics 28

Nordlendings and Sorlendings 36

School and a Big World 41

Making Do 44

Lefse in the Wintertime 50

Confirmation and Dancing 52

Almost a Grownup 57

Interlude: The Sandheis

Elmer's Burden 67

Native Sons 79

Part Two: Muriel's Story

Womanhood 85

Disgraces 92

A Summer's Dream 99

The Baby 111

Like Nothing Happened 119

Proving 125

Moving Forward 137

A Farm Family 142

Benchmarks 150

Pleading 156

Boldness 164

Uncle Chet................................. 173

Return to the Farm 177

Farm Family 184

Losing Ground 190

Ashes and Dust........................... 195

Resilience................................. 201

Everyday Places........................... 210

Afterword... 219

Acknowledgments

Bibliography

Index

About the Authors

About the Press

INTRODUCTION

MURIEL HENRICKSON SANDHEI thought herself an ordinary woman. Born in 1921 on a farm near Fort Ransom, North Dakota, she was of Norwegian descent in a mostly Norwegian American community, contained in a region that was largely the same, save for a scattering of Swedes and other northern Europeans. Muriel's family raised grain crops, ten milk cows, ten hogs, and twenty or so chickens—modest, but enough. She spent her early years helping her mother and older sisters in the house and garden, attending country school, and going to a Lutheran church in town every Sunday. She was expected to marry a farmer and become a wife, mother, domestic role model, and overall good Christian woman in her community, all of which she did. If one looks at Muriel's everyday life and only the subjects that were polite to discuss in Fort Ransom in the early to mid-1900s, she lived an ordinary life. A Norwegian American farm girl growing up in North Dakota in the 1920s and 1930s is indeed a typical story. A farm woman balancing children and church activities during the 1940s–1960s is also common. Yet this book honors a woman who made extraordinarily bold decisions seem natural. When tragedy or turmoil entered her life, Muriel acted with quiet resolve and moved forward.

You will read two distinct parts to Muriel's life story, Part One being an account of Muriel's girlhood. She was the second-youngest of nine children born from 1906 to 1924 to John and Josephine Henrickson. John emigrated from Norway to Fort Ransom at age twelve with his older brothers and his parents, who were ages seventy and fifty-nine at the time of immigration. Josephine Nelson, Muriel's mother, was born to Norwegian immigrants in Minnesota, but raised in Fort Ransom by a couple who adopted her at age seven following the death of her mother. The authors have every reason to believe Muriel's growing-up years were generally good by the standards of her day, and that the Fort Ransom community thought highly of the Henricksons as salt-of-the-earth people. Notably, John was active in conservative-to-moderate politics during the state's progressive reform era, in which the Nonpartisan League rose to prominence. He served in the North Dakota House of Representatives 1926–1927. However, the authors believe that he was more of a farmer than a politician and that his conservatism in most aspects of life defined his character more than his political activism in his forties and fifties.

Much of the narrative contained in Part One could apply to almost any girl growing up in a small, robustly Norwegian American enclave in North Dakota in the 1920s–1930s. The geography of Fort Ransom is distinguishable, though, as it is located in the wooded valley of the Sheyenne River. Starting near McClusky in central North Dakota and meandering about six hundred miles, the Sheyenne passes Fort Ransom two-thirds of the way to its mouth at the larger Red River near Fargo. Carved by flowing waters over the course of centuries, the valley around Fort Ransom has a homey, uniquely nestled feeling in a state known for its vast, windblown plains.

Fort Ransom was established as a military post in 1867 to protect settlers and railroad workers as they built the Northern Pacific Railroad between Fargo and Bismarck in northeastern Dakota Territory. It served as a fort through 1872 and was founded as a village in 1878, with some buildings remaining from military days and a few new dwellings. As one of the few villages in North Dakota without a grain elevator or railroad running through it, Fort Ransom had at least two positive attributes that most others did not: an established site in a protected river valley and a flour mill. The three-story flour and feed mill was built next to the dam, northwest of the downtown, in 1881. For nearly the next forty years, farmers came from miles

The John and Josephine Henrickson family, circa 1927. Back, left to right: **Ethel, Palmer, Harold, Mildred, Luther, and Bernice. Front, left to right: Muriel, John, Andor (Pud), Josephine, and Frances.** (Courtesy Tom Sandhei)

around to have their wheat ground into bags of Hold the Fort flour and to grind their oats and barley into cattle feed.[1]

Fort Ransom was incorporated in the 1970s, well after this story's conclusion. Until that time, it had undefined boundaries and was part of Fort Ransom Township, which by personal accounts consisted of more farm-dwellers than townspeople. The village's perimeter varied based on the person asked. United States Census figures were specific to the township, and the authors did not take on the significant task of researching and defining Fort Ransom proper through the decades. Therefore, the historic population of "consistently about 100" is an estimate based upon anecdotal conversations with some

---

[1] Snorri Thorfinnson, *Fort Ransom Area History, 1878–1978* (Fort Ransom Community Club, 1978), 55. Walker's Flour Mill was in operation from 1881 to 1919.

of the oldest-living people who grew up around Fort Ransom. According to Census records, the entire population of Ransom County, Dakota Territory, was 537 in 1880. The records from 1890, which would have been specific to Fort Ransom Township, were lost in a fire. Therefore, the first reliable accounting of the township's population came through the Census of 1900. Population figures from 1900–1960 follow:

> 1900: 402
> 1910: 574
> 1920: 616
> 1930: 468
> 1940: 465
> 1950: 407
> 1960: 323

Following Part One, the Interlude provides insight into the Sandheis, the family that Muriel married into at age eighteen. Christian "C.A." Sandhei and his wife, Elise Olson, were both born in Norway, he in 1879 and she in 1890. C.A. emigrated with no immediate family in 1900, and was indentured to a Fort Ransom farmer—a fellow Norwegian immigrant—to help pay for his journey to the United States. After fulfilling his obligation, C.A. attended college, received his teaching certificate, and taught school in Fort Ransom from 1905-09. In 1907, he filed his claim on 160 acres south of Bucyrus in Adams County, southwestern North Dakota. He spent enough time there in the coming years to meet the government's homesteading requirements. He also married Elise, who was raised on a farm near Fort Ransom, in 1909. Soon afterward, they set off for Bucyrus, and Elise had their first child. In 1911, they returned to Fort Ransom, where C.A. taught school and Elise had two more children. But in the fall of 1914, the family moved back to Bucyrus to live permanently. The family had three more children, one of whom died shortly after birth. Even with three sons helping farm the homestead, making an adequate living was a challenge in semi-arid Adams County. The Sandheis remained on the homestead until 1936-37, after a series of catastrophic farming years during the Depression prompted them to return to their Fort Ransom roots. Elmer, the middle son of C.A. and Elise, was 24 years old when the family moved to a farm on the west prairie above Fort Ransom. As C.A. groomed Elmer to farm, Elmer began courting Muriel, nine years his junior.

Muriel's parents, John and Josephine, and Elmer's parents, C.A. and Elise, knew and liked one another. They were neighbors, they went to the same church, and their children were comparable in age. What's more, C.A., Elise and John were all born in Nord Rana in northern Norway. In Norway, Rana is a municipality of comparable size to a North Dakota county. The Fort Ransom area drew many of its immigrants from Nord Rana in general, and Mo I Rana specifically. Mo is the town—locally referred to as Mo, but called Mo I Rana outside the region to distinguish it from other places named Mo. In Fort Ransom, the distinction between northern and southern Norwegians was clear through the mid-19th century, as anecdotally noted in this story of Muriel's life.

The authors have not done extensive research on the origins of Fort Ransom's Norwegian population, but preliminary research and conversations with the locals indicate the majority of Fort Ransomites were from northern Norway. In general, the northern Norwegians in Fort Ransom attended Standing Rock Lutheran Church—part of the United Norwegian Lutheran Church (UNLC) of America, which descended from the official Church of Norway. The southern Norwegian minority attended Stiklestad Lutheran Church less than a mile away. Stiklestad was part of the plainer, more conservative Hauge synod. The liturgy and pedagogy of Standing Rock and Stiklestad became more similar after 1917, when the two synods merged. They also shared a pastor from 1930 until 1968, when fire destroyed the Stiklestad Church and the congregation dissolved. The authors found no anecdotal evidence supporting any outward contentiousness or discrimination between northern and southern Norwegians in Fort Ransom. In fact, they seemed to feel a common pride in being Norwegian and in being from Fort Ransom. First and second-generation

Norwegian Americans in Fort Ransom treated their internal separation as natural, as though northern Norwegians felt a comfortable kinship toward other northern Norwegians, and southern Norwegians toward other southern Norwegians.

Part Two of this book is uniquely Muriel's story of love, trauma, grief and resolve. It begins with a shift in her plans and dreams as she finishes high school in 1937–1938 during the depths of the Great Depression, and then her rapid thrust into adulthood. At the same time that her family faced imminent foreclosure on their farm, she found herself unmarried and pregnant. She set off for Montana, which began as the great adventure of her early life and ended in tragedy. You, the reader, are invited to share in her experiences when over and over again in the ensuing decades, Muriel's story revealed that life was what she made it. Perhaps if nothing traumatic or rapidly transformative had occurred in her early to middle adulthood, she would have led a perfectly acceptable, ordinary life as a North Dakota farmwife of the mid-20th century. If the crux of the narrative was that an unfairly high number of terrible and difficult things happened to Muriel, the authors would not feel compelled to share her story with readers a century later. In 1940, 1950, or 1960, few people would have faulted Muriel for crumbling, making safer decisions, or seeking to be saved. Rather, the authors are telling her story because she lived courageously and responded boldly in situations that could have wilted her.

The telling of this story is made possible by the memories of Muriel's four adult children, as well as their cousins and friends from Fort Ransom; by the historical research conducted by the authors; by oral histories provided by Josephine Henrickson and other Fort Ransom residents to the State Historical Society of North Dakota and Barnes County Historical Society; and by C.A.'s daybooks, which C.A. kept religiously from 1936 to 1969. "Daybook" is the term he used for his daily journal, which consisted of a combination of weather reports, comings and goings at the Sandhei home, family and community news of the day, and, on occasion, poetry and his views on farming and politics. These daybooks, which are in family hands, are rich sources of information on everyday life and offer insights into family dynamics, priorities, and points of view.

Muriel's children believe that she coped with painful memories by keeping them in an internal box that only she could access. She shared very few facts or feelings about the loss of people she loved or the difficulties she faced, because according to the cultural norms Muriel knew, those sorts of topics were unmentionable. Asking her would have been considered insensitive and disrespectful. Her sharing them freely would have been judged as impolite, imposing, and unnecessary. Muriel's children believe her commitment to their future success sustained and drove her above all else. Her determination to start them on the path to a good life became the legacy they would carry on and admire. Faced with the decision of whether to tell the life story of a mom who grieved and remembered privately, Muriel's son believed her story was her most important gift to share. He found his co-author in a woman raised on a farm twenty miles from where Muriel grew up, fifty years after her. This story is their honoring of an extraordinary woman and the people, culture, and places that shaped her life.

Tricia Velure and Tom Sandhei

PART ONE

The Henricksons

MURIEL

JULY 29, 1921, WAS MEANT for rocking in a chair in the shade of the front porch with a glass of cool lemonade. In the high nineties, it was not the hottest day of the year in Fort Ransom, North Dakota, but even the most willful farmer rolled up his sleeves. John Henrickson, in soiled bib overalls and a light blue cotton shirt, came home earlier than usual that day, given that it was harvest season. But the crew had finished a dusty day of threshing at a neighbor's place that afternoon, and his wife, Josephine, was about to have their eighth baby. His three boys could stay with the threshing crew and help them move to the next ripe wheat field.

When John left home with Harold, Luther, and Palmer that morning, Dr. Gronvold had just arrived in his wagon from town. Dr. Gronvold had delivered all of Josephine's babies except her first, Mildred, who Josephine's sister Lizzie had attended.[2] Inside the tiny ground-floor bedroom in their white, wood-frame farmhouse, Josephine was exhausted from labor and the heat, which was palpable by 9:00 a.m. The nearest screen door was in the kitchen two rooms away, offering nothing but a whisper of a draft between the rooms. Dr. Gronvold, a quiet man with a take-charge nature, began giving orders: "Mildred, get some water boiling on the stove. Ethel, bring some clean towels and sheets."

---

[2] Josie Henrickson, interview by Larry Sprunk, October 3, 1974, North Dakota Oral History Project Records, Collection 10157, audio recording, State Historical Society of North Dakota, Bismarck. Josephine was addressed as "Josie" in this interview, and the recording is filed as such.

Fifteen-year-old Mildred and eight-year-old Ethel were their mom's eldest daughters and best helpers, especially at keeping the other children occupied outdoors. This day was no exception. Josephine and the doctor were alone all morning and much of the afternoon, save a few check-ins by Mildred, who was following instructions to do so.

When John arrived home, the girls raced to tell him there was no baby yet, but they were sure it would be soon. His body was lethargic from the heat and hard work, and he took his time washing up at the pump. He took a long, eager drink from the dipper and stood still a few moments, taking in the giggles of his girls, playing tag in the yard. He filled the dipper again, drank it more slowly this time, and made his way toward the porch on the side of the house, where his chair awaited. He gave himself five minutes to rock and close his eyes, before fixing the adjacent pasture fence, which the calves had torn down the day before. The fence would need to wait, though. Hearing the baby's first strong cry from his chair, he smiled, waited while Mildred went inside to attend her mom and Dr. Gronvold, and walked toward the front door. His girls beat him to the door, and anxiously debated with him about whether they had a new sister or brother. "Sister!" They all shrieked, stomping their feet and folding their hands, hoping their prayers would be answered. "I think a brother," he teased, more to get a rise out of them than to speak his truth. In fact, he just wanted a healthy baby and, in a few years, another good worker on the farm. Mildred opened the door two minutes later and said she was sworn to secrecy. Laughing, she let her father in and kept the rest outside, telling them their turn would come next.

John walked through the small parlor, slowly opened the slightly-ajar door to his and Josephine's bedroom, and laid his eyes on their new daughter. "Muriel," Josephine told him without hesitation, as he sat down on the bed. "Hello, Muriel," he said gently to this fair-skinned girl with translucent fuzz on her round head. "She's a beauty."

The parents admired their new addition to the family for several minutes, deciding her features were a perfect mix of Henrickson and Nelson, after Josephine's family. Mildred worked around them, carrying away the soiled linens and opening every window in the house as widely as she could, trying to coax the stale air out of the house. But the sisters' persistent knocks on the front door signaled that they could no longer be held off. John stood up to make room for Ethel, Bernice, and Frances, and chuckled as they walked in with ear-to-ear smiles, all eyes on Muriel. They oohed and aahed and gently kissed her on the forehead, one by one. Needing no cautionary words from their mother, they knew Muriel was fragile, and that they would need to take turns holding her, with help from Mildred. Admiringly, John excused himself from the room, saying he was going out to mend fence and would be in for supper at dusk. Mildred took her cue to go start supper, trailing her father out of the bedroom.

As Josephine let the girls take turns holding their sister, Ethel went first, but graciously gave Muriel up when Mildred called for her help in the kitchen. Next in line was five-year-old Bernice, whose baby-holding posture made it clear that she outranked three-year-old Frances as lead mother hen. Little Frances seemed to care most that her mother still loved her as much as Muriel, and Josephine accommodated her with a brief cuddle amidst the sweltering heat, as only a toddler would request. Ten minutes later, Dr. Gronvold shoed all the girls out, checked Muriel's heartbeat and placed her in the cradle next to the bed, and ordered Josephine to rest. Tomorrow morning, Josephine's life would continue as normal.

The next morning, the 5'2" Josephine, still slight of frame after having eight babies, was already back at work without complaint. After all, this was late July, the peak of the harvest season in North Dakota. In the Henricksons' garden and the surrounding fields, grains and vegetables were ripe, and every able body was needed to complete the work. Josephine prided herself on being a "good worker," as she had heard John describe her to the neighbors, a "big help" to him around the farm and the "perfect role model" for her daughters around the house. That day, Josephine enjoyed the breakfast that Mildred took so much pride in making, with just a little bit of guidance, before getting on with the harvest.

JOHN AND JOSEPHINE

*J*OHN AND JOSEPHINE HENRICKSON, six years apart in age, never played together or went to the same school, but his family knew her family, as every family knew each other in Fort Ransom. The fact that they attended the same church service every Sunday further enhanced their familiarity. While John and Josephine remembered their first encounter well—it was memorable—they were not formally introduced. As children at the time, they were to be seen, not heard.[3]

The youngest of Henrik and Barbara Olson's eleven children, John was born "Johannes" on March 14, 1876, when his parents were fifty-eight and forty-seven years old. Henrik farmed near Mo I Rana, Norway, a fjord community just below the Arctic Circle. Mining, hunting, fishing, and boatbuilding were more common occupations than farming in Mo I Rana, where the dark winters were long and the mild summers were brief. Henrik's modest farm in the valley included a small house, a barn and chicken coop, and a bit of cropland—too little to support eleven children, he found out.

Ole, the second-oldest son, left Norway for Fort Ransom, Dakota Territory, in 1882, following his cousin Cornelius Rufsvold. Lars followed his brother Ole in 1886, only to die of pneumonia the next year. In 1888, Henrik and Barbara immigrated to Fort Ransom, bringing with them their oldest son Peder, who was thirty-five and unmarried, twenty-year-old Adolph, seventeen-year-old Gregor, and

[3] Josie Henrickson, interview. This interview is the source of many of the details provided in this chapter.

twelve-year-old Johannes. Henrik, an old man at age seventy, wanted to help establish his sons in a more promising place than Norway, even if it meant traversing an ocean and half the United States.

Like many Norwegians of their day, Henrik and his family came to America to make a better life. Farming the northern Great Plains was the most widely advertised opportunity at that time, as settlers had filled areas to the east and south. Dakota Territory was promoted as a mecca for wheat and the home of bonanza farms. The Homestead Act lured newcomers with farmland for hard-working pioneers.

Fort Ransom attracted such an abundance of Norwegian immigrants that the area was dubbed, "Little Norway." This place even resembled home, with its wooded hills and streams trickling into the Sheyenne River—a setting unlike almost any other on the vast, open plains of Dakota Territory. The lush summer forest teemed with wild game, cutting trails until humans wore their own. Bushes filled with gooseberries, chokecherries, Juneberries, and wild plums, while adjacent grain fields carpeted the valley floor in hues of green, then gold. The deciduous hardwoods painted the valley all shades of yellow, orange, and red each fall. During the frigid winters, the ice and snow transformed the river into an ice-skating rink, and the steep hills into a skiing and sledding playground.

The Henricksons arrived via train in Lisbon, Dakota Territory, in June 1888. Fort Ransom was another fifteen miles to the northwest by wagon or foot, and the family set out walking the well-worn trail at dawn the next morning. By mid-afternoon, the foot-sore family found what they believed might be their son and brother Ole's house, dug into the bluffs above the Sheyenne River at Fort Ransom.

"Ole lives on the next farm to the north, but come in and rest. Have some coffee," said their new neighbor, Peder Nelson.

Peder and his wife, Christine, were eager for fresh news from Norway and stories from the newcomers' journey. Just as importantly, they discovered who they knew in common in Mo I Rana, where Peder and Christine had also spent their early years. Peder said little about Fort Ransom, as Ole would share everything they needed to know.

Nor did he introduce the young children, who were too busy eaves-dropping to make a peep from the far corner of the one-room house.

After a short visit, the Henricksons continued on to Ole's farm. Never had Johannes, whose name was Americanized to John, seen such tearful emotion from his steady mother than when she said goodbye to his two sisters in Norway or when she laid eyes on Ole in Fort Ransom. She was overjoyed to have her sons in one place again. Temporarily, they would all live with Ole, his wife, and their two young children in their log home overlooking the valley. Soon enough, Henrik and Barbara's older sons would settle down on their own farms, while young John would remain with Ole and their aging parents.

John's brothers indeed established themselves on other farms nearby. After their father died in 1892, their mother and sixteen-year-old John floated among the brother's households. John was of great help to his brothers until his cousin Cornelius Rufsvold took him on to help with his 240 acres, an extensive acreage around Fort Ransom. Being unmarried, John lived with Cornelius, his wife Christine, and their children in their comfortable house in Springer Township, on the east prairie above Fort Ransom. Their home had a fresh coat of gray paint trimmed in white, finished off with a front porch perfect for watching the vast sunsets and greeting visitors, as well as a side porch for the men to come and go. Christine appreciated the fancy Victorian scrollwork atop the posts on the porches, and devotedly tended the flowers planted around the perimeter.

Having lived and worked on the Rufsvold farm, expectations of John were high. He was industrious, well-liked, and one of the best-looking young men in Fort Ransom. His mother and Christine reminded him that now was his time to settle down with a pretty wife, before he became an old bachelor farmer.

***

Fort Ransom was the only place Josephine Nelson ever remembered living. Born on June 9, 1882, near Paynesville, Minnesota, her parents were Norwegian immigrants Peder and Christine Nelson. Josephine was just one year old when the family journeyed farther west to settle near Fort Ransom. The Nelsons had four more children in Fort Ransom before Christine died following childbirth in 1889. Feeling unable to care for his children, Peder sent them to live with different families in the area. He married his second wife, Anne, a couple years later, and they had three of their own sons. The couple also brought home three of Peder's other children.

Seven-year-old Josephine, the eldest, did not return to Peder's house. She had been living with Jacob and Maren Mikkelson on the west prairie above Fort Ransom and had come to think of them as her parents.[4] The Mikkelsons had no biological children, and they were taken with hazel-eyed, soft-featured Josephine, with brown ringlets streaming down her back. In fact, Maren believed it was her Christian calling to mother this young girl.

Josephine became well versed in the Bible under Maren's tutelage and sat perfectly still next to Maren during church services every Sunday. As the congregation took their seats after singing each hymn, Josephine sometimes leaned forward and glanced toward Jacob on the other side of the room with the men. She wished she could go sit on his lap, as she liked to do at home. In those moments, Maren gently put her hand on Josephine's shoulder, and the little girl promptly sat up straight. Josephine was also no bother at ladies' aid meetings. Maren had helped assemble the wives of the Standing Rock congregation to form the Zion Ladies' Aid in 1886, considering it her earthly role to do something special for the Lord. Josephine listened and learned about the ladies' aid raising money for the hospital in nearby Lisbon and the salary of a Lutheran missionary in Madagascar, among other holy causes.[5]

---

[4] Melford Rufsvold, phone interview with Tom Sandhei, 18 February 2020.

[5] "A Brief History of the Zion Ladies' Aid for 75th Anniversary," *Favorite Recipes of Members of the Zion Ladies' Aid* (Fort Ransom, North Dakota, 1959), 1-4. "Mickelson" was the surname spelling used in that history.

John and Josephine Henrickson (front) wed in Fort Ransom on June 9, 1904. Witnesses (back) were Henry and Anna Rufsvold. (Courtesy Jerry Sorby)

Additionally, Maren taught Josephine to spin, knit, sew, and embroider; all essential skills for a young lady of the time to have, Maren told her. By the time Josephine was sixteen, she spun wool for stockings and mittens nearly as well as Maren did, and was such a fine seamstress that women as far away as Lisbon sought her out for dress-making. One of those women, who was married to a Lisbon attorney, hired her as a housekeeper for a few years, and Josephine experienced town life in a large four-square house. She enjoyed and appreciated the finery she was exposed to, yet she was a farm girl at heart. Longing to live in the country, Josephine returned to the Mikkelsons' house, where she continued to sew dresses while Maren encouraged her in finding a husband.

Josephine pined after only one man: the handsome, light-brown-haired John with gray-blue eyes. She had known him since his first day in Fort Ransom, when she watched him from the corner of her parents' house while their parents visited about Mo I Rana. Now she saw him in church every Sunday and whenever she delivered a new dress to Mrs. Rufsvold. By the summer of 1903, John finally started paying notice to Josephine. He came to court her, and received the Mikkelsons' immediate permission. Maren knew John's kindhearted mother through their common devotion to church activities, not to mention his association with the Rufsvolds. At Christmas time, the courting progressed to engagement. The young couple would marry in June.

A FARM IN THE VALLEY

JOHN WAS TWENTY-EIGHT AND Josephine was twenty-two when they wed in June 1904. John was still working on the Rufsvold farm in exchange for room, board, and help from Cornelius's sons on his own eighty acres, located next to theirs on the east prairie above Fort Ransom. John had owned the acreage since 1899, and it was a good start for him.[6] Yet he knew he would soon need more acres to support a wife and family. And memories of his upbringing in the woods of Norway fed his yearning to live in the valley, amongst the trees.

In 1910, John finally bought the valley farmstead he wanted. It was in Springer Township, just a mile west of Cornelius's farm and two miles east of Fort Ransom on the east bank of the Sheyenne River. At eighty acres, it brought John's total acreage to 160, which was typical of the area. Here John and Josephine built a basic wood-frame house to replace the dilapidated log cabin invaded by daylight between every log.[7] Painted white with white trim, the new house had two stories and three bedrooms—enough for the three young children the couple now had. It also included a big enough porch for

[6] Fort Ransom 125th Anniversary Book Committee, ed. *Fort Ransom Community History, 1878–2003*, 184, 376, 465; Ransom County, North Dakota, Document No. 4852; John H. Henrickson and Thomas J. Sinnott, 14 October 1899; Register of Deeds, Ransom County; Josie Henrickson, interview. In combination with Census records, these sources provided the authors with John's whereabouts during this time period.

[7] Fort Ransom 125th Anniversary Book Committee, ed. *Fort Ransom Community History, 1878–2003*, 376; Ransom County, North Dakota, Document No. 32056; John H. Henrickson and Adams & Frees Company, 11 October 1910; Register of Deeds, Ransom County.

John's rocking chair and views from every side toward the established barn, chicken coop, granary, and woodshed.

When Muriel was born in 1921, she joined four sisters and three brothers. The serious but good-natured John taught the boys how to farm. Josephine, who was nurturing yet firm, taught her girls how to set the table, wash dishes, retrieve water, shake rugs, sweep floors, and, over time, how to cook and bake. All the children had their designated duties and grew into more roles as they matured.

Sometimes a hired man lived with the family. Bernard Skonseng stayed with them for several months in 1910, when the children were too young to work, and Axel Nelson lived there in 1920, when John's boys were on the brink of being able to do most of the work he could do. Hired men like Bernard and Axel were young men who left Norway with little money and no spouse. Their formal education was minimal, and they spoke little to no English until the Henrick-

John and Josephine moved to their farm in Springer Township, two miles east of Fort Ransom, in 1910. (Courtesy Tom Sandhei)

son children taught them words and phrases. These young men were simply trying to get started. A nice family like the Henricksons, with a warm home and reliable meals, made the transition possible.

With help from the children as they grew—and sometimes a hired man—John milked by hand at 6:00 a.m. and 6:00 p.m. The children especially loved the adventure of going across the river to retrieve the ten cows during the nice-weather months. A quarter mile from the Henrickson farm, there was a cable strung across the river with a pulley and a platform attached to it. The lucky boy chosen to herd the cows on any given day attached himself to the pulley at the edge of the river and rode across the cable to the other side, laughing all the way! After herding the cows to the river, he reattached himself to the pulley and crossed again.

Then the children collected milk in pails and separated the cream using a hand cranked DeLaval separator, which had spinning disks that kept the milk on the bottom and forced the thicker cream to the top. Cream cans—metal containers with lids that held about ten gallons—stored the excess cream that they hauled to the general store in Fort Ransom on "open nights" every Tuesday and Saturday. That was when all the stores stayed open late, and local farm families like the Henricksons came to town to trade cream for sugar, yeast, coffee, and spices.

John and Josephine purchased very few groceries because they grew most of their own food and butchered their own meat. They did nearly all their business in Fort Ransom, which consisted of a general store, one or two grocery stores depending on the year, a café, bank, blacksmith, auto repair shop, post office, and, until 1919, Walker's Mill, which ground wheat into flour.

Life on the farm was dictated by the seasons. In addition to milking year-round, feeding and watering were twice-daily chores during the cold months, when the cows could not graze on fresh grass. Hay was stored upstairs in the barn and pitched down to the mangers below through strategically placed holes in the floor. Watering generally only required letting the cows outside, as the barn was located just above the riverbank. But during the winter, John had to chop a hole in the ice before the cattle could drink.

The handful of horses also needed tending twice daily. Horses pulled every piece of farm equipment and every wagon and sleigh for the family. With so many cows and horses, cleaning the barn was a once-daily chore. John and the boys pitched the cow manure onto a stone boat—a flat wooden platform on skids—for a team of horses to pull away. The manure was stored in a pile, loaded into a manure spreader, and distributed over the grain fields as fertilizer.

Next to the barn was the chicken coop, with twenty or so chickens. The Henrickson girls moved quickly to snatch the eggs from the nest each morning, yet their hands and arms nearly always showcased at least one mark from a hen peck. Eggs were one of the few constant fresh foods, and any eggs the family did not eat; they traded at the general store. Josephine led the butchering process whenever John suggested a chicken dinner. With no hesitation, she caught two or three young chickens, chopped off their heads, and plunged the bodies into scalding-hot water to loosen the feathers. The Henrickson children—boys and girls alike—plucked the feathers, gutted the chickens, and disposed of the innards. Whether the sight of a headless chicken running in circles was worse than the stench of a scalded chicken was debatable, but the rich, buttery taste of freshly fried chicken made this unpopular job worthwhile.

The family's ten pigs were another source of food and income. Twice daily, the boys slopped the hogs with the potato peelings and other food scraps collected by their mom and sisters in a pail in the kitchen. The pail also held excess liquids like skimmed milk and the water used to boil potatoes, so the mixture truly defined "slop." That, along with a bit of corn and small grains, made up the hogs' main diet. Four or five times a year, John and the boys butchered a pig to make ham, salted pork, bacon, and chops. Josephine and the girls rendered the lard.

While the animals required year-round attention, the fields required intense effort from the time the frost lifted each April to the time the ground froze each November. Growing grains involved not only planting and harvesting, but also fertilizing and picking rocks. Rocks rose to the surface constantly, with plowing, cultivating, and Mother Nature's freeze-and-thaw cycle. The stone boat's main purpose was to haul away rocks from the fields. Situated on skids just a few inches off the ground, rolling the bigger rocks onto the stone boat was fairly easy. John and the boys threw the smaller rocks onto it.

Spring's planting involved plowing, disking and harrowing the soil into a healthy black seed bed where the seeds would sprout and grow as soon as they received moisture. As John completed spring's work, his next task was haying—cutting grass and sweet clover from the hay fields and ditches so that his cattle and horses would have food for the winter. The first hay crop was ready to harvest in June. John and the boys mowed, raked, and stacked the hay into stacks, shaped like a loaf of homemade bread. The rounded top shed water, so that the hay would dry in preparation for loading onto hayracks and hauling to the barn, where it was stored and used through the winter. John hoped for three hay cuttings each summer, but as a smart Norwegian farmer in North Dakota, he counted on only two.

The late summer brought ripe crops, ready for harvest. A binder cut, gathered, and tied the wheat, oats, or barley into bundles, all in one operation. John and the boys, assisted by neighbors who they helped in return, gathered five or six bundles into neat rows called shocks. Shocking was hard manual labor that needed to be done as soon as possible after cutting. If rain delayed that work, the grain sprouted on the ground and went to ruin.

The last phase of the harvest ritual was threshing. This was the most intense and exciting time of the year, and it was a family and community affair. It united a crew of a dozen or so men around a threshing machine for a threshing bee. The machine was so large and expensive that several farms shared it. Like every family, the Henricksons waited with great anticipation for the threshing crew to arrive at their fields. Two men ran the steam engine, which connected to and ran the threshing machine with a long drive belt. They made sure all the parts were properly oiled and maintained throughout the threshing process. Then there were the field pitchers who pitched the bundles from the shocks into hayracks, and a team of younger boys who drove the horses that pulled the bundle wagons to the site of the threshing machine. The boys thought this was fun and felt like grownups. The spike pitchers were stationed at the threshing machine, where they unloaded the bundles of grain and pitched them into the threshing machine to separate the grain from the straw. Finally, the grain traveled from the thresher's spout into grain wagons. Walker's Mill ground some of the wheat into flour until it closed in 1919. Extra wheat and nearly all the barley was stored in the granary at home. When the price was right or John needed the income, he sold it at the nearest grain elevator in Englevale, about eleven miles away. He kept the oats to feed his hogs and cattle.

Winter brought welcome relief from the ceaseless work of the growing season. While the chores of milking, cleaning the barn, refreshing the straw, and feeding the animals were always present, the daylight hours were too few and the temperatures too cold to work outdoors any longer than necessary.

One of the few welcomed jobs for John and the boys during the long winters was chopping and gathering firewood. The Sheyenne River Valley was lush with ash, oak, elm, dogwood, cottonwood, and box elder. This abundance of trees provided ample fuel for heating the house and cooking the meals. John took his boys along with him out into the woods, pointing out each variety of tree and the pros and cons of each one as firewood. Ash was the preferred hardwood, they learned. Its grain was straight, making it easiest to split, and it burned slowly and cleanly, leaving little residue. Oak and elm made good fuel too, but their gnarly grain made them harder to split. Fortunately, there was plenty of ash in the Sheyenne Valley.

"Use only what you need," John always said, reminding them that the farmers on the east and west prairies only wished for such good wood nearby. "They have to go looking for trees," he said.

John also taught the boys how to use the crosscut saw—"the best saw for cutting wood," he told them. It was about five feet long with deep, sharp teeth and a handle on each end—requiring two men working alternately, in rhythm, to pull the saw through the log. First John taught Harold the back-and-forth motion. Once Harold had proven himself, John let Luther be the second man on the saw, standing right behind him until Luther learned the motion.

"The best wood-splitters can hold a log with one hand and wield the ax with the other," John told them as he showed that he, himself, was one of the best. "They can split any log, even when it doesn't balance on the chopping block."

"I learned from my father and brothers in Mo," he said, their eyes dancing at the mention of this far-away land where their father did half his growing up. "I made this ax handle myself when I was thirteen," John added, "It's from a tree very near here. I made it to look like my father's ax, which came over on the ship with us from Norway."

John designated Palmer, the youngest, as lead hauler and stacker. "This is a big responsibility. Stacking it right keeps the wood dry. Only dry wood burns clean," John explained as he showed Palmer the right way inside the woodshed north of the house.

The Henrickson boys knew their woodcutting prowess was more important to their father than their skill at any other single task. John supervised every one of them, every time, at every step of the process, until they proved themselves capable and responsible. If he taught his sons well, as his father had taught him, he knew they would keep all their fingers. The first time Harold and Luther went off into the woods by themselves without their father, they smiled at each other with wide eyes, like they had been entrusted with their father's most-prized possession. They walked extra tall that day, knowing they were almost men, trudging through fresh snow into the same woods their father had trod as a teenager.

MOTHERING

WHETHER REAL OR PERCEIVED AS she grew and heard stories from her siblings, Muriel always insisted she could remember being two, and the reason she knew this is because she remembered the day Pud was born. Josephine gave birth to her ninth child on January 2, 1924. The temperature hovered around negative twenty degrees outside, and inside the wood stove roared red to compete with the invading draft. The men stayed out in the barn while Dr. Gronvold again ran the show, but the weather was too cold to send the girls outside to play. The upstairs bedrooms were cold as well, without getting under the bedcovers. First, Mildred kept her sisters busy doing extra kitchen chores and sweeping. Then their father and brothers came in for the supper the girls prepared, consisting of thick slices of Josephine's bread, dunked in fresh cream and sprinkled with white sugar. Mealtime was even quicker and quieter than usual. Everyone, especially the boys, were uncomfortable with the thought of what was happening just two rooms away from them, which they would not talk about now or ever.

Instead, John told his children lively stories of winter in Norway when he was a boy. They had heard about snow shoeing and tobogganing and watching the northern lights dance before, but still they found a few questions to ask. "Are the hills taller in Norway than in Fort Ransom?" "Why are the northern lights so bright in Norway?" "Will we go to Norway someday?"

Luther refreshed the wood in the stove, while Mildred and Ethel finished washing the dishes. Wanting no downtime, Mildred began playing the piano, and John led the family in singing every song they could think of, some twice. Muriel noticed that her sisters' voices were soft and pretty, but her father's voice was the loudest and best. She loved to sing and imagined when she would be old enough to know the words and sing confidently like her father and play the piano as well as Mildred did. That—and taking care of the new baby—was the most fun she could imagine.

A vigorous cry brought an abrupt end to the music. While Mildred went into the bedroom to help Dr. Gronvold, John herded the children into the kitchen. Sitting around the table, he gave his girls a grin and quick tease of, "Sister or brother?" Their unanimous answer this time was, "Brother!" Bernice explained, "We've had four girls in a row. It's time for a boy."

Mildred came and went a couple of times with water and arms full of linens, not even glancing at her father and siblings, to her sisters' dismay. The wait was finally over on Mildred's third trip out of their parents' room. They followed her to the bedroom, where John stood with the baby in his arms. "Meet your brother, girls," said Josephine. "This is Andor. After your uncle."

Muriel, Frances, and Bernice did not know they had an uncle Andor, and Mildred shook her head "no" at them to avert any questions. John handed the baby to Ethel, signaling to the girls that oldest to youngest, they had to wait their turn. Andor was so heavily swaddled that they could not get as much of a look at him as they wanted. "Leave him covered, girls. We don't want him to catch cold in this weather," Josephine said kindly, but firmly.

This was when Muriel's training as a mother began. Regardless of whether she was actually helping or simply attending her mom and sisters as they changed him, bathed him, calmed him, and fed him; she relished this role. She was allowed to hold him while sitting in the big chair with armrests until one of them fussed, which she was determined not to do. As Andor grew in the coming months, he became what her siblings called "pudgy," a word Muriel did not understand, other than to think it was funny. "Pud," her tiny voice said instead one day, and the moniker stuck. From then on, Andor was Pud to his family and everyone in Fort Ransom.[8] He was the final child born to John and Josephine, and to Muriel, he was hers.

---

[8] Muriel's children believe "Pud" was short for "Pudgy," based on stories told about him. The exact origin of his nickname is unknown.

ALWAYS WORKING

IN EVERY IMPORTANT WAY, THE Henricksons exemplified what it meant to be a good Norwegian-American farm family. Their children were more seen than heard. They worked alongside their parents, obediently. From the moment young Muriel could remember, she watched her mom and older sisters to know what to do—and the clear message was to work. They made three meals a day, they kept the house clean, and they washed the clothes. If the task had to do with food or the house, it most likely was happening at the direction of Josephine and Mildred. "Idle hands are the devil's workshop," their mother regularly said if one of the girls was dawdling while the others were working.

Muriel learned chores at the same time that she learned nursery rhymes and the alphabet. After setting the table, Bernice played the comical finger chant "Tommeltott" with Muriel, lightly pinching each of Muriel's fingers while singing:

Tommeltott (Thumb)
Slikkepott (Lick the pot)
Langemann (Long man)
Gullebran (Gold band)
Lille petter spellermann (Little Peter Fiddleman)

Muriel howled and wiggled at the end, as Bernice held tight onto her pinky. Then they went on about their work. Indoors, Muriel felt constantly surrounded by motion. "Please get out of the way, Muriel," she heard at least daily.

Josephine started the stove and the coffee pot before sunrise, while John and the boys milked the cows and carried water. Morning and night, the boys carried drinking water and cooking water from the well near the barn, across the yard from the house. They also carried milk from the well, where it was kept cold in a sealed container at the end of a heavy cord. Carrying water and milk, along with feeding the fire with fresh wood, were the boys' only steady jobs around the house.

The girls were up at sunrise to pick eggs and help in the kitchen. Oatmeal was the family's most common breakfast, but at least once a week, Josephine made eggs, with the whites still runny and translucent. White bread was a staple at every meal, sometimes toasted at breakfast. Josephine baked bread several times a week to keep up with the family's appetites and was constantly preparing for the next meal. Muriel's favorite was bread with cream and sugar, mostly because it was sweet and rich, but also because the boys debated to earn the crusty, buttery end slice from the bread loaf, which soaked up the most cream. Bread and cream brought out the most animated conversation at the Henricksons' table.

At all times of the day, Josephine kept a pot of coffee hot on the stove. John and Josephine drank it with breakfast, and any men around the place came in for mid-morning coffee and afternoon coffee. This included John, any hired help, and any visiting neighbors who stopped when they saw John in the yard.

Wash water for doing the dishes and laundry was collected in the cistern. It was a large, concrete tank located under the kitchen floor. Rainwater fell on the roof, traveled through a network of eave troughs and gutters, and drained into the cistern, which Josephine and the girls pumped by hand on wash day each Monday. Each Henrickson had only a few clothes, but multiplied by eleven, there was a lot of laundry. There were also cloth diapers from 1906–1925, plus dishtowels and pillowcases. The Maytag washing machine was set up in the kitchen near the hand pump from the cistern. If a dry spell depleted the water supply, the older girls carried it from the well.

The washing machine was powered by a small gasoline engine with a flexible metal pipe to carry the exhaust outdoors through a small opening in an exterior wall. Once the clothes were washed, they ran through a wringer mounted atop the washer, powered by a hand crank. This process wrung most of the water out of the clothes, prior to hanging them on a clothesline west of the house. During the coldest months, the clothes freeze-dried outdoors. On days of snow or rain, they hung on racks indoors, creating a maze for the young girls to weave through until Josephine reminded them, "The house isn't a playground."

Each Tuesday, Josephine, Mildred, and Ethel used two thick, black sad irons in rotation, to iron every article of clothing down to the underclothes. As soon as one sad iron cooled down, they traded it for the hot one from the cook stove. The stove was kept hot for every chore from ironing, to cooking, to heating water for washing dishes. Around it was the warmest spot in the house, making it an especially popular gathering place in the winter. But even on hot summer days, the stove was in constant use, making the kitchen too dangerous a place for any shenanigans.

Summertime was a burst of lettuce, radishes, peas, corn, string beans, cucumbers, rutabaga, tomatoes, carrots, potatoes, and onions from the family' garden just south of the house. The Henrickson children gobbled down Josephine's leaf lettuce in cream and vinegar as though it was candy. Muriel watched closely as her older siblings ate their corn on the cob, wondering if the buttery kernels were sticking to their fingernails as they were to her own.

The summertime treats seemed to come in rapid succession, starting with rhubarb, then strawberries, raspberries, and melons from the garden. The girls followed Josephine with pails into the surrounding hills, picking Juneberries, chokecherries, plums, and apples. Muriel was constantly trying to catch up as she climbed hillsides and stepped over branches and wished she could reach as many berries as her taller sisters could. Instead, she picked leaves and tiny insects off the fruit as it collected in the pails. Her fingers were stained in purples and reds that deepened as she worked. As she sucked each sticky fingertip, she tasted the tangy nectar to the back of her tongue. "Why do we eat chokecherries?" Muriel asked Josephine after her entire face puckered from biting into one of the tiny blue-black berries.

"We don't eat chokecherries," her mother said plainly. "We eat chokecherry jam, which tastes good because we add sugar."

The first vegetables canned each summer were the peas and beans. The older girls knew what to do as well as Josephine did, picking the ripe pods from the vines, collecting them in a pail, and shelling the peas from the pods by hand. Muriel loved when Josephine and the older girls tended the garden, because that was when she got Pud all to herself, undisturbed, on a blanket spread across the grass. She played Tommeltott with him the way that Bernice did with her, and he giggled in delight.

Picking peas and beans was a daily task for a couple of weeks, as they ripened at different rates. Some were eaten fresh at dinner or suppertime, and others were reserved for canning. The peas to be canned were rinsed with cold water and then blanched, in which they were partially cooked in water that was not quite hot enough to boil. Then Josephine filled quart-size Mason jars not-quite full, twisted metal lids tight onto the jars, and placed them in a pressure cooker atop the stove, which brought the jars to a high enough temperature to seal the lids. As the jars cooled following their "bath" in the pressure cooker, the girls quietly waited within earshot for the lids to "pop." Wide eyes and nods came with each pop, signaling the pressure inside the jar had dropped—essentially sucking the lid down to make an airtight seal. The canning process was repeated for pickles, jams, jellies, fruit sauces, and every vegetable that could be preserved. The canning process occupied days and weeks around the house, as the men and boys harvested the wheat and other grains from the surrounding fields.

As a young girl, Muriel already sensed that harvest was both the most exciting and most tiring time of the year. Never was there more work to do. Josephine and the girls fed the threshing crew for three days, for which preparations started nearly a week earlier to make the bread, scalloped potatoes with ham, roast beef and pork roast served with mashed potatoes, and pies and cookies to feed the crew and the family. Alongside those preparations, Mildred was making the first batch of applesauce one day and pickles the next. After feeding everyone, Josephine and Ethel washed stacks of dishes, more than Muriel had ever seen, while Mildred and the other girls washed cucumbers. "More pickles?" Muriel asked.

"Yes, we are making more pickles," Mildred said. "And tomorrow, we will can again."

And so, the pace of work continued, and Muriel spent much of her time with Pud. She loved watching the activity around her almost as much as taking care of her baby brother. She did not realize it would come to an end. One day, talk of school began at the breakfast table. Mildred was to leave the next day for teacher's college, and Harold and Luther for high school. The others were returning to Springer School № 2, half a mile down the road from the Henrickson farm. "Can I go to school?" Muriel asked, causing her siblings to laugh.

"Not yet, Muriel," her mother said. "Three more years. Frances will be home with you for one more year. You'll be good friends."

After the girls finished the breakfast dishes, Muriel left Pud long enough to follow Mildred upstairs, and for the first time in her young life, she saw a suitcase. Mildred opened it and started gathering her clothes. "Where are you going?" Muriel enquired with sad eyes.

"I'm going to a town called Valley City, thirty-five miles away. It takes about an hour to drive there. I'm going to learn to be a teacher. But I'll be here all day today, and I'll still come home to see you sometimes."

Muriel now wanted to be older, to go to school, and to take care of Pud. She wanted to know how to do everything Mildred and their mother knew how to do. Mildred let her stay to help organize her things, and together they walked down the stairs, Muriel trying to step exactly where Mildred did, to get to work.

POLITICS

WHEN MURIEL WAS BORN IN 1921, the world was still sighing in relief that the Great War and the Spanish Flu pandemic were over. She was not to know these events or the aftermath as a little girl, of course. Those topics were not discussed, and she herself only knew peace and health. She also was not to know the changes that automobiles and radios were making to her parents' lives; for her, they simply existed. She did not know that her mother could not vote just a few years earlier, or that alcohol even existed, because her parents lived in temperance. All she knew was the farm where she lived, a few neighbors' farms from visiting, and the Norwegian Lutheran town of Fort Ransom, where she sat in church on Sunday mornings, and witnessed trade firsthand while holding onto her mother's skirt on open nights. Muriel's childhood was limited in worldview, even as it was boundless in sky and hillsides to freely explore. All of these details were unbeknownst to her at the time.

What her parents lived with, though, was that in just one and a half years, one thousand soldiers from North Dakota had lost their lives in the Great War. Two of them were Josephine's own brothers—Andor, a half-brother from the same father, and Christ, her full brother, whose birth coincided with their mother's death. Josephine did not grow up in the same home with them, as she grew up with the Mikkelsons. Yet they were her brothers, and their deaths in April and July 1919—five and eight months after the war officially ended—tore Josephine apart inside. Andor died of tuberculosis at a military hospital in Massachusetts after returning to the U.S. from France. Tall and slender, with thick blond hair and piercing light blue eyes, Andor was twenty-four years old when he died. The family would never know the cause of thirty-year-old Christ's death; they only knew that he was wounded in France and was sick when he left on a ship bound for Hoboken, New Jersey, on July 13, 1919. He died at a hospital in New Jersey later that month. Christ was quieter and attracted less notice than Andor, and she worried that his final moments were lonely, even nondescript. Had he died of Spanish Flu, like half of the soldiers who did not survive the war?

In America, the estimate was 675,000 deaths from the flu epidemic of 1918–1920; worldwide it was at least twenty million, perhaps even forty million or more.[9] Josephine could not fathom such numbers from her Fort Ransom home, although she lived the flu epidemic firsthand. One by one, everyone in the house contracted the flu in late 1918. With Dr. Gronvold thinly stretched as he visited sick folks across the community, Josephine's only choice was to nurse John and the children herself, which she successfully did.[10] As for Andor and Christ, she prayed they were with the angels, and thought of them in happy times at home. She rarely spoke of them; her children need only know that their uncles were brave, good men. One day when young Andor was old enough to understand, perhaps she would tell him more about his uncle.

Major progress for women in America came shortly after the war. North Dakota ratified the 19th amendment in December 1919, and it was adopted in August 1920, ushering in full voting rights for white women nationwide. Josephine voted for the first time in the 1920 elections, when her and John's preferred candidate for Governor lost, but their votes for President Harding helped him easily win North Dakota. John was perfectly comfortable taking Josephine to

---

[9] "Unit 5: Set 4. The Spanish Flu in North Dakota—Introduction." State Historical Society of North Dakota—North Dakota Studies, accessed November 10, 2020, https://www.history.nd.gov/textbook/unit5_4_intro_flu.html.
[10] Josie Henrickson, interview.

the polls for the first time. Really, he did not see the point in making any more commotion over it.

Of much more importance to John and Josephine was temperance. They saw no place for alcohol in the world, and were very pleased that prohibition, which had been in effect in North Dakota since statehood, became the law nationwide in January 1920. In their minds, that should have been the end of the conversation. Of course, that was not to be the case, as they heard rumors of bootlegging and booze runs to Canada, which continued for the next thirteen years of prohibition. Even a few Fort Ransomites were claimed to be booze runners. Warnings against alcohol and its accompanying social ills were often part of Reverend Sandanger's Sunday message. John and Josephine did not need to speak of the issue at home, as they believed going to church and not exposing their children to alcohol sent the necessary message.

Between the births of Frances and Muriel, John felt notably modern when he purchased his first Model T. Shortly after Muriel came along, he bought his first battery-powered radio. He was nowhere near the first in Fort Ransom to own a car or radio, but he also was not the last—and that was the logical place to be, he thought. He and Josephine gathered the family around the radio to listen to news and programs out of Fargo, and to President Coolidge's first-ever broadcast from the White House in December 1923, just four months after he took office following President Harding's death of a heart attack. By the end of the decade, *Amos 'N Andy* was a family favorite, along with the happy piano and band tunes. Vacuum tubes enabled the radio to pluck the signal out of the air, which John thought was an absolute miracle of science after Harold and Luther's explanation. The batteries needed to be recharged, though, so he became a regular at the hardware store in Lisbon, which offered the nearest charging line. Lisbon, population 1,650 with a Main Street at least two blocks long, was a fifteen-mile drive each way. That was the farthest John traveled with any regularity. When he brought one or two of the children along to Lisbon, they considered it a highlight of their year, like no other place they had seen.

How foreign the car and radio were to John, Josephine, and their generation of Norwegian immigrants around Fort Ransom. "Contraptions" was the blanket term John used for modern technologies. For Muriel's older siblings, the excitement around these contraptions went along with the shorter women's hairstyles, freer-fitting clothing, even knickers, according to the papers! None of the Henricksons wore knickers, but once the first girl in Lisbon had a pair, it would only be a matter of time in Fort Ransom, John said to Josephine in a tone of judgment, though not disgust. These were the ideas of a generation of young men and women who were more equal, mobile, and connected to popular culture than ever before.

All of the newfangled notions and technologies came along as John read news stories about the manufacturing boom, soaring employment, and national prosperity. This was heartening news, to be sure, but, "What about farming?" he regularly wondered aloud at the table. "What about North Dakota? Costs are going up, and wheat prices are going down."

John felt less in control of his financial destiny than ever before. In fact, he realized his disillusionment might compare to that of his father before he decided to leave Norway. John was frustrated, yes, but the biggest difference was that he still believed the farming economy would improve, and he had no intention of leaving Fort Ransom. He also had young children to raise, and as long as they continued to have a warm house and abundant food, staying put was the right decision. He thought he would not like any other place nearly so much as his farm and Fort Ransom. And so, he tried to affect change the only productive way he knew how—through politics.

John had initially supported the Nonpartisan League (NPL), a political movement born of the desire for more local, farmer control in 1915. More control over his own destiny was an appealing message to John, and he believed that could begin to be accomplished through the NPL's plan for a North Dakota Mill and Elevator Association. It was the moderate, farmer-centered answer to securing higher grain prices. However, after that plan failed to materialize over the next several years, and the NPL lost its moderate sensibilities, John joined a different movement that felt more reasonable, more American. The Independent Voter's Association (IVA), which opposed what John called "socialist corruption," took control of the North Dakota House of Representatives in 1920, the first election in which women could vote. In October 1921, just three months after Muriel's birth, the IVA forced a recall election in which their endorsed candidate, Ragnvald Nestos, ran for governor and beat seated Governor Lynn Frazier, an NPLer.

John was hopeful that with Nestos's victory in North Dakota and a strong American economy, the State Mill and Elevator would become successful. But years came and went without any progress for farmers resulting from the State Mill and Elevator. Neither the weather nor the crops were great, and grain prices were low and getting lower. Local banks began to foreclose on farmers who could no longer make payments on their loans, and then the banks themselves began to fail. John firmly held this was primarily the result of a nationwide deflation of agriculture prices.

Urged on by his neighbors and his disgust with failed farm policies, John decided to run for State Representative from District 14 in 1926. His platform, like that of his party, was to put farming on par with manufacturing in terms of American priority. Josephine and the Henrickson children grew accustomed to John's political talk when he was at home and to his absence while he visited other farmers in the district. In fact, he spoke more during that time period than he ever had, and with more excitement. At age four, Muriel thought her dad was the smartest dad anywhere, and very handsome in his suit, which he formerly only wore to church.

Her brothers admired their father, and at the same time, his political distractions meant they were responsible for more farm work, some of which was trial by fire. Harold, who graduated high school in the spring of 1926, and Luther, a year behind him, bore the brunt of John's regular absences that summer, and had to address any issues that arose around the house or with the livestock. One of the more difficult chores was hauling water from the river. Because the well had only enough water for the household, the water for the cattle had to be hauled from low spots in the river, where the water had pooled. Retrieving and hauling the water was a job for at least two experienced men, with a third person standing in the wagon, if possible. Luther was the most experienced, as Harold had never shown an interest in farming, but this year it was up to the two of them, with Palmer as their helper. Harold dipped each bucket in the water, then he handed it to Luther, who stood on a plank precariously protruding through the spokes of the wagon wheel. If the horses got spooked, Luther's job got even more dangerous. When that happened one August day, he flew through the air and landed hard on his back five feet away. His brothers instantly rushed toward him, as Luther could not speak. They could see him forming the words with his mouth, but none of them came out. "Go get Ma," Harold feverishly yelled at Palmer.

"I'm. Okay . . . I'm okay," Luther yelled as Palmer was running away. "I had the wind . . . knocked out . . . of me."

They agreed to say nothing about this event to their parents, ever. They needed to prove to their father that his trust in them was well placed. More importantly, their mother was busy canning and filling the root cellar for winter; her knowing would only worry her every time they hauled water from the river.

Harold left for Valley City Teachers' College two weeks later. Frances became the newest Henrickson at Springer School № 2, where all of John and Josephine's children attended through the eighth grade. Muriel and Pud were still too young to go to school, despite Muriel's lobbying her mother for two days before school started. "I'll be good," she said. "I'll listen to the teacher. I'll learn fast."

Muriel cried a few tears in silence the next morning, mostly for the loss of her constant friend, Frances. She did not understand but refrained from asking her mother why Luther was still home after the others left.

What only the older children knew was that John had decided Luther must stay home to work on the farm that fall. Education was important, but in the hierarchy, farming was the necessity, especially in tough economic times like these. When John won his election that November, Luther was to stay home for the next two years, the length of John's term in the North Dakota House of Representatives. Palmer also stayed home to help Luther the second year. John's time in the Legislature sent him to Bismarck, the farthest distance he had been from Fort Ransom since arriving in 1888. He was in Bismarck from January into March 1927, part of January 1928, and on other occasions for meetings. Luther was in charge of the farm during his father's absence, drove his mother to town as needed, and assigned work to Palmer. The family spoke very little of John when he was in Bismarck other than on the days he left home, when the younger children were especially curious to hear their mother's retelling of John's adventures.

"Andy Anderson gave your father a ride to Englevale in his big truck," she told the attentive children, whose wide eyes expressed their opinion that Andy had a very neat job. After explaining that Andy delivered goods from the train to the stores in Fort Ransom, she continued, "Englevale is where your father boards the small train to ride east to Fargo. There he gets off that train, gets on a bigger train, and rides west to Bismarck."

It was during one of these retellings in John's absence that Luther and Palmer entered the house in the worst panic that any of the family had witnessed before. There was no time to shelter the young children from the immediate scene of a distraught Luther, wincing in pain and holding up his right hand, blood dripping onto the floor as he walked into the kitchen. "His finger got caught in the chain of the corn binder!" Palmer shouted.

Ethel hurried the children upstairs, sparing them the worst of the blood. They huddled in the girls' bedroom in stunned silence, hoping to overhear any news that might escape the lips of their mother, Mildred, or Palmer. They were frightened of any sound from Luther. "Will he be alright?" Frances asked Ethel in a hushed voice.

"He will," Ethel said. "People survive without fingers."

Mildred soon came upstairs and announced that Luther was minus part of his right ring finger. Palmer and their mother were taking him to the doctor in Lisbon, and Luther would be just fine after the doctor dressed his hand. At breakfast the next morning, Josephine told the children Luther was resting in her bed. "He's going to be alright," she said. "He just needs to rest a few days, so the rest of us will need to help Palmer outside."

Muriel listened closely for other updates and waited for Luther to say something—anything—about it in the days ahead. When their father returned, she waited for a discussion of Luther's finger. She heard no such conversation then or ever. Muriel came to understand in that experience that some things hurt too much to talk about.

NORDLENDINGS AND SORLENDINGS

TWO RELIGIONS WERE PRACTICED ACTIVELY in the Henrickson household: hard work and the Lutheran faith. Going to church every Sunday morning was what they did. Attending Sunday school was the expectation from age four or five until grade eight, when young teenagers transitioned to reading for the minister for two years, which concluded with their confirmation into the faith—a rite of passage. Fulfilling all these requirements was the Christian thing to do. John and Josephine had followed these Christian rules without question, and they expected their children to do the same. First and foremost, they wanted their offspring to have strict moral codes and Godly hearts. Almost as important, as the Henrickson children heard through chatter about a few other families, they did not want to give their neighbors any reason to gossip. All the good Fort Ransom families went to church.

The Henrickson's church had always been Standing Rock, which was formed in 1882 under the United Norwegian Lutheran Church (UNLC) of America. Nearly all Standing Rock members at that time were immigrants of *northern* Norway (Nordlendings), who had belonged to the official Church of Norway. When John and Josephine arrived as youth in Fort Ransom, they attended services in people's homes or local schoolhouses, in a rotation. The congregation built the white, wood-frame church building, with a spire reminiscent of their churches in Norway, in the northwest corner of town in 1898. The men sat on the right side of the church, and the women and children sat on the left, according to customs that nobody at Standing Rock publicly questioned. The long pews, purchased with funds raised by the Zion Ladies' Aid, were always full. Eventually, the church was so packed on Sunday mornings that the congregation rebuilt the church in 1908 to accommodate the growing membership. Pastor Ole Anderson preached at Standing Rock in his heavy black robe with a stiff, white collar for thirty years, completely in Norwegian, which all his congregants spoke.

The majority of Sorlendings in Fort Ransom, who came from *southern* Norway, went to Stiklestad Lutheran Church, located across town from Standing Rock. Organized in 1887, Stiklestad was part of the Hauge Synod, formed in the spirit of Hans Hauge's reform movement that began in Oslo, Norway, a century earlier. The Hauge Synod emphasized personal discipline, followed simpler liturgy than the UNLC, and held that ministers should be plain clothed in suits, like the other men of the congregation. Haugeans opposed dancing, drinking alcohol, and playing cards. Like at Standing Rock, though, the language of church was Norwegian, and the men sat on the right side of the aisle, separate from their wives and children. The Stiklestad faithful completed construction of their own white, wood-frame church with spire in 1897, a year ahead of Standing Rock.

The need for two congregations was equally clear to the early members of Standing Rock and Stiklestad. The activities that Standing Rock folks saw as amusements, Stiklestad members believed were sins. But outside of church and their central difference in Lutheran philosophy, these fellow Norwegians were friendly and said nothing negative aloud about one another. After all, a common language and desire to live in harmony united them in their new valley community.

By the time Pastor Gustav Sandanger came to serve Standing Rock in 1919, the reason for division was becoming less clear. The UNLC and Hauge synods had merged to form the Evangelical Lutheran Church two years earlier, placing Standing Rock and Stiklestad under the same denomination of Lutherans. And so, Standing

Rock, the larger of the congregations, made the Christian gesture to invite Stiklestad to consolidate into one congregation in 1919. Stiklestad politely declined, citing its pastor-sharing arrangement with the

Standing Rock Lutheran Church in Fort Ransom, circa 1912.
(Courtesy North Dakota Institute for Regional Studies, Fargo)

Preston and Waldheim congregations in the country, between Fort Ransom and Kathryn. But the seed of change was planted. [11]

While the Henricksons did not read the Bible at home, the children recited the bedtime prayer, "Now I lay me down to sleep, I pray the Lord my Soul to keep. If I die before I wake, I pray the Lord my Soul to take." At mealtime, Josephine led the children in the Norwegian table prayer:

> I Jesu navn
> Gar vi til bord
> At spise drikke
> Paa dit Ord
> Deg Gud til aere
> Oss til gavn
> Sa faar vi mat
> I Jesu navn
> Amen. [12]

Muriel grew accustomed to her mother imparting the faith at home and the church being the center of community activity. For her, as of age five, this meant putting on her nicest dress and attending Sunday school for an hour before the church service started. She learned new songs, hung on every word her teacher said, and loved being in a class with a dozen other children her age. For her father, going to church seemed to mean shaking hands and visiting with the menfolk after the service, and performing in the Nokken men's choir. "Nokken," he explained to the children, was a mythical, water-

---

[11] "A Brief History of the Zion Ladies' Aid for 75th Anniversary," *Favorite Recipes of Members of the Zion Ladies' Aid* (Fort Ransom, North Dakota, 1959), 1–4. Fort Ransom 125th Anniversary Book Committee, ed. *Fort Ransom Community History, 1878–2003*, 123. Anecdotally, the authors heard from numerous sources that men sat on the opposite side of the aisle as women and children at Standing Rock, as was commonly the case at Norwegian Lutheran churches in North Dakota in the early 20th century. No known written records exist on this subject for the Standing Rock congregation. General information about the UNLC and Hauge synods, particularly in relation to Standing Rock and Stiklestad, is courtesy of Pastor Bradley Edin, who served Standing Rock, and Lay Pastor Al Grothe, who attended Stiklestad during his entire youth.

[12] Translated to English, the prayer reads, "In Jesus name; To the table we go; To eat and drink; According to his word; To God the honor; Us the gain; So, receive the food; In Jesus name, Amen."

fall-dwelling sprite in Norwegian folklore. The Nokken sang sweet and exquisite music to good listeners at the waterfall.

For her mother, it was teaching Sunday school and attending monthly meetings of the Zion Ladies' Aid, which led to special events that the ladies' aid planned. Aid meetings were on Josephine's schedule without exception; in fact, she served as secretary for several years. Just as she had grown up regularly attending aid meetings with her mother, Josephine brought her own young daughters along to meetings, with the caveat they sit quietly alongside her or play nicely outside with the other girls who would come to the meeting. Muriel loved hearing the women speak Norwegian about topics she understood, unlike what Pastor Sandanger talked about from the pulpit each Sunday. The women divvied up duties and planned menus for the church auction sale, Bible camp, and the ice cream social, when they might also decide to serve pie or cake. The aid then used the funds they raised to buy necessities for the church and make donations. Muriel listened closely to the charitable causes they selected, from Concordia College in Moorhead, Minnesota, to Lutheran missionaries serving in other countries.[13]

As soon as each Henrickson girl was old enough, she helped serve lunch at the auction each June and the ice cream social in August. Muriel wanted so badly to be old enough, which seemed to be about twelve, "based on maturity," her mother explained. Unsure of the specific meaning, Muriel believed that behaving as much like a grown-up as possible was sure to advance her cause. In the meantime, she observed her Sunday school teacher helping the students who struggled to stand still, her older sisters following the orders of the women in the church kitchen, and her mother serving food alongside the other women of the church, always with kindness and thanks.

---

[13] Zion Ladies' Aid meeting minutes transitioned from Norwegian to English as of November 1941. The only known mention of the language spoken at meetings was, "Discussion whether we should discontinue using the Norwegian language at meetings," on December 9, 1948. Zion Ladies' Aid meeting minutes, Standing Rock Lutheran Church, Fort Ransom, North Dakota, 234.

SCHOOL AND A BIG WORLD

IN THE FALL OF 1927, EAGER Muriel started first grade at Springer School № 2, where her sister Mildred was the new teacher. Located down the road a half-mile east of the Henrickson farm, the walk was short and the views were familiar, but this was a long-awaited adventure for Muriel. Mildred had walked Muriel to the school a few days before classes started, just the two of them, to satisfy Muriel's curiosity. Fifteen years older than her youngest sister, Mildred became even more interesting that day. She became Miss Henrickson, showing a new student what and where everything was in her classroom. Muriel started memorizing continents by sight on the globe, and asked Mildred to point to Fort Ransom and Mo I Rana, which were the centers of their family's universe.

Springer was a one-room school serving twenty-five students from grades one through eight—including all of John and Josephine's children between the 1910s and 1930s. Many people called it the Henrickson school, because it was so near John's farm and was the school where all the Henrickson children attended. The building was one story, about twenty-five by fifty feet, and painted white from top to bottom. The school's small entryway, called the cloak room, had a south-facing door to avoid the strong north and east winds. The interior door further minimized the cold draft into the classroom in winter months, and the transom above the door was kept open when the temperatures were warmer. Entering the classroom, Muriel saw a chalkboard covering the entire front wall, the teacher's desk at the head of the room, a potbelly stove at the back, and more school desks than she could count. "Do I know that many kids?" she wondered, thinking of all the boys and girls in her Sunday school. The south-facing wall had four large windows to welcome the natural light. Already Muriel gazed outside at the tree trunks and branches, thinking of the fun she would have playing hide-and-seek with her schoolmates during recess.

Like her siblings and most of her friends, Muriel started the first grade speaking better Norwegian than English. "Good morning" was "*Godmorgen*" at the Henrickson home. Her parents spoke Norwegian almost exclusively to one another, and much of the time with the children. Mildred's job—Miss Henrickson's job—was to teach her pupils proper English. That was the language of school. Really, she was to teach her students how to be *Americans*. Toward that end, she focused on reading, writing and arithmetic. Her students must exhibit good grammar and penmanship, master the spelling of difficult words like "exhibit," read *The Adventures of Tom Sawyer* and other great works of American literature, and commit the states and multiplication tables to memory.

In many ways, the one-room school provided an effective learning environment. Younger children, like Muriel, listened to the instruction of the older students, and those older students often tutored the younger ones. Muriel was inquisitive, smart, and eager to help Miss Henrickson teach those who did not catch on as quickly as she did. She loved the fact that her sister was the teacher. Miss Henrickson knew everything there was to know about language and literature, Muriel thought, so she listened intently and wanted to know everything about sentence structure and storytelling.

Muriel also loved the social aspect, even though visiting occasionally got her into trouble. It was not so serious that she was kept inside during recess. Rather, it was mostly scolding, and it usually happened during arithmetic, which Muriel found rather dull. Sometimes she wished for more children to talk, laugh and play with at school. She especially wanted the company of her cousins Clarice and

Ardis, who went to a different country school a few miles away. But, Muriel also felt that even if she had more friends, her closest friend would still be her sister Frances. There was nobody she would rather be with to climb trees, pick wildflowers, or bounce from the seat of the teeter-totter.

"You'll always be my best friend," Muriel told her.

"No matter what," Frances agreed.

When Miss Henrickson said, "Time for lunch," Muriel and Frances shot up from their desks. They pulled the sandwiches out of their sacks and compared lunches with the other girls. Muriel and her sisters packed their own sandwiches, favoring peanut butter and chokecherry jelly to any meat. In the winter, Muriel liked to bring chicken soup or beef stew, which heated on top of the wood stove at school all morning. Each child had a Mason jar full of water for the day, and Muriel knew hers from the worn pink ribbon tied around the top.

No matter the season, Muriel rushed to eat so that she could play outdoors, where the woods, hills, and river held endless potential in her imagination. The Sheyenne Valley of her youth was every bit as enchanting as Winnie the Pooh's Ashdown Forest. The freedom to explore was just as great as Tom Sawyer's Mississippi River. For that precious lunch hour each day, time was suspended in the country air, like dandelion seeds in a soft spring breeze.

MAKING DO

MURIEL WAS ABOUT TO ENTER the third grade at Springer School № 2 when she realized what "making do" meant. All summer long in 1929, she heard the statement, "We need rain." At church, on open nights, and around the kitchen table, the sentiment was put in practical terms: "I've never seen the river so low." "If we don't get rain this week, we'll have no crop at all." The weeks passed, and Muriel saw the drought firsthand in the garden. The dirt was gray and dusty. The vegetable leaves were crisp to the touch. When the boys hauled water from the river each morning, she and her sisters gave the plants a drink, perking them up until the afternoon sun dried them up again.

Even her father looked parched. His frown lines were deepening. He spoke fewer words at dinnertime—only that the wheat crop was terrible. Political talk had vanished since he had chosen not to run for a second term in the North Dakota Legislature. Following John's lead, the whole family said less. Muriel learned no details about their financial woes. She simply knew not to expect candy on open nights or new shoes just because her toes poked through the current pair. "We will make do," Josephine said when she noticed the holes in Muriel's shoes.

That was as close a mention to hardship as was uttered at the Henrickson's house. The silence on the subject spoke loudly. So, when the Great Crash happened in the stock market that fall, Muriel tried her darndest to overhear the adult conversations around her for clues about what it meant. She overheard nothing about the stock market, but in the process, she caught that crop prices were worse than ever. "The price of wheat was $2.20/bushel after the war. Now we're lucky to get $1.00," her father told a neighbor who stopped by one Saturday morning for coffee, while Muriel and Frances sat at the top of the stairway, playing in silence with their ragdolls.[14]

"How is everybody gonna make it another year?" the neighbor replied, as Muriel and Frances locked eyes. That unanswered question was to hover over the Henrickson farm like a raincloud.

At school, an eighth-grade boy asked Miss Henrickson about the crash, and she stammered for several seconds. "The stock market is for investors in New York City. We will wait to see if the downturn affects North Dakota," she replied.

Muriel went about her days with her usual cheerful spirit. At the same time, she was mature for her age—the other moms all told her so—and she was more inquisitive than her peers. She took note that she was not told to change anything. Work routines stayed the same. She had enough to eat, and she was warm enough. Yet she sensed a subtle reduction of food on her parents' plates, and perhaps even less food on the table overall. "I like the neck best," Josephine said about the tiny piece of chicken she put on her plate.

Muriel wondered if her mother truly preferred the neck, but she followed the lead of her siblings in not asking. They also began eating cream of wheat more often, which Muriel liked, so she did not question the reason. Making do was so subtle and gradual that one day, it was implicitly normal. Most of the time in the coming years, life continued to be perfectly good.

Muriel was learning to play the piano, and she enjoyed it so much that it consumed more of her spare time than anything else. The piano was always there, she needed nobody's help or companionship to play, and her mother approved as long as Muriel's schoolwork and house chores were done. It was a perfect friend for a girl whose

---

[14] "Crop Production Historical Track Records," United States Department of Agriculture, page 207, accessed December 28, 2020, https://www.nass.usda.gov/Publications/Todays_Reports/reports/croptr18.pdf

captivation with music began the first time she sang "Mary Had a Little Lamb." She stood at the end of the piano while Bernice practiced it on the piano and taught her the words. On long winter nights, their mother, Mildred, and Ethel liked to read; their father preferred playing whist with the three oldest boys, and Muriel and Bernice took turns playing piano. Bernice, who was six years older, played "Josephine" and several waltzes with ease. Muriel was making fast progress to catch up. By age twelve, she played nearly as well as Bernice.

Joy in play—play of many kinds—danced inside Muriel, more than in any of her sisters or brothers. Her hazel eyes lit up like her mother's when she smiled or laughed. In the wintertime, Muriel was the instigator for tobogganing. When she said, "Let's go," her excitement was so infectious that at least two siblings nearly always bundled up in their wool overclothes and followed her out the door. The ideal sledding hill—long and steep with a treeless path—was just across the road. The children took turns pulling the wooden toboggan, which their father had made as a teenager and kept waxed ever since.

By the spring of 1934, Muriel completed her final year at Springer № 2. She finished eight grades in seven years and was beyond eager to expand her horizons at the high school in Fort Ransom. She longed for academic challenges nearly as much as she wished to expand her social circle. At Springer, the number of students had dwindled every year, as farm families had left one by one. A couple of grades had only one student. In high school, Muriel would be in her cousin Clarice's class, and she would walk to and from town with Frances, the only person with whom she shared any secrets.

On hot summer Sundays, Muriel and Frances spurred their siblings down to the river to swim, carefree, in the murky water, with only the faintest current in the years of little rain. They had all learned to paddle and float before they started school. "I need to trust you by the river," Josephine had repeated many times.

Their favorite swimming spot was near the cable line across the river, where they crossed to bring the cows home for milking. Here the children took turns mounting the platform attached to the pulley, then jumping into the middle of the river. The familiar, "Aah!" preceding the splash was Muriel's favorite sound of summer.

The best swimming days were when their Rufsvold cousins joined them. The children all wore versions of the same black bathing suit, sewn from material and a pattern that Josephine and her sister Lizzie bought together. While the cousins swam and laughed, the

Muriel as a young teen in her bathing suit, ready for a swim in the Sheyenne River. Circa 1934. *(Courtesy Tom Sandhei)*

parents sprawled out on old quilts on the shady riverbank, sipping lemonade and reminiscing in Norwegian. When the children got hungry, they joined the adults, and Josephine and Lizzie unpacked the bread loaves and jams from the picnic baskets. These were happy afternoons, when worries seemed distant, if only for a few hours.

John and Josephine kept their troubles to themselves. Like many of their neighbors, they were barely holding onto the farm. Year after year in the 1930s, prices for the meager grain harvest stayed low. Severe drought visited in the summer of 1934, along with dust storms so fierce they forced the family inside the house for entire days. With black prairie dust blowing through every crevice in their valley house, Josephine placed damp rags along the windowsills, and John kept a lantern lit all day. The only thriving greenery were tumbleweeds, which John begrudgingly hayed on calmer days. The hay contained just enough grass to make it palatable for the hungry cattle the next winter, as long as it was moistened before feeding. The Henricksons' saving grace was their ability to raise their own beef, pork, chicken and produce in the valley. Living next to the river, they could haul enough water to keep the garden productive. They always grew enough vegetables to survive the next winter.

Muriel became accustomed to spending hours a day in the garden. Soaked in sweat and stained with grasshopper spit on her legs and skirt, she felt very unladylike. Sweat was new to her. It confused and embarrassed her. Her first inclination was to watch her sisters for cues, which were to wash herself longer at the pump twice a day. But perspiration was not the only perplexing issue. Everything about her body seemed to be suddenly changing. She suspected she was "filling out" and "becoming a woman," as she had heard in passing from her mom and aunts in reference to her sisters and cousins. "Is Ma going to talk to me about it?" she asked Frances once. Getting a definitive "no" in response, Muriel kept similar wonderings to herself as she watered and weeded.

Inside the house, Muriel used a needle and thread almost daily, learning most of what she knew from her mother. Muriel had seen examples of Josephine's finer work on Sunday dresses, but everyday clothes consumed most of the girls' time. Muriel became as efficient as her sisters at sewing, patching, and mending. They darned socks until more of each sock was patched than original. When the cuffs and collars of shirts were threadbare on one side, the girls removed and reversed them and sewed them back on.

"You do excellent work," the exacting Josephine told Muriel one day. Such effusive praise startled Muriel, who did her best to keep pedaling the Singer sewing machine. She was accustomed to kindness and warmth. Acclaim was less familiar. "Thank you, Ma," she responded when she finished her even hem on her father's work shirt.

Josephine and John grew increasingly reticent through the 1930s, save glimmers of joy at riverside picnics, parlor piano performances, and their children's educational achievements. Making do was stoic work. But they never lowered their high standards for a job well-done or a proper household. And they never mentioned the possibility of losing the farm, except maybe to the older boys, who would never tell their sisters.

"You are learning how to lead your own household, Muriel," her mother went so far to say. "You need to be ready to help on your husband's farm someday."

Muriel did not know about that. She might instead want to become a teacher, like Mildred. But for now, Muriel drew comfort from her mother's inference that they would be staying on the farm. She liked proving herself as smart and capable. In fact, Muriel was confident in her own abilities. Her confidence even had a way of feeding her playfulness. Depression or not, she emitted the brightest light in the household.

LEFSE IN THE WINTERTIME

PARALLEL TO MAKING DO, SAMENESS was a theme of Muriel's youth. The Henricksons tended to eat oatmeal for breakfast and meat and potatoes for dinner and supper. They went to Fort Ransom for church and Sunday school every Sunday. They went to town again on Tuesday and Saturday nights to sell their cream and eggs. The children walked to country school a stone's throw away, and then to high school in Fort Ransom. Washday was every Monday, and ironing day was every Tuesday. Baths were every Saturday night before going to town. This recurring pattern marked every day and every week.

One notable exception to the mundaneness of life was when Josephine and her girls made lefse. Always prepared for Thanksgiving, Christmas, and Easter, lefse-making too had its pattern. If there were other special occasions, like Mildred's twenty-fifth birthday, they made potato lefse. Yet the infrequency of it broke up the routine.

Muriel learned the distinctiveness of each kind of lefse from her mother and older sisters as they made the dough, as though she was being entrusted with special knowledge, which only the most fortunate girls had the privilege to learn. First, there was *potato* lefse—or, simply, lefse. The Henrickson women made more potato lefse than either of the other two kinds. Potatoes were boiled, mashed, and mixed with flour and butter. The dough was rolled out over and over until it was thin as a fingernail. Then each slice was baked a few seconds, until golden with light brown bubbles, on the surface of the cast iron stovetop. As they waited for the lefse to cool before stacking it and putting it away for the holiday, every person got to eat one piece of warm lefse, spread with butter and sprinkled lightly with white sugar.

The second type of lefse was *Hardanger*, which was made for holidays only. It got its name from the beloved fjord along the Atlantic coastline of southern Norway. A fjord, Mildred told Muriel, was a long, narrow inlet with steep sides, created by a glacier. Hardanger lefse was not made with potatoes, but rather was flour-based with a sweeter, more fragile dough. "Add just enough flour so that it rolls thin," Josephine repeated. "Just enough" was a feeling, Muriel learned. Then the girls rolled it and followed the same baking process as they used for potato lefse, placing each piece delicately and directly on the stovetop. If a piece tore or got too dark, Josephine let the girls try it with butter, sugar, and a sprinkling of cinnamon.

The third type of lefse was *krina*, named for the wooden tool that creates the pattern in this lefse. Made with white flour and wheat or graham flour, the special ingredient in this lefse is lard, and there are three added steps not included in potato or Hardanger lefse. After the dough was rolled and baked like the others, the lefse was left to cool. The Henrickson girls then spread a roux over the top and created the krina pattern on each lefse, making it look like a fork had been rolled over the top in a pretty design. Then back to the stovetop it went to set, and into the oven to bake a bit longer. Krina lefse was best with butter and brown sugar. Using white sugar or cinnamon would be sacrilegious, the older girls told Muriel. She nodded affirmatively even though she did not understand. Then she hoped for a torn piece of it as well. Like Hardanger lefse, krina lefse was a special treat reserved for holidays.

One sunny summer day while digging potatoes, Muriel asked her mother, "Can we make lefse today?" Getting no response, she added, "Or someday soon?"

"We cannot make lefse in the summertime," Josephine said. "The house would get too hot."

That was the best reasoning for sameness that Muriel had ever heard. It explained why some things, like lefse, were special.

CONFIRMATION AND DANCING

ACCORDING TO THE STRICTEST LUTHERANS in Fort Ransom—namely the Stiklestad faithful—dancing was a sin. As for the Henricksons and most of their Standing Rock peers, they believed that when a young person was old and thoughtful enough to profess his or her faith, he or she may tastefully dance. The confirmation ceremony, complete with First Communion, was the time of that profession. Happening at age fourteen or fifteen, it came after two years of intensive study. All Lutheran youth were expected to be confirmed, and of course, that was virtually all the youth in Fort Ransom. How confirmation entitled them to dancing rights, Muriel was unclear. But one should not question such things. "A good thing is a good thing," she told herself.

Nonetheless, dancing was a very popular social activity in Fort Ransom. Each Friday night year-round, the town halls in Fort Ransom, Nome, and Kathryn rotated as dance host. The town buzzed with cars and the happy chatter of well-dressed young people. Some of the men started their night at one of the newly legal beer joints. Some women talked inside cars on Main Street. But by 8:00 p.m., the biggest crowd was at the hall. A local band, usually led by a pianist or accordionist, played two-steps, waltzes, polkas, and schottisches from 8:00 p.m. to midnight. Catching glimpses from afar of a few dances at the Fort Ransom hall, the jolliness swirling inside called to Muriel. "You aren't missing much," her mother assured her. "You'll see."

Never had Muriel seen her parents dance or heard them talk about dancing. She had not known her siblings to dance either. "If they're allowed to dance, why don't they?" she and Frances contemplated a few times but did not arrive at any logical answer. The two of them could hardly wait to dance.

Frances's confirmation, and subsequently her time to dance, arrived two years earlier than Muriel's would. Confirmed in the spring of 1933, Frances told Muriel everything she needed to know about "reading for the minister," which referred to the classes and studies that prepared them for confirmation. "Sit in a spot where Pastor Sandanger can't make direct eye contact with you," Frances advised. "Memorize everything he tells you to learn the first three weeks," she continued. "Raise your hand a lot those first few weeks. Give long answers. Then he'll stop calling on you."

Muriel absorbed all of this advice as she prepared to read for the minister that fall, when she was an eighth grader. A month before, on her twelfth birthday, her mother also informed her that she was old enough to start helping at the church's ice cream social. Muriel happily filled the men's water glasses at the social that August, and just as enthusiastically cleared tables at the end of the day. This series of life events was all adding up to the moment she had been anticipating; when she was finally mature enough to be called a young lady.

Muriel and a dozen classmates read for Pastor Sandanger every Saturday from 10:00 a.m. to noon during the school year. Her confirmation class included both Standing Rock and Stiklestad members. In 1930, after Stiklestad's pastor died, Pastor Sandanger had agreed to serve both congregations. He preached at Standing Rock one week in his traditional robe and collar, and at Stiklestad in his plain suit the next. His understanding was that Standing Rock members would attend Stiklestad services, and vice versa. After all, they were all Norwegians by heritage, they all spoke Norwegian, and they graciously greeted one another around town. However, attending Standing Rock and Stiklestad as though they were one and the same proved too radical for some of the old-timers. In silent opposition, they went to church every other week. The Henricksons, with three children still needing to be confirmed when the change took place, continued to attend services every Sunday.

The merger of the two confirmation classes made no difference to Muriel. She saw most of the same faces at school that she saw at confirmation class, and all their parents or grandparents had come from Norway. Going to church at both Standing Rock and Stiklestad made complete sense to her.

Around this same time, family units began sitting together at church rather than separated by gender. This change also was logical to Muriel, who had wondered, but had not asked, why they ever sat separately to begin with. She and Frances had concluded men and women are equal; it was as simple as that. As the Henricksons walked from their car to the church on the first morning of the switch, John spoke the first words Muriel had heard from him on the subject: "I don't know why we're changing something that's worked my whole life. But today I will sit with you and feel no differently about the sermon than I did last week."[15]

Changes aside, Pastor Sandanger led the same rigorous and extensive course of memorization that he had become known for. He expected his confirmands to recite numerous passages from the Bible and Luther's Catechism, which included the Lord's Prayer, Ten Commandments, Apostle's Creed, the Eucharist (or Rite of Holy Communion), and the Rite of Baptism. In addition to the actual texts, each pupil needed to memorize detailed descriptions of what each passage meant. Muriel found memorizing rather easy, but she thought reading for the minister was as dull as math. Only the dangling carrot of future dances kept her focused for those two years.

A new white linen dress was also on her mind as confirmation Sunday neared. At least a couple of the other girls in her class were

---

[15] The seating arrangement at Standing Rock in the 1930s is the authors' educated guess after anecdotal conversations with numerous Fort Ransom sources. No known written records exist on this subject for the Standing Rock or Stiklestad congregations. Commentary from a member of Preston Lutheran Church, located a few miles north of Fort Ransom, indicates that men and women sat separately into the 1930s: Fort Ransom 125th Anniversary Book Committee, ed. Fort Ransom Community History, 1878–2003, 204.

getting new confirmation dresses. Muriel envisioned a V-neck dress just past her knees, with flouncy cap sleeves and a gathered waistline. Maybe she could make it herself after school let out for the year, she thought. Before that day came, though, her mother approached her at the sewing machine with another option. "You might be wishing for a brand-new dress for Confirmation Day, but I think you will like this just as much," Josephine said, half-smiling while holding up Frances's confirmation dress. "How about we add a new collar and a sash at the waist?"

Of course, she was not getting a new dress. How could she have thought such an absurd thing? The girls getting new dresses did not have older sisters. Muriel had four! Muriel hid her disappointment and thanked her mother. The next day, Josephine and Muriel got started on remaking the dress. She would wear it with her white stockings and Frances's white shoes, which might have started as Bernice's shoes. Muriel decided to make it the best hand-me-down dress it could be, so much so that nobody would know it was remade.

Confirmation Sunday came in June 1935, when the peonies were blooming all over Fort Ransom. White, pastel pink, and true pink blooms graced the altar at the front of the sanctuary. Every Standing Rock pew was full, lined with the confirmands' extended families. All of Muriel's siblings were in attendance, including Harold and his new wife Borghil, who had also grown up on a farm near Fort Ransom. Muriel knew virtually everyone in the church, all 250 people. Most of them were fanning themselves with their programs as the temperature climbed with each new body that entered.

While Muriel was self-assured and excited, Frances had cautioned her that Pastor Sandanger was not just going to hand each confirmand a sheet of paper and shake hands. Muriel had witnessed with her older siblings that a test was involved, in front of the whole congregation. So, Pastor Sandanger had urged them in their final class to be prepared for any question about what they had learned over the past two years. "Do not get ahead of yourself. Do not embarrass your parents," he had said. "Give this somber occasion the seriousness it deserves."

At long last, the confirmands—the girls in white or pastel dresses, the boys in gray or black suits—lined up around the altar. Each waited his or her turn to be called upon to answer at least one question. No one knew what questions would be asked. One by one, the students responded to the questions. Some were too quiet to be heard from the pews, but most were correct or close to it. One boy was so hot and nervous, that he fainted. His mortified mother attended to him, he recovered quickly, and the service continued without further incident. Much to her parents' pride, Muriel gave an accurate and articulate answer to Pastor Sandanger's question. He handed her a certificate of confirmation, nodded approvingly, and shook her hand. Strangely, even the two students who had not answered the pastor correctly were given certificates of confirmation. Frances had told her that would happen. They decided the rebuke from embarrassed parents was probably punishment enough for the youth who gave wrong answers. Besides, this subject fell into the broad category of things one did not question.

Muriel went home with her certificate and something far more valuable to her: permission to dance! She said nothing of the sort at the chicken dinner in her honor. Her parents were as content as she could remember. They played croquet that afternoon in the plush green grass, watered by plentiful rains that spring. Afterward, they ate angel food cake with whipped cream and strawberries from the garden. It was a rare, almost perfect, day. There was no reason to talk about dancing yet.

Muriel waited until bedtime to go to Frances in hushed excitement. "When is the next dance?!" she exclaimed. They started planning for Muriel's first dance that night.

ALMOST A GROWNUP

MURIEL STARTED HER FRESHMAN YEAR of high school in Fort Ransom in the fall of 1934. She was a teenager now, almost a grownup, with an excitement for more friends, more interesting classes, and the town buzz. There was an allure to knowing that on any given day, a different mix of people were coming and going on Main Street. Who might she see that day? What news might her teachers and thirteen classmates bring to school? What books would she get to read—anything by Virginia Woolf, whose writing Mildred had previously deemed "a bit too mature" for her? She did not know what the books were about; she just knew she was ready to read what adults could read. Life was about to get more interesting, Muriel mused.

Fort Ransom School was a one-story white building with a basement, situated across the street from Standing Rock Church. The main level was split into four classrooms—first through fourth grade in the southwest corner, fifth through eighth grade in the southeast corner, and the high school in the two rooms on the north side. The basement had storage space and the coal furnace. At least four Springer schools would have fit inside Fort Ransom School. It was big to Muriel, who had never been farther than Lisbon a few times, and had never seen another high school besides the huge one there.

Muriel was the youngest in a class of fourteen students, all of whom she knew from Springer № 2 or church. While it was hard for her to imagine, high school was only starting to become common. Mildred and Harold had both graduated from Lisbon, because Fort

Ransom only offered one to three years of high school in their day, depending on how many students were interested in a given year. The first high school class graduated from Fort Ransom in 1930.[16] Palmer and Ethel graduated in Fort Ransom together in 1931, as Palmer was kept out of school in 1927–1928 while their father served in the Legislature. Bernice graduated in 1933, and Frances was two grades ahead of Muriel.

School was a three-mile walk down a familiar country road and the town streets. Muriel's stride in her black saddle shoes gave the impression that she was always on a mission, even in pleasant weather. Frances had to keep up. Winding past barren fields after months of drought, enveloped in all directions by golden hills, the sisters talked mostly about boys and radio shows. Some days as they passed by the ruins of the old ski jump, they imagined daring young men jumping in front of cheering crowds. Early Norwegian settlers had carved out a twenty-foot-wide strip down the hill and built the jumping structure, making a spot to continue what they had loved to do in the Old Country. Muriel wished she could have seen the ski-jumping for herself. Her curiosity extended far and wide—far back to the Native American tribes who had once lived here, and far away to the prairie towns beyond these hills, where trains stopped every day, taking people to Fargo and Minneapolis. She could only imagine how big the world was.

The girls looked into the yards of the farms they passed, waving at anyone who was outside. When they met a car, they stepped off the road, turned away from the trail of dust, and resumed their walk after it settled. Finally, they entered town, passing Stiklestad Church on their left and a line of neat, white houses in a row on their right. The café owner, grocer, blacksmith, and auto repairman were just starting the day on Main Street.

Crossing the bridge over the Sheyenne, they headed north toward the school, just a quarter-mile ahead. Other girls and boys

---

[16] Fort Ransom 125th Anniversary Book Committee, ed. *Fort Ransom Community History, 1878–2003*, 141.

usually caught up to Muriel and Frances by this time to laugh and compare homework. This was the thirty-five-minute routine Muriel settled comfortably into for the next four years. On the coldest days, John hitched up the team of horses to take them to school.

Muriel was instantly one of the popular girls in the high school. She had all the qualities of a popular girl, starting with being pretty. Her fair skin set off her dark brown hair, bobbed an inch below her ears. She smiled easily and broadly, showing straight, white teeth with a slight gap in front. Adults had always commented on the gap, calling it "cute," akin to cute dimples or cute freckles, Muriel supposed. Reaching a hundred pounds and five feet, three inches her freshman year, she felt about the right size in comparison to her friends, as long as she stopped growing. Some days her body felt ahead of her clothes, or at odds with her desire to run around as she always had. After confiding in Frances, she at least believed her body was normal. "I want to be a woman," Muriel said. "I just want to be done *becoming* a woman."

Besides being pretty, Muriel was smart, fun, outgoing, and musical to boot. She wore those qualities confidently, but not vainly. Whether playing the piano, singing in the choir, or acting in a school play, her enthusiasm was palpable. The altos beside her mouthed the words more than they sang. Muriel harmonized like the melody was asking her a question, and she knew the answer. Without trying to be, she was one of the most charming girls in any setting. Girls saw her as a leader on the stage and in the classroom. Boys thought she was fun, and quite a few had a crush on her. All her classmates sought her out for help with English homework.

Muriel was equally well-liked among her teachers. Most of her classmates dreaded Mr. Skonnard's English class. Known for keeping a yardstick on top of his desk, he demanded students' complete attention and clear command of the English language in both reading and writing. Muriel did not even have to try to pay attention in Mr. Skonnard's class. His high expectations provided the challenge she wanted after leaving Springer, where the series of teachers spent so much time teaching down to the masses that Muriel's abilities went mostly untested. Mr. Skonnard did not include any Virginia Woolf in his curriculum, but he treated proper grammar like the perfect combination of art and science. It could be plain and beautiful, precise and playful.

Mr. Skonnard saw so much potential in Muriel that he started encouraging her college aspirations before she even finished her freshman year. This was music to her ears at a time when she found herself distracted by the big world outside when it seemed too small inside. Staring out the window in her other classes, she imagined her outstretched arms feeling the leaves as she walked up the hill, or the crunch of snow under her feet skiing down. She dreamt of all the dancing in her future. She thought of moving to Valley City for college. Still, she paid enough attention to get almost straight As.

The next four years could not pass quickly enough for Muriel. School stimulated her socially and intellectually, but more importantly, it was her steppingstone to what was next. Muriel felt the tiredness that visited her parents for extended periods. Too little harvest proved a heavy burden. She formed her own conclusions from the news on the radio—that the times were hard, and her role in them was to keep working and following her mother's instructions until she graduated from high school.

Meanwhile, Muriel looked forward to the next dance. Her mother had indeed been wrong about dancing. Muriel had been *missing out*, and getting confirmed was the best thing she had ever accomplished, because it meant going to dances. At first, Muriel was only allowed to go with Frances in Fort Ransom. The next year, after she turned fifteen, she could ride along with Frances to dances in other towns. When she turned sixteen, she could go with other friends to dances. These rules were tolerable for Muriel, who at least saw the progression in her freedom. She learned dance styles lickety-split, and she danced to nearly every song at every dance. She had her pick of partners, and she did have her regulars, but she liked the variety.

While her popularity as a dance partner grew, so did the number of potential suitors. She knew some boys from school, and others were from neighboring towns. A few of them caught her eye, but never for long. She went on one date each with a handful of boys, mainly for a ride to a dance and a free Coke.

"Socializing is your weakness," her mother commented regularly. But, socializing never got in the way of Muriel's responsibilities. She came home after dances, went to church with the family every Sunday, and consistently did all of her chores and schoolwork. From Muriel's perspective, she was proving herself worthy and capable of college, just as Mildred had fifteen years before her.

The sameness of Depression-era life continued, save the dances, until the winter of Muriel's junior year. One Saturday night in February, she saw someone new at the dance hall in Fort Ransom. At well over six feet tall, with broad shoulders, a square jawline, and a sweep of thick, dark hair, he could not be missed. He was the most handsome man Muriel had seen in her life. She continued to dance while she eyed him on the perimeter, making small talk with Elmer Anderson.

At the next dance in Fort Ransom two weeks later, he was there again. Dressed in pleated gray pants and a light blue sweater that matched his eyes, he looked neat and even more handsome. Like the last time, he talked with Elmer Anderson, and he never danced. He came up in Muriel's conversation with her friends while the band was on break. They all had a crush on him, but Muriel indicated nothing more than a passing interest. "He must be ten years older than we are," she said.

Later that night, Muriel took her own break for one dance to walk toward the water station past Elmer Anderson, who she had known her entire life. "Hello, Elmer," she said, hoping she was walking slowly enough so that he would engage.

"You took a dance off! Did you finally get tired?" he teased.

"I get thirsty sometimes!" she said with a huge smile.

"Well, I know I can't keep you off the dance floor for long, but this is Elmer Sandhei. He's living on Hilmer Nelson's place west of town," said Elmer Anderson. "His parents will come with his younger brother and sister in the spring," he added with a mischievous grin.

"It's very nice to meet you, Elmer. I'm Muriel," she said to the red-faced newcomer.

Pausing consciously, but not awkwardly, the new Elmer said, "It's nice to meet you, too."

"See you again soon," Muriel said, and bee-lined for the water she had mentioned but was not thirsty for.

Muriel's heart was racing. In a fleeting second, she had decided that a brief encounter might intrigue him. She also had not wanted to make her interest too obvious. And could he see her blushing? Had she handled that correctly? Should she avoid the Elmers for the rest of the night? The questions flooded her brain as she forced herself to drink a glass of water. No sooner had she finished than one of her regular dance partners pulled on her arm. The moment was over, and she made sure not to look in Elmer's direction the rest of the night.

She discreetly watched for Elmer in church each Sunday afterward. Every Sunday, she left disappointed, but he did continue to come to some dances, and the mystique around him grew—at least for Muriel. She found herself thinking about him at school, on her walks to and from school, while she sewed, and as she went to bed. She did not mention anything to her parents, but she heard around school that the Sandheis had lived here twenty-five years ago.

Finally, one Sunday just before school let out for the year, Elmer was in church. In fact, he was there with his parents, his younger brother, and his little sister. "The Sandheis are in church," John whispered to Josephine as the new family sat down. After the service, the Sandheis became the most sought-after people who Muriel could ever recall coming to church. Her father approached Elmer's father with a hardy handshake and a smile, like they were long-lost close friends. That day, when Muriel least expected it, she met all the Sandheis.

The Sandheis, as Muriel learned on the drive home from church, had lived in Fort Ransom long ago, and decided to come back. From then on, she saw the whole family on open nights and in church every Sunday. Elmer was at most dances, and even came to a basket social that summer at Young People's Hall, where all the church youth activities were held. Muriel desperately wished he would bid on her basket, so that the two of them could sit at a table for two and enjoy the lunch she and Josephine had prepared. Really, she did not care about the eating, but she wanted him to somehow know exactly how she would decorate her basket and tie her bow, and pick hers above all the others. Instead, Elmer held back, allowing other men to bid while he observed. Friendly but reserved, he was no more eager to bid on a basket than he was to dance. Elmer was different; he intrigued her.

Muriel knew it was a silly crush and would never come to anything, Still, the more she danced with everybody but Elmer and tried to forget him, the more she thought about him. Her next strategy was to remind herself this was her last year of high school, and next year she would be going to college. She had not talked with her parents about it per se, but they knew how good of a student she was. They knew she had ambition. Besides, Mildred, Harold, and Palmer had gone to college in Valley City.

Muriel could not have been more surprised when her parents asked to talk with her one Sunday afternoon that fall of 1937 after all the harvesting and canning were done. Her mouth grew dry, and her heart raced as she sat down at the kitchen table. At first, her father beat around the bush, talking about the worst farming years he had ever known. She was taken aback that he would talk to *her* about *that*. He had always treated her like a favorite and said he was proud of her. But farming? That was what he talked to the neighbors or Luther about.

Then the real reason for the sit-down became clear. "We understand you might want to go to college." John said. "Before you get your heart set on that, we just want you to know that we don't have the money for college just now."

Silence followed. Muriel held back the tears as complete disappointment set in. She knew there was nothing she could say to change her father's mind. As he got up from the table, her mother followed. The conversation was over. Her dreams of going to college and becoming a teacher were crushed.

INTERLUDE

The Sandheis

ELMER'S BURDEN

ELMER SANDHEI WAS TWO YEARS old when his family departed Fort Ransom in 1914. They were bound for Bucyrus, North Dakota, more than eight hours away in the southwest corner along the North Dakota-South Dakota border of the state. With barely a tree in sight, the hills rolled gently toward infinity, like waves flowing on an open sea. Bucyrus first captivated his father in 1907, when he arrived to stake his claim as a homesteader along the South Dakota border, eight miles south of town. C.A. traveled back and forth between Fort Ransom to teach school and Bucyrus to farm over the next several years. He began living full-time at the homestead only after he had a wife and three children to put down his roots.

Four hard-scrabble homesteads dotted every square mile, delivering skimpy returns to those determined to prove up. Some, like the Sandheis, achieved the feat of proving up and stayed. They lived dirt-poor, tending the idea of next year. Every year provided barely enough returns to justify another. Few people, however, survived the 1930s. On the morning of November 17, 1936, twenty-four-year-old Elmer hugged his mother, shook his father's hand, and left the only home he had ever known. The family intended to start over, and Elmer alone had to bear the initial burden. He was returning to Fort Ransom.

Elmer knew Fort Ransom as his parents' hometown, where he had visited his grandparents a handful of times during the summer. Elmer's mom, Elise Olson, had left Mo I Rana, Norway, with her parents when she was three years old in 1893, bound for Fort Ransom. Grandma and Grandpa Olson still lived on the farm they started at that time, set on the west prairie above town. Their son Oscar—Elmer's bachelor uncle—lived with them and did most of the farming, as kindly Grandpa Olson was every bit his age of seventy-nine. Seven years his junior, Grandma Olson was fun to talk to and seldom sat down. Elmer liked all of them, and appreciated them being his lifeline until spring. Really, though, he hardly knew them.

Elmer's dad, Christian, who everyone called C.A., came alone from Mo I Rana to Fort Ransom at age twenty-one in 1900. Indentured to a farmer who had paid for C.A.'s voyage to America, C.A. worked off his debt while learning English. He teetered between plans to farm or teach, and promptly got his teaching certificate. C.A. then tried to farm *and* teach. During the school term, he taught at the town school in Fort Ransom, and during the summer, he took the train to Bucyrus and walked or caught a wagon ride south to the homestead.

After marrying Elise on her parents' farm in the spring of 1909, the pair left Fort Ransom for good, or so they thought. They had their first child, Harold, in their tarpaper shack at the Adams County homestead nine months later. They broke more ground, raised a garden, and eked out enough of a living to stay for all of 1910. After the dry spring and summer of 1911, though, C.A. again decided to teach in Fort Ransom, where the income was steady and Elise had her mother nearby. Elmer knew that was the reason why he and his younger sister Alfhild were born in Fort Ransom—so that C.A. could make money to invest in the homestead. Elmer's associations to Fort Ransom were nothing more than tidbits and the grandparents whom he occasionally took the train to go visit.

Leaving the homestead in his black 1928 Chevy, Elmer was not yet able to think of what was next. Feeling numb and barren like the frozen brown earth surrounding him, he took the familiar road to Hettinger, the nearest big town at 1,200 people. He lost all sense of time until the tires bounced over the railroad tracks. He pulled into the gas station, where the familiar station attendant knew from the over-packed car that this was the last time they would see one another. "Good luck to you, young man," the attendant commented as Elmer handed him $1.50 with a nod and thanks. "Soon, there won't be anyone left around here."

He might be right, Elmer thought. In Elmer's recollection, his school years on the homestead were abundant ones. They milked ten cows and kept five pigs, two dozen chickens, and up to eight workhorses at any one time. They fed the livestock with their own hay and oats in the winter and pastured the cows and horses in the summer. Sure, there were a few sparse rainfall years, when the livestock survived with less grass and the family had a smaller wheat and oats harvest, but he always had plenty to eat, and the family seemed to have money.

That all changed in the 1930s. Low crop prices, throngs of grasshoppers, and dust storms exacerbated three especially dry years in 1933, 1934, and 1936. In 1936, the worst summer of all, the Sand-

Elmer with his 1928 Chevy at the family's homestead south of Bucyrus, North Dakota, in the mid-1930s. (Courtesy Tom Sandhei)

heis received only three inches of rain. The crops were an utter failure. Most of the cattle in the Sandheis' vicinity had to be disposed of. In July, C.A. traded two cows for hay from a Minnesota farmer. Elmer could still hear his dad saying, "You're saving their lives. As you can see, there's no fodder of any kind to be found around here."

After months of witnessing livestock and hope waste away, Elmer felt an overwhelming urge to escape. The designated day was finally upon him. Elmer stopped only at the gas gauge's urging that afternoon. He ate the cured beef sandwich his mother sent as he drove eastward across the grey-brown plains and nursed the canteen of water. He wished for coffee after the second sandwich, but had none. His mind stayed vacant on the straight road through the countryside, dotted here and there with farms whose houses and barns seemed asleep. A smattering of cows and horses stirred, but he saw no people. Finally, he started registering the landmarks his father had vividly described to him, and saw his own farm, situated just off the gravel road in a mature grove of trees. He pulled into the driveway, parked in front of the house, and exhaled the months of awaited relief from desolation.

Elmer had an hour before the darkness set in to bring in his clothes and bedding, light a couple of lamps, and start a fire to start warming up the house. It was a two-story white house, every room small and dingy-white, with one bedroom on the main level and two bedrooms upstairs. Elmer closed the door at the base of the steps, as he would live completely on the main level that winter. The owners, Hilmer and Dagmar Nelson, had left him a table, chairs, and a few basic furnishings. Hilmer had left several days ago to join his sister Dagmar in Wisconsin, where she worked as a bookkeeper and he started as a laborer at the same manufacturing company.

The farm consisted of a cattle barn, chicken coop, granary, and corn crib in a neat cluster southwest of the house, all painted in a deep, barn red. In between the outbuildings and the house was a small white workshop, and the outhouse stood at the edge of the tree grove out back. The farmstead was part of a 160-acre parcel on the west prairie, situated two miles west of Fort Ransom atop the Sheyenne Valley. Elmer's dad had rented it in the hopes that farming in eastern North Dakota would prove better than in western North Dakota. In a letter before the decision was made on Fort Ransom, Grandma Olson passed along Grandpa's description of the 1936 harvest around Fort Ransom as "next to nothing." But, she lobbied, "The livestock had enough to eat and drink. You'll have some trees for protection from the elements, and you'll have family here. We'll be here to help in every way we can."

Grandpa and Grandma Olson were expecting Elmer for supper. Conveniently, they lived just half a mile away. But that night, crossing the road seemed too far to have to go. He wished he could ignore his hunger, not have to talk to anyone, and just go to bed. He wanted to sleep off the old homestead and start fresh on his own tomorrow.

Instead, he drove to his grandparents' house, where Grandma Olson could hardly wait to feed him a huge supper of ham and potatoes and hear all about his drive, his plans, and the family back in Bucyrus. The conversation was livelier than Elmer was accustomed to, and he liked it. His grandma invited him to a second helping of everything, which he accepted. His grandpa added a fresh log to the stove before Elmer ever felt a chill. After supper, his grandma brought warm rice pudding with raisins to the table in glass goblets. "We're going to put some meat on those bones this winter," she commented.

The dinner scene was entirely different from the one he knew on the homestead. He and his siblings typically ate in near-silence, and they devoured the meal put in front of them. C.A. waited until the house noticeably cooled before putting more lignite in the stove. Meat was becoming a treat, and dessert was reserved for holidays. But that night, Elmer drove back to his new home feeling stuffed. His grandma was right; his 6'4" frame frame really could afford to gain a few pounds. He caught himself smiling as he thought back on her lighthearted way of saying he was skinny.

The next morning, Elmer awoke with a start at dawn to get the barn ready for the three cows and seven horses that the livestock hauler would drop off in the next couple of hours. He and his dad had determined that all the surviving cows and horses, save one milk cow, had to winter with Elmer in Fort Ransom, or face near-certain death in Bucyrus. Elmer's main job was to tend to them until the rest of the family moved to Fort Ransom in the spring of 1937. As Elmer walked out the front door, Uncle Oscar was just pulling into the yard with hay and feed and, to Elmer's delight, a small thermos of coffee. "Ma needs the thermos back, so drink up," Oscar said with a smile.

Elmer followed the order, and thought it was the best cup of coffee he had tasted. "Egg coffee," Oscar clarified. Elmer knew he was rather old for spoiling, but he could get used to his grandma's special treatment. For all he knew, mixing coffee grounds with a raw egg was not special in Fort Ransom. Maybe ham suppers and egg coffee were common fare here. Elmer had no concept of norms outside of Adams County.

Oscar and Elmer got to work, and by the time they finished setting up, the livestock hauler was backing up to the barn. Elmer greeted him with a handshake and confirmation he was at the right place. As he started to unload the cows and horses, Elmer saw Oscar's shocked expression. Oscar said nothing and blinked his moist eyes hard. The emaciated livestock emerged slowly, with distended bones and hollow eyes. A somber Elmer patted each of them on the neck, saying, "Okay, girls. You're gonna be okay now. C'mon. Come get some oats."

Elmer was accustomed to seeing malnourished livestock. He detested it, and he wished he could change it. Nonetheless, his shock had faded away. Now, witnessing Oscar's horror, Elmer suddenly felt sick to his stomach. He wondered, had the drought hardened him? In that moment, Elmer resolved that getting the three cows and seven horses healthy again was his full-time job. The neighbors had no doubt seen their share of thin cattle after 1934 and '36, but apparently nothing like these sad creatures from western North Dakota. He worked out the feeding plans with Oscar.

So began Elmer's first winter as a farmer in his own right, in an unfamiliar place that he already believed was better than the God-forsaken place he had come from. In the days and weeks that followed, he enjoyed three meals a day in Grandma Olson's kitchen. He even added a few pounds of "meat on those bones," as she predicted. And he made good on his aim to put weight on the livestock while he got the barn and workshop set up to his liking.

By the time the New Year came around, twenty-four-year-old Elmer knew his routine and noticed he had time on his hands. His grandma always invited him to stay longer and play a few hands of rummy or whist. His uncle and grandpa introduced him to the neighbors—Carl Thompson, Ole Olson, Art Anderson, and Elmer Anderson. Elmer found Carl particularly interesting, mostly for his stories about the great times he had as a young man with C.A., Elmer's father. Elmer had only heard his father's version in a scholarly bent, whereas Carl made C.A. sound almost fun and carefree. Still, in spite of his grandparents' good intentions to keep him company, Elmer wanted a bit more variety.

Elmer's new friends sensed his restlessness and knew firsthand all about it. So, they invited him into town to play pool at Collette's Café. There were no drinking establishments in town, and Elmer was not much of a drinker anyway. He took a liking to pool, appreciating the focus it required and the natural comradery it provided. His main competitor was Emil Pederson, who also became his closest friend. The two young men were the best pool players and most likeable guys around, though they both downplayed compliments from anyone who said they were the best at anything.

One Saturday afternoon in February, Elmer Anderson came into Collette's as Emil and Elmer were finishing a pool game. Elmer Anderson, always fun loving, told them he and his wife Mildred were going to the dance at the hall that night. They should come along, he said, "for a change of scenery." Emil had other plans. Elmer also resisted at first, citing "no dancing skills whatsoever."

"You don't have to dance. There will be lots of us at the back just talking and watching," Elmer Anderson retorted, adding, "There will also be lots of single girls there."

His inhibitions worn down, Elmer relented with a glint in his eyes, "Okay, okay. This will probably be the first and last time."

Elmer went home to prepare himself. He was always presentable in public, as his parents had taught him. He never left home without washing his face and combing his hair, and he sat down at his grandma's table with freshly washed hands. But he generally only shaved every other day, sometimes stretching into the third day. He had only put on his nice gray slacks and white button-town shirt twice—for Thanksgiving and Christmas—since arriving in Fort Ransom. That afternoon, he bathed as he always did on Saturday, and then carefully shaved, slicked his dark hair back with Brylcreem, and put on his dressy outfit. He added the light blue sweater that his grandma had knitted him for Christmas, but quickly took it off, thinking it reeked of trying too hard. He took a last look in the small, hazy bedroom mirror and left for supper at his grandparents' house.

"Don't you look nice!" his grandma greeted him as he let himself in the door. "You must have a date tonight."

"No, Grandma," Elmer blushed. "Elmer talked me into going with him and his wife Mildred to the dance tonight."

"Oh!" she said. "That'll be fun for you."

Elmer's grandpa and uncle overheard talk of the dance and asked nothing else about it, just like they never asked him about his pool playing at Collette's. They were happy that Elmer was having a good time, like a young man should, but neither dances nor pool were their scene. The Olsons did their open night business on Tuesdays and Saturdays and came straight home. Every other Sunday, when church was at Standing Rock, they drove into town for church. Those were their routine outings.

As Elmer exited his grandparents' house that night, his grandma gave his wool coat a last-minute dusting off with her hands and wished, "Have fun tonight, Elmer. I know you'll be good."

Elmer was unsure what exactly she meant, other than to be on his best behavior, which he thought he nearly always was. He supposed she just worried about him. The only thing he was nervous about as he drove into town was his two left feet. He had no intention of dancing and hoped he would not somehow be talked into it. His plan was to shoot the breeze with Elmer and any other guys he knew there and see if there were any pretty single girls from Fort Ransom. He probably would not talk to any of them, but at least he would know who they were.

He met his friends at the hall just after 8:00, and already the dance floor was full. Neither Elmer was a dancer, as it turned out, so they hung back and talked over the orchestra music. Elmer met as many people that night as he had met altogether in the previous three months. If he would have been tested on their names, he would have failed, but most of them had heard about him. His last name got him an instant pat on the shoulder from the older men he met, who asked the same general questions. "Your dad is a great man. How is he doing? When is he coming back to Fort Ransom?"

Others said, "Oh! You're Hans and Petrine Olson's grandson! I've heard so much about you."

Elmer did not ask for the details of what Grandma Olson had shared. He knew from people's tones that his Sandhei name and Olson relatives were enough to give him instant credibility in Fort Ransom. They liked him by association. This was a new feeling for him. Of course, his family was respected in Adams County, but Elmer had played a role in that. Here, he had done almost nothing yet to earn a good reputation. He had not even gone to church, other than to the Christmas service with his grandparents.

Elmer kept busy enough meeting people and talking with Elmer Anderson that he had only noticed a few girls whirling around the dance floor. According to Elmer Anderson, two of them had boyfriends, one he did not know (so she must be from another town), and the fourth was a girl named Muriel Henrickson. She was petite and wore a navy-blue dress dotted with pink flowers that gathered at her small waist and barely passed her knees. She had an easy smile. Dancing all night, with a different partner to every song, she struck him as fun, even flirty. She danced with other girls, and when she did, she led. Muriel skimmed the dance floor, with energy springing up from her feet.

"Muriel is in high school!" Elmer Anderson yelled over the music. "I don't even know if she's a senior! But she is quite the dancer, and she is popular. Should I introduce you?"

"No, not tonight," Elmer said, and that was that.

He drove away thinking about two girls that night. By the time he made it home, though, only Muriel was on his mind. Sure, she was younger than he was, but she could not be that much younger. Muriel popped into his mind when he woke up, while he worked, and when he went to bed for two weeks, until the next dance in Fort Ransom. This time, Elmer Anderson had no problem talking Elmer into going along.

Elmer put as much or more effort into getting ready that Saturday. His grandma handed over his freshly ironed gray slacks and white shirt with a grin, but no comment, after dinner. He even added the light blue sweater to his outfit, which she was so proud to see when he came over for supper before the dance. "It matches your eyes to a tee!" she said, covering her smile with her hands to hide a few absent teeth. At the dance, several of the women he had met two weeks earlier approached him with almost the same compliment, confirming for him that the sweater was a good addition.

Elmer really only cared about one girl's opinion, though. He wondered if he would meet Muriel that night. He was not sure how, because he did not want to make his interest obvious, nor want to dance. Instead, he wished for the meeting to happen naturally. And so, with no real plan, he stood next to Elmer Anderson again, and just like two weeks before, he met some new people who came and went from their conversation. A few asked if he was a dancer. "No experience," was his polite reply. "I'm more of a talker."

More than two hours into the dance, when the two Elmers were standing alone, the moment came more naturally than Elmer could have scripted it. As Muriel walked past them on her way to the water cooler, she said hello. Elmer did not really hear what Elmer Anderson said in response, but whatever it was got a stop-you-in-your-tracks smile from Muriel, who had a cute little gap between her two front teeth. Then came the introduction.

"It's very nice to meet you, Elmer," she said with a voice much bigger than her tiny frame. "I'm Muriel."

Elmer felt his face turn red, and he hoped the words he said really came out as, "It's nice to meet you, too."

Then Muriel brought her hand up as if to wave goodbye, and the moment was over. The two Elmers stood silently with boyish grins, making sure she was far away before they spoke another word.

"She's fifteen years old, Elmer. She's a junior in high school," Elmer Anderson said, as though his new friend was about to get himself into trouble.

"Fifteen? Wow. Okay," Elmer said. "I might have to wait a bit on that one."

Waiting, in fact, was the central theme of Elmer's first six months in Fort Ransom. While he continued to attend most of the dances and always saw Muriel there, he did not talk with her again, and did not even consider it. He just thought about her—the same way he had thought about the cute new girl at country school who had made the eighth grade worthwhile, or the beautiful woman who had begged him to waltz at the one dance he had attended in Hettinger. For the time being, Muriel was too young to pursue, and no other girl he saw interested him. And so, he continued the rotation of working, playing pool, and going to his grandparents' house. With the onset of spring, he started to work longer hours at both farms, helping his grandpa and Oscar with their work to earn his keep, while setting up his dad's place to prepare for the family's arrival at planting time.

On the first warm day in April, Elmer and Oscar hauled over the chickens and hogs that they had saved for C.A.'s place. The cows and horses looked up in surprise at the new arrivals, but quickly went back to swishing their tails in the warm sunshine as they nibbled the first shoots of emerging green grass. The animals were not only healthy, but content. As the livestock settled in and Elmer and Oscar paused at the fence next to the barn, Oscar patted his nephew twice on the shoulder. Elmer had done his job.

NATIVE SONS

IT WAS MOTHER'S DAY 1937, and the Sandheis were determined to make it their first day back in church at Standing Rock. Elise and nine-year-old Elsa Mae had been in Fort Ransom since April, when they caught a ride with another neighbor leaving Bucyrus, but C.A. and fourteen-year-old Chester had arrived just two days ago in the 1922 Chevy. They were barely settled in at the Nelson place and even less on top of all the work to be done on the farm. Still, going to church as a family came first. They must make a good impression. Led by C.A. in his double-breasted gray suit and Elise in a navy dress with matching jacket and hat, the family sat down next to Grandpa and Grandma Olson, who complimented Elsa Mae on her pink floral dress and matching hair bow and the boys on their suits and ties. C.A. and Elise quietly greeted a few familiar faces near them, and whispered to each other as they identified a few old friends in the crowd. It felt like home, even if the homecoming was bittersweet.

C.A. could not be seen as a failure. Yes, he had returned to the place he had left twenty-three years ago for something better. Unfortunately, he had no more pennies to his name now than before. On the other hand, C.A. had experienced a great adventure at the Bucyrus homestead. He had grazed cattle in America's widest-open country and seen buffalo bones and coal veins in the hillsides. He had also survived the worst sustained drought in history and made the wise choice to leave before it potentially got even worse. He had brought his family, perfectly well-dressed and cared for, back to their roots and Elise's family. This day was not humiliating, but it was humbling.

After church, it became clear to the Sandheis that Fort Ransom was always welcoming to its native sons. "I've heard only good things about all of you," Pastor Sandanger said to C.A. in the greeting line. "You're not just one of ours; you're one of us."

Seemingly every old friend of C.A. and Elise approached the family outside the church that day, all saying how wonderful it was to have them back home, and many of them saying what a nice young man Elmer was. Elmer did not know most of these people and had no idea what nice things they were referring to. Outside of Christmas, he had not even gone to church.

Many of C.A.'s former students from Fort Ransom School greeted them as well. Elmer knew his dad as a farmer, not as a teacher, because C.A.'s last year of teaching was 1913–1914, when Elmer was a toddler. But C.A. had taught school for seven years in Fort Ransom, and he seemed to have been a very popular teacher. Common comments outside the church that day were "I learned more from you than anyone" and "You were the hardest teacher, but also the most interesting." Elmer was not surprised. His dad was hard on him too, and still C.A. had taught him almost everything he knew.

One family that approached the Sandheis held more interest than the others, from Elmer's point of view. He was hoping Muriel's father might have been a friend of C.A., and indeed he was. Elmer did not know why that friendship was important to him, given that he had not talked to Muriel since the night he met her, and she was too young for him to pursue. Nevertheless, his heart skipped a beat when she walked his way with her parents and brother. The fathers were not just friends; they were great friends and close in age. C.A. introduced the whole family to Josephine and John Henrickson, who then presented Muriel and Andor, who went by "Pud"—no explanation given. Muriel and Elmer nodded at each other with grins, signaling to their parents they knew each other. "We met at a dance," Muriel said. "Hi, Elmer."

"Hi, Muriel," he said, blushing again, which went unnoticed in the excitement of the reunion.

Josephine and Elise were as happy to see one another as their husbands were. They exchanged highlights on their grown children, including Elise and C.A.'s Harold and Alfhild, who were teaching in western North Dakota, and too many Henricksons for Elmer to follow. From the conversation's perimeter, the children listened politely to their mothers' stories of knowing each other "forever" through church. Elmer was doing his best to take mental notes of the details, even though he may never have the occasion to utilize them.

As of that day, the C.A. Sandheis officially became part of Fort Ransom again. Adults treated them like they'd been there all along, and the youth seemed to intuitively know to welcome Elmer, Chester, and Elsa Mae into the fold. Optimism sprang fresh.

The C.A. and Elise Sandhei family, circa 1941. Back, left to right: Elmer, Harold, Chester. Front, left to right: Elsa Mae, C.A., Elise, and Alfhild. (Courtesy Tom Sandhei)

PART TWO

Muriel's Story

WOMANHOOD

MURIEL, BARELY A SENIOR IN high school in 1937 when her father informed her that she would not be going to college, was on the brink of womanhood. She was not going to be a college student or teacher, as she had wished. But perhaps she could pursue stenography work in Minneapolis, as Frances and Bernice had, and move in with them. Maybe she would meet Prince Charming at a dance, and he would sweep her off her feet and into his own life. She did not know what was to come.

With college out of the question, Muriel saw no point in aiming for straight As. Grades would not matter if she was to become a seamstress, waitress, or farmwife. Besides, she would probably still get Bs doing the bare minimum. With a new, carefree outlook, Muriel set out to give minimal effort and have more fun. She stopped studying for tests. She made excuses to her mother about delays after school.

Three weeks after Muriel began coasting, Mr. Skonnard suspected this was more than a case of senioritis. He pulled Muriel aside after school and spoke right to the heart of the problem. "I'm noticing a change in you, Muriel. I'm concerned. Valley City Teachers' College will be concerned if you keep this up much longer."

Facing criticism from her favorite teacher, Muriel was so horrified that she instantly divulged that she would not be going to college. Mr. Skonnard let her speak without interruption. When she finished, he waited for her breath to slow and the silence to hang in the air for a few seconds.

"This all makes sense now, Muriel. I understand why your parents are unable to send you to college. And I know you must feel like your studies are suddenly less important," Mr. Skonnard said. "But why let the short term ruin the long term? You've been working your whole life for this year. Don't throw all of that work away now. Finish school the way you started. Show us who you really are. You are a bright young woman with some of the best grades in school. You are an optimist. Just because college is unattainable right now, doesn't mean it's unattainable forever."

Muriel paused and thought. Maybe college was just one good farming year away. She and Mr. Skonnard proceeded to have an honest, adult conversation. They talked about school and hopes and dreams. Thanking him and walking out the school door fifteen minutes later, she felt her optimism swell. From that moment on, school itself became fun again. She enjoyed her classes, knowing that they might serve her one day in ways she could not yet imagine. Her attitude at home improved because she knew the situation was beyond her parents' control. Doing her best at school and at home in no way limited her weekend entertainment, either. By day she skied or trekked through the woods with Clarice and Ardis, and by night they danced in Fort Ransom or a few miles away in Kathryn, Nome, or Englevale. Life as a senior was good, Muriel thought. Mr. Skonnard's advice to make the most of this year was just what she needed to hear.

Of course, while Muriel's dance card was full of boys who had asked her on dates, the one man she wanted to ask her still had not. She dreamt daily of walking or dancing with Elmer Sandhei, but she realized the feelings were possibly one-sided. And so, while she regularly eyed Elmer standing in the back at dances, she looked for others who might strike her fancy just as much. She saw him at church every Sunday too, but in conversations afterward, the women generally gathered in their small circles, and the men in theirs. She and Elmer seldom came face to face. When they did, they gave each other a smile and the basic, "Hello. How are you? Well."

Muriel appreciated Elmer's proper use of "well" rather than "good," and concluded he must be smart and worldly. All the young and middle-aged men seemed to seek him out, so she also perceived him to be a great conversationalist. Nobody else held Muriel's curiosity the way that Elmer did.

Muriel (right) and Ardis Rufsvold regularly skied the hills around Fort Ransom. Circa 1938. (Courtesy Tom Sandhei)

When Muriel graduated in May 1938, she had done what she had set out to do the previous fall. The Depression had not spoiled her senior year. She had fun and still received college-worthy grades. "Well done, Muriel. I'm proud of you," Mr. Skonnard said.

Mr. Skonnard shared his praise with her parents, which to them was nearly as good as Jesus himself commending Muriel. By the middle of summer, his words had travelled to all of her siblings, Pastor Sandanger, and Elmer's parents—among others. Muriel was a "top student" and a "nice girl"—and those were just the qualities she had heard about. That summer, her parents gave her the autonomy to go to every dance and outing she was invited to, from picnics to swimming to fireworks. Her mother only asked who she was going with, and the answer was almost always Clarice and Ardis, who as cousins, were pre-approved. Also, if Pud wanted to go along, Muriel had to bring him. Pud was an easy passenger, and half the time, including Pud meant picking up his friend Chester Sandhei. Those arrangements were more than agreeable to Muriel, who hoped for an extra sighting of Elmer. For all of these benefits, Muriel silently thanked Mr. Skonnard. Right or wrong, she thought his approval had set her up for this new level of freedom.

The flurry of activity essentially cancelled out her disappointment that for at least a year, she was to remain at home with her parents, Luther, and Pud. Mildred was about to marry Loubert Rufsvold, a local farmer, leaving Muriel as Josephine's only kitchen and garden helper. Muriel only hoped to not be on her way to being an Old Maid.

Finally, days after she turned seventeen, Muriel got the sign she had been waiting for on a hot, humid open night in Fort Ransom. Somehow, she and Elmer were the last two left in a group gathered on Main Street as the sun sank past the hills, and they just kept talking. Muriel made sure to indicate she was staying on the farm for a while, but she thought most of what she shared about herself was blather. She was unaccustomed to nervousness. What came naturally to her was curiosity, so she settled into asking Elmer questions about his life. He told her about the homestead in Bucyrus and how desolate it was compared to Fort Ransom. He talked about hunting rabbits and teaching his parents how to use the radio. They laughed loudly about their parents' amazement at telephones and sound in movies. As their nerves faded in the darkness, he said he would see her at the next dance.

Indeed, they did see each other, and Muriel decided to walk past Elmer. Before she knew it, she heard herself saying, "I need to cool off. Should we talk outside?"

Elmer asked Muriel on a date that night. The next Saturday, Elmer picked her up, greeted her parents, and took her to a movie in Lisbon. The next Saturday, they went again. The courtship was on. Muriel's parents could not have been happier about the new pair. In the year and a half since the Sandheis had been back in Fort Ransom, the parents had grown closer, the children had visited back and forth at each other's houses, and Pud and Chester had become close friends. They went to church together, they saw each other at every school function, and Muriel's father referred to them as "good Norwegians—some of the best."

Her parents agreed that Elmer and Muriel's age difference was of little concern, as Elmer was "mature," and Muriel was "just the right age" to find a nice man. They trusted Elmer explicitly. He became one of the family in the coming months. When he came to pick up Muriel, he came ten minutes early, just so he could talk to John and Luther. Her parents said nothing on the topic of dancing, but it was not lost on Muriel that they probably were pleased that he was not a dancer. They no longer needed to wonder about the intentions of Muriel's dance partners. Now she had good, dependable Elmer.

Elmer teased Muriel that maybe he really was a good dancer. "You haven't seen my skills, so how do you know?" he said, laughing. "Either way, I'm too tall for you to dance with."

And so, the Scenic Theater in Lisbon became their favorite date spot. They made the fifteen-mile trek on the dirt road most weekends, lured by movie stars like Clark Gable, Katharine Hepburn, and James Stewart. Muriel did not care what movie they saw; she enjoyed the car ride with Elmer just as much or more than any movie. They talked about every topic under the sun, agreed on most subjects, and shared inside jokes about Fort Ransom. "Thank goodness you aren't one of those Stiklestad Lutherans," Muriel teased.

Months passed, and Muriel's thoughts of college faded. By the spring of 1939, her relationship with Elmer was getting serious enough so that they had talked about their future. He even came to Josephine's Easter dinner. Muriel suspected that once she turned eighteen, Elmer might ask her to marry him. Her daydream now was a wedding, wearing a white satin dress with a lace inlet around the neck and slight puff at the shoulders, holding a bouquet of pink roses. She imagined the two-tier white cake, topped with a Kewpie bride and groom. While Elmer focused on a place to live, Muriel thought of the piano, sewing machine, and silverware.

Toiling in the garden every day, mother and daughter were an efficient pair in need of a larger team. They worked in near-silence, innately sensing what the other was doing. Muriel weaved and bent over the cucumbers and other vining plants, leaving the straight, visible rows of radishes and carrots to her mother. Mostly thinking of Elmer, Muriel's other main wish was for the companionship of her sisters, particularly Frances, who lightened the work and the humid summer air. She remarked how Josephine often had the same thought at the same time, standing up straight and noting in her own way, "We're one woman short again."

Already shorthanded, Muriel realized one muggy August day: How on earth would Josephine make it on her own after Muriel was married? She could not get married and leave her mother alone on the farm. Muriel waited to raise the concern with Elmer, though. He had enough issues already. His father could not farm without him and Chester any more than John could function without Luther and Pud. Their dads were in their sixties! The sons were doing the bulk of the physical labor. A barrage of problems raced through Muriel's head, until the answer on the Henrickson farm became painfully evident. She sensed from her father and Luther's rumblings that they were going to lose the farm.

Muriel felt as though she had missed the announcement. First, it was implied, and then it was assumed. Around here, that was the way to handle an unpleasant topic. She learned from Elmer, of all people, that Luther was making plans to leave the next spring for parts unknown. Muriel did not know what was going on inside her own house. Would her parents move to town? Did they want her to get married, so she was no longer their responsibility? At home, Muriel acted like life was normal, because her mother and father said nothing about any imminent changes. But her worry grew, and the only person she confided in was Elmer. They shared everything. He wanted to marry her, but knew his dad wanted him to stay on the farm. She assumed her parents would be thrilled if they got married but was unsure of the timing. Meanwhile, halfway around the world, Adolf Hitler had started a war in Europe. Was America going to get involved? The uncertainty swirled, and Elmer and Muriel let it, at least for now.

DISGRACES

THERE WERE TWO WORDS THAT were only whispered in Fort Ransom: "Catholic" and "expecting." A third word—"pregnant"—was considered profanity. Muriel only knew one Catholic family in town, the Collettes, who owned Collette's Café and the new tavern. "They go to church in Lisbon," her parents explained. She was not certain of any girls who had gotten pregnant before marriage. But she had heard gossip about a few babies who were born a bit too soon after a wedding. She had also wondered about the sudden departure of a girl to an aunt's house in Fargo. All she knew for certain was that expecting a baby before marriage was the biggest of all disgraces. Even married women were "expecting," and it was impolite to discuss.

In early December 1939, a fear of the biggest disgrace overcame Muriel. At first, she told herself that her math was probably wrong. But after three consecutive mornings with a nauseous stomach, her body was confirming what she already suspected. She was expecting! Her good Lutheran parents had raised her properly. She went to church every Sunday. Everyone in Fort Ransom thought she was a nice girl. Yet, here she was, unmarried and soon to have a baby.

After the certainty sank in, Muriel blurted the news to Elmer on their next date. He sat in silence for a moment, looking out the car window as the motor idled and Muriel awaited a word, a gesture, or any comfort he could find to give her. He hugged her, and they agreed to keep the baby a secret until they had some time to think. Their situation would be a total scandal if anyone in Fort Ransom found out about it.

Christmas and the New Year came and went. Muriel felt like "expecting" was practically written across her forehead, but no one suspected it. She and Elmer started to plan their future. First, Elmer was going to do right by Muriel. They would go away and get married, he told her. He would find a farming job, like Luther had done for the next summer. He even gently enquired with Luther, who gave no indication of catching on to his sister's predicament. But no specific plan panned out, and they were running out of time.

They decided to tell their parents in late February. Muriel confessed the news to her mother first. As hard as that was, she anticipated Josephine being the kindest of any adult. Muriel's instinct was right. Josephine gently listened and reassured her that they would figure out how to handle it. "You and Elmer just need to get married right away. And maybe get away," Josephine said. "Our family has never been the subject of gossip, and that doesn't need to change now."

Before that, though, they had to tell Muriel's father. Coupled with his farm finance troubles, the timing was terrible. Never had Muriel dreaded a conversation more. Her feistiness had shrunk under the weight of her secret. What a foreign feeling this was to a girl who previously had been confident.

Muriel came down from her bedroom when she knew Josephine had delivered afternoon coffee to John at the table. Standing before him, she looked into the eyes of the father she had always adored. As apologetically as she could, she said, "Elmer and I are going to have a baby. We're going to get married."

John sat up straight and banged his cup down on the table. "Shameful," he uttered as he turned away.

It was the first unkind word he had said to her in her entire life. Bowing her head, Muriel stood stiffly and waited for any other words to come. Her heart nearly pounded out of her chest in the cold silence. Muriel glanced at her expressionless mother and knew to get out of her father's sight that instant.

When Josephine came to her bedside several minutes later, she provided the plan. "You can't stay here in your condition," she said calmly, touching Muriel's shoulder. "We will find somewhere for you to go and get married. I'll reach out to Bernice, and to my sisters if need be. Until then, you stay close to me."

A week later, Bernice wrote home from Minneapolis with a better prospect than anyone could have anticipated. Bernice's roommate had a brother, Ralph, living in Billings, Montana. Ralph had a connection to a big rancher looking for someone who was good with horses and livestock.[17] Muriel got the information to Elmer before the day was out, and the next morning, Elmer phoned Charles Pelton, who owned a ranch near Fishtail in south central Montana. The Peltons kept 1,300 sheep, 40 cattle, 30 horses, and a few feeder pigs on 5,000 acres. Five thousand! Accustomed to 160 acres, give or take, Elmer was impressed.

Elmer had never worked with sheep before, but he knew cows and horses well, and thought of himself as a fast learner. Charles—quickly insisting on "Charley"—was more than satisfied with Elmer's credentials. Elmer then indicated that he had a bride-to-be; might there be work for her? In fact, yes. Charley's wife Gladys could use a steady farm girl's help in the kitchen and garden. Elmer pressed on with the delicacy of the situation, and Charley practically stopped him before he started. If the young pair could work hard, they had jobs and comfortable quarters awaiting them in Montana. The particulars would be figured out in person.

With plans in place, it was Elmer's turn to tell his parents the news. Knowing that Chester would now be the one pressured to stay on the farm, Elmer told his brother first, while they cleaned barn stalls. Chester grinned and did not know what to say, but he agreed

---

[17] Gary Henrickson, phone interview with Tom Sandhei, 18 October 2020. Bill Pelton, phone interview with Tricia Velure, 16 October 2020. Extensive research exposed no definite connections between the Sandheis or Henricksons to Elmer and Muriel's known destination and place of residence in Montana. The most plausible connection found is through Bernice's roommate Nora Holman, whose brother Ralph was living and working in Billings according to the 1940 Census, and who was living in Absarokee, Montana, by 1945. Nora married Bernice and Muriel's brother Palmer in 1945, and Gary is their son. The Peltons knew Ralph Holman, according to Bill Pelton, but it is unclear if they knew him as far back as 1940. Bill Pelton is the grandson of Charles Pelton.

to stay away from afternoon coffee. Elmer was more worried about how his father would react to the news of him leaving home than he was the reason why. In the eyes of Fort Ransomites, unwed pregnancy was the woman's responsibility. As long as Elmer did right by Muriel, he was fulfilling his duty.

"I have news . . . Muriel is going to have a baby," Elmer told his parents. "We're going to Montana to get married. I've already lined up work for us there."

C.A. stared at Elmer, and then over him, at the kitchen wall. No words could convey the disappointment of a Norwegian father toward his wayward child—even if that child was twenty-eight years old. In C.A.'s point of view, Elmer was supposed to stay on this farm forever, just like his uncle Oscar was doing. In an even worse blow, Elmer's departure was on account of a girl. C.A. stood up from the table, put on his coat, and walked outside. Elise, finally able to share her feelings, clenched Elmer's hand. In no rush, they shared the table, and Elmer told his mother all he knew.

Final preparations ensued for Elmer and Muriel, each on their respective farms on opposite sides of Fort Ransom. They packed all their clothes, for both summer and winter, and told no one else outside of their houses. The story in Fort Ransom was to be that the young couple had eloped to Montana, which in essence was true.

On the morning of March 16, 1940, Elmer hauled hay with his brother Chester like he had so many times before. Wasting no time after they finished, Elmer packed his 1936 Chevy with the minimum of belongings and said his farewells. His father shook his hand firmly and emptily wished his son well. C.A. had not mentioned Muriel's name since Elmer delivered the news. His mother's face was warm, and she hugged him tightly. As they released, she said, "Drive safely. Call when you get to the ranch."

Muriel, on the other hand, had a tearful goodbye with her mother and Pud. Her father refused to say goodbye at all and was in the barn before Elmer drove up. Completely devastated, Muriel looked at Josephine as if to ask if he was coming but knew in her heart he was not. About to leave home forever, she could not make things right. Her father's "shameful" rebuke echoed inside her. There was nothing more to say. Muriel turned to her Elmer, who nodded in deference to his future mother-in-law and led his fiancé to the car.

The couple silently turned out of the muddy driveway, gazing through the windshield at their future. Muriel gently pressed her handkerchief to her cheek as one tear dropped, then another. Around them, water droplets tried to fall from the ice-covered tree branches, touched lightly by the nearly-noon sun. Spring was coming.

The trip west was solemn, yet the anticipation could not be denied as they got on Highway 10, heading west to Montana.[18] The paved road was a first for Muriel. Few cars were on the road. They stopped in Jamestown, Bismarck, and Dickinson to stretch their legs and eat the sandwiches and potato lefse that Josephine sent with them. The soggy barrenness of North Dakota in March stretched before them. The ditches were full of dirty snow, while the black soil was making an appearance in the surrounding fields.

Crossing the border into Montana, her adventure with Elmer now felt official. This was easily the farthest away from home that Muriel had been in her lifetime. They were about to make their first major stop: Glendive, Montana. The couple spent their first night together in a motel. The next morning, they went to church and introduced themselves to Pastor E. E. Tollefson after the service. Pastor Tollefson summoned them to the parsonage for coffee later that afternoon. Elmer and Muriel passed time at the local lunch counter and were right on time for the polite preaching session at the parsonage. Mrs. Pelton, such a "good Christian woman," had "generously" phoned him to express her and her husband's support of the marriage, he said. Once the couple expressed their earnestness, Pastor Tollefson announced that Mr. and Mrs. Erick Walseth, esteemed elders in the parish, had agreed to serve as their witnesses the next day.

---

[18] Construction of the Interstate Highway System in North Dakota did not begin until the 1950s. Highway 10 was the main east-to-west road across North Dakota. It was a paved two-lane road in 1940.

**Elmer and Muriel in what the authors believe is their wedding photo.
The couple married in Glendive, Montana, on March 18, 1940.**
(Courtesy Tom Sandhei)

Muriel's heart raced as she and Elmer walked into the courthouse the next morning. He was handsome in a solid gray suit and plaid silk tie in gray and burgundy. She did not even care that hers was a baby blue hand-me-down, a bit dowdy for the occasion. It was a far cry from the white satin dress of her dreams, but an adventure with Elmer in Montana was far superior to the same-old stiffness of life in Fort Ransom. As the clerk signed the marriage license, Muriel wore true excitement on her face, something she had not felt since she learned she was expecting! Before lunch on March 18, 1940, Muriel became Mrs. Elmer Sandhei. Young and in love, the couple shook hands with the three strangers at their wedding ceremony and hurried to their car.

A SUMMER'S DREAM

WITHIN A FEW MINUTES OF saying, "I do," Elmer and Muriel continued their journey toward south central Montana. Daylight could not be wasted with so many hours of driving ahead of them. Muriel's perpetual smile had spread to Elmer's face by this point, and the adrenaline made Elmer's foot a bit heavier as they sped away from Glendive. Talking and laughing, they paid almost no attention for the first hour on the road. Then, as the vastness of the countryside grew and their conversation waned, Muriel found music on KGHL out of Billings. Through their newlywed eyes and ears, this was splendor. This was their new life.

They pulled off the road in the mid-afternoon to stretch and eat the last two pieces of Josephine's lefse. Just when they thought life could not get any better, they saw mountains—snow-covered mountains, no less! Neither one of them had seen hills bigger than the ones in Fort Ransom until passing through Medora just a couple days ago. Muriel suddenly felt the world taking her breath away and wondered if Elmer sensed it as deeply as she did.

They drove until darkness set in, and then stopped in Billings to find a hot meal and a motel room. But the honeymoon was brief. After breakfast the next morning, they set out on the last leg of the journey. Charley and Gladys Pelton were expecting them for dinner at noon.

Passing the Stillwater County seat of Columbus, and then Absarokee, the directions Gladys sent in her letter were getting more detailed as the mountains became closer and larger. Hundreds of sheep peacefully grazed in the barely green pastures surrounding the muddy road. Horses swung their tails happily in the spring sunshine, and cows gazed at the car like it was a stranger of little consequence. Drawing near the Pelton ranch, Elmer and Muriel passed Fishtail—an even smaller village than Fort Ransom—and made their final turn onto West Rosebud Road.

They drove right up to the Pelton ranch, and they could barely believe their eyes. Before them was the most beautiful house—a huge cobblestone foursquare with a crisp white front porch along the whole length of the house! Silent awe overtook them.

Then Muriel let out a happy, "Aah!" and Elmer laughed. She put her hand over his hand on his lap and squeezed tightly.

The Peltons came to the car with smiles and warm hellos. In their late forties, Charley and Gladys introduced their oldest child George, age twenty-three, who lived and worked on the ranch with his wife Forestine and one-year-old daughter Kathleen. Charley and Gladys's other children: Miriam "Mim," age sixteen, Robert, age fourteen, and Marilyn, age six—were all in school. Another sibling, Lois (who went by Marjorie, her middle name), was Muriel's age, and she was preparing to become a teacher at Eastern Montana Normal School in Billings. A hired hand named Tommy, from Missouri, was out nursing a sick sheep.[19]

George, who was several inches shorter than Elmer and about the same weight, helped his new friend carry the luggage into the house. Round-faced with combed-over dark brown hair and kind

---

[19] 1940 United States Federal Census, database with images, Ancestry (https://www.ancestry.com/discoveryui-content/view/77667793:2442?indiv=try&o_vc=Record%3aOtherRecord&rhSource=6224: downloaded 21 October 2020), Sixteenth Census of the United States, S.D. No. 2 E.D. No. 48-29 Sheet No. 1A, Enumerated 13 April 1940, Henry E. Waldo, Enumerator; Brownell, Joan L., "Pelton House," *National Register of Historic Places Registration Form* (Washington, DC: U.S. Department of the Interior, National Park Service), Sections 7–8; Bill Pelton, Phone interview with Tricia Velure, 16 October 2020. Pelton family and Pelton ranch information throughout this chapter is weaved together and drawn from those three sources and reviewed by Bill Pelton, son of George and grandson of Charles.

Elmer and Muriel in front of the home of Charlie and Gladys Pelton near Fishtail, Montana, in the spring of 1940. Muriel is visibly pregnant with her first child. (Courtesy Ed Hamilton)

blue eyes, George gave Muriel an approachable, trustworthy feeling. Forestine, with fire-engine-red hair almost to her shoulders, seemed reserved and sweet as she showed Muriel to the washroom—*a real bathroom* with a tub and sink and flushing toilet. The young couples were to share the smaller, white one-story house, less than twenty yards south of the main house. Muriel certainly did not consider it small; it was larger than her house back home. But compared to the house next to it, it was a cabin.

Before the newlyweds-turned-ranch-hands could even exchange their first impressions, it was time to eat. George and Forestine, with Kathleen in her arms, walked them over to the big house. Elmer and Muriel maintained their composure; now was no time to be country bumpkins. George, who was friendly and warm, told them how the family had lived in the white house while the big house was built in 1927–1928. Cobblestones were everywhere around here, so it only made sense to build a cobblestone house. He pointed to the two-stall garage for his Ford and his father's Oldsmobile, a scenario completely unfathomable to the young, calm, nodding couple from North Dakota. Neither one had grown up with a garage on the place, let alone a two-car garage. George then mentioned the apple orchard out front and a barren garden spot that intrigued Muriel. Walking up onto the porch and through the front door, Muriel was instantly captivated by the massive cobblestone fireplace in the living room to her left, flanked by a full length of cabinets. To her right were Charley and Gladys, welcoming her and Elmer to dinner.

It was Tuesday at noon, and they sat around the largest table in the biggest dining room she had ever been in. Thank goodness for the familiar, "Come, Lord Jesus, be our guest; let these gifts to us be blessed, Amen." Mixed with the aroma of fresh bread and roast beef surrounding them, there was comfort here. Muriel felt a bit unworldly, but she was confident in her intelligence and domestic capabilities. The table was lively with conversation, and the Peltons already felt like friends. They wanted to know all about Muriel and Elmer's families and farming operations back in Fort Ransom. Though smaller in acreage, Elmer explained, they got more rain and raised more crops in fertile black soil. Like elsewhere, the Depression had hit hard, and everyone was ready for better times ahead.

"Hopefully Hitler doesn't have other plans for us," George said, as Elmer nodded in agreement and Charley changed the subject.

Muriel listened more than usual, taking it all in. George and Forestine, with little Kathleen, seemed like a vision one year into her future. Charley and Gladys were the elders, but they were ten and seventeen years younger than her own parents—a palpable difference now that Muriel had begun to absorb their more-forward thinking in their modern home. After dinner, the ladies cleared the table and brought the dishes to the kitchen, where Muriel found running water and electricity! Just like in Fort Ransom, electricity had not reached this part of Montana yet—except the Pelton ranch, that is. Charley had wired the house and had his own light plant installed, beamed Gladys. She made the statement more out of happiness than boastfulness, thought Muriel.

As the ladies did the dishes, Gladys and Forestine asked Muriel about the wedding and the baby, but just the right amount, she thought. Then Gladys brought her up to speed on the children she would help care for and her responsibilities around the house and ranch. Watching their husbands tour the ranch out the window, the women embarked on their own tour.

Muriel saw the whole house, including the four bedrooms and bathroom upstairs. She told them how lovely it all was but did not go so far as to say she had never seen anything like it. Then they showed her the finished basement and went outside through the back porch, which "is the perfect sleeping porch for the children on hot summer nights," Gladys said. Pointing in the direction of the place where Charley's brother Art lived, Gladys told her how she and Charley had come to Montana in 1918, stayed with his brother for a time, and moved to this ranch in 1922.

The walk was leisurely on this nice spring day, and Muriel loved the vividness of Gladys's stories. They stopped short of the barn and outbuildings where the men were, and the 1,300 sheep were just a mention. This tour was to get Muriel acquainted with the ranch in general, and more specifically with the houses and yard, where she would be spending most of her time. Gladys described a vegetable crop similar to what Muriel's mom grew as they passed the garden spot and pointed out the flowerbeds around the two houses. "Peonies are my favorite," she said as she pointed to a few tiny shoots peeking out of the soil. "I have a dozen peony bushes."

"Charley calls her the peony queen," Forestine softly added with admiration, and all three of them smiled. Muriel already knew she liked these women.

Forestine took over guiding in the house that they would be sharing. It had a roomy, open front porch with a cement base and pillars at each end. Inside, it was more modest than the big house, but still it had electricity, a central furnace, and running water. They walked through a large living room, kitchen with a combination wood/coal stove, and three bedrooms—each with its own closet. Muriel's mind raced! She was sure the two women could detect her wide eyes as they spoke and she listened, trying to catch every minute detail.

That night in bed, Muriel and Elmer stayed up late sharing all they had learned with each other. "How do the Peltons make money?" Muriel asked, thinking of her own father being slowly foreclosed upon, and overhearing conversations everywhere about, "barely making ends meet."

"Lots of wool," Elmer said. "Wanna hear my favorite thing I heard all day? . . . I complimented Charley on his boots," he told Muriel, who'd also noticed his shiny black cowboy boots. "Charley told me, 'Sheep paid for these boots.'"

The couple laughed. Then Elmer continued with the story of Charley's dad being a banker. He supposed Charley started out with enough means to invest through the 1920s and 1930s, even as their neighbors went out of business. Charley owned 920 acres in 1933, he had told Elmer, but today he owned 5,240.[20]

"He wasn't bragging," Elmer said. "I think he just wanted me to understand how big the operation is, so I'm prepared for it all. It's a lot of responsibility."

The sheer amount of physical labor to be done on the ranch began to set in for both of them the next day. Muriel gave herself over to the busy household, where she quickly assimilated into the Pelton's cooking, baking, dishwashing, and general cleaning chores. She was easily charmed by the Pelton girls, who she began to love like they were her own sisters. Sixteen-year-old Mim, whom Muriel would have gravitated toward just a few months ago, now seemed light-years younger. Gladys quickly recognized and appreciated Muriel's domestic skills. The sudden onset of adulthood was not lost on Muriel; she felt herself exuding "married and expecting" as she worked.

Elmer kept busy with all the tasks of caring for the horses and milk cows, which he was entrusted with from day two onward. He appreciated not having to chip ice off the pond for the livestock each morning, as he did in North Dakota. Here they drank from Rosebud Creek, which was rushing with the spring ice and snow melt.

By late April, Elmer started working his first lambing season. The Peltons did shed lambing—far different from pasture lambing, he learned, because the owners could go to bed at home every night. Ranchers whose herds lambed on the open range lived miles from home in a sheep wagon this time of year. Tommy's year-round bed was also the sheep wagon, but here it was parked near the lambing shed, about a quarter mile from the big house. It stayed there all win-

---

[20] The number of farms with 700–999 acres decreased from 113 in 1935 to 76 in 1940 in Stillwater County, Montana. The number of farms with 1,000 or more acres only decreased from 233 in 1935 to 226 in 1940 in Stillwater County. "United States Department of Agriculture Census of Agriculture Historical Archive—Montana." County Table III—Number of Farms, 1940 and 1935, accessed May 12, 2020, http://usda.mannlib. cornell.edu/usda/AgCensusImages/1940/01/38/1266/Table-03.pdf. "National Register of Historic Places Registration Form, Pelton House, Stillwater Co, MT." United States Department of the Interior, National Park Service, Section 8, Page 13, accessed May 12, 2020, https://mhs.mt.gov/Portals/11/shpo/docs/NRnoms/STco_Pelton_House.pdf.

ter and through the lambing and shearing seasons. When the Peltons trailed the sheep into the mountains in June, the wagon went along, so that Tommy had a roof over his head while tending sheep camp for the summer. Essentially, it was a canvas tent on wheels, with a bed, a stove, and a table—everything a shepherd needed.

Lambing continued for several weeks, all day and all night. Elmer got up from bed at midnight to assist Tommy and learn the ropes. If a ewe had difficulty with birth, they helped her. If there was a sick sheep or lamb, they nursed it back to health. Overall, shed lambing in Montana felt a lot like calving season back home, Elmer thought, except on a much bigger scale. On a good night, he went back to bed in fifteen minutes; on a bad night, not at all. Regardless, he started milking before sunrise. This life was simultaneously exhilarating and exhausting.

Lambing also brought docking. Before each mom and her baby left the lambing shed, the men branded matching numbers on them and cut off the lamb's tails and testicles to prevent fly and maggot infestations when the weather warmed.

As lambing dragged on, the crocuses bloomed. Just as in North Dakota, they were the first flowers to appear. Here they splashed the May pastures in an intense violet, contrasted by the snow-topped mountains above and the rising grass all around. New life sprouted across the surrounding meadows every day, including the alfalfa Elmer seeded for hay. The Peltons had 150 acres of irrigated hay ground, a luxury by Elmer's standards. He had never seen irrigation before!

"Hopefully Mother Nature will be the irrigator this year," Charley said with a wink.

The bustle on the ranch shifted from lambing and docking to shearing. Elmer felt anxious to try his hand at these next unfamiliar activities. Would he know what to do? Would he work quickly enough? All the local ranchers got together to share labor, George told him. The closest comparison Elmer could imagine was a threshing crew back home. In the morning, one group of men worked with horses and dogs to gather the sheep. Another group sheared on wooden floor planks next to the lambing shed. Another transferred, bagged, and stomped the wool down into the bags. And another sewed up the three-hundred-pound bags and placed them in wagons for transporting. On day one of shearing at a neighboring ranch, Elmer tried his hand at all these tasks. The men joked around about the "rookie" on the crew, but their nods after he got the hang of each job made him feel fairly capable. At the end of that day, Elmer was tired but mesmerized by all that he had been a part of.

This was Elmer's favorite experience on the ranch so far, he told Muriel in bed that night. Bedtime was their brief time to exchange what they had learned and seen that day, and every day there was a new story. "It's so great," were his words that night, but Muriel heard his meaning: "We're living in another world, like we're dreaming."

Muriel and Elmer were happy in Montana. It was hard to imagine from here that a war was raging in Europe. Norway had just fallen to Nazi Germany, along with five other countries within a month. Maybe George was right about Hitler—that his plan was to keep going until he finally provoked the United States to get involved. War talk was not good bedtime conversation, but it was hard not to think about, even in the charm of a sheep ranch.

Muriel saw shearing day for herself when the men worked the Pelton's sheep, because the Pelton women were responsible for feeding everyone that day. For two days leading up to it, Gladys, Forestine, Muriel, and Gladys's girls baked bread and pies. They cooked a huge beef roast, mashed two full kettles of potatoes, and baked beans and corn as side dishes. Gladys made the gravy. The men got their choice of apple or mincemeat pie. The temperature was just right for the men to roll up their sleeves, so they were happy to dish up outside from a big picnic table. Some fit around other tables the women had set up; others plopped down on the fresh grass. There was talking and laughter, but no leisure in this picnic. The men were in a rush to get back to the sheep.

This day was a tiring one for Muriel. Kitchen preparations began at 6:00 a.m., the women took a five-minute pause for coffee around 10:00 a.m., and the men lined up for food at noon. The afternoon was consumed with dishwashing, bringing coffee and sweetbreads to the men, storing the leftovers, and preparing supper. When Gladys or Forestine asked Muriel how she was feeling, she only said, "I can't complain," and politely smiled. In the absence of her own mom, Gladys was Muriel's mentor, and gave her great comfort. Forestine, just two years older than Muriel, was a good friend, generous with roomy dresses and gentle guidance when she sensed Muriel having a pain or overexerting herself. So, Muriel did not want to trouble them with her petty grievances about pregnancy. But when Elmer asked in bed that night how she was doing, she responded with an honest, "I'm beat. I feel fat."

Elmer told her his shearing stories, which Muriel could tell he was especially proud to share now that he had some experience. That day, he had seen Charley's paint branding for the first time. His brand was a blue horseshoe, painted atop the lamb's wool with the opening facing forward. "When Charley branded, that opening faced straight ahead every time," he said. "When everyone else branded, they weren't quite as fussy. I bet that drives Charley crazy!"

"How did you do?" she asked.

"I only painted a few, and I made sure all my horseshoes opened to the front!" he said. They laughed and fell asleep.

The next day, Tommy led the sheep into the spring meadows. Ten days later, after they had grazed and settled into summer, Tommy trailed the sheep onto the summer range, which was in the highest elevations, thirty miles from the ranch. George followed on his horse, with a pack horse alongside him with supplies. Charley and Elmer went in back of him with a team of horses pulling the sheep wagon. Elmer tried to take in every detail of the surrounding mountains as Charley had the reins and told him stories, hoping he would remember it all to tell Muriel that night. Such was the bedtime routine they had settled into; there was almost no other time for the newlyweds to talk alone.

As the calendar turned to July, Elmer was excited to be charged with a task he not only felt confident about but liked. He might have enjoyed haying better than anything else, in fact. "You're every bit as experienced at it as George and I are," Charley assured him. So, on July 3, Elmer hooked up the team to the mower, and led them out to the thirty-acre alfalfa field, the Pelton's largest. A crop of deep green and purple spread out before him, and the sweet, earthy scent filled his nostrils. The smell of home greeted Elmer, calming him, yet urging him on. Even the horses seemed eager; he could hear their loud snorts. He paused for just a moment, then gave them a quick cluck as he lightly slapped the driving reins across their backs. They needed no convincing.

He went down one row, then another, until the horses, Elmer's hands, and the earth below them were in steady rhythm. His mind wandered several times toward home, where Chester might be doing the very same task today. He was thrilled to be out there all day long, and to have Muriel bring him lunch for the first time. This was one of the few times they were ever alone during the day on the ranch, and the conversation went back and forth about all the new characters in their lives—people they had known for less than four months but felt completely at home with. At the end of the day, Elmer felt a familiar exhaustion that told him where he would be sore the next day— across his upper back, down his shoulders and biceps. It all felt right.

Sore or not, July 4 was a big day. The entire family, including Elmer and Muriel, filled the Ford and the Oldsmobile by 8:00 a.m. for their longest trip of the summer. The Red Lodge Rodeo started that day, and the Peltons had been attending every year since it started in 1929. Red Lodge was an hour's drive across the mountains—what George and Forestine called hills—on dusty gravel roads. George told them all about Red Lodge being the entry to Beartooth Highway, which took tourists over the rugged Beartooth Mountains into Yellowstone National Park. Thousands of people would be in Red Lodge for the parade and the rodeo, George said, and he, his dad, and

Robert would also shop for new boots. Elmer and Muriel decided to check out the downtown until the parade started.

This was the greatest Fourth of July, Elmer and Muriel agreed, before even seeing the parade or rodeo. They felt a world—not just one state—away from Fort Ransom, holding hands to make sure they stayed together as they walked amongst thousands of people. Muriel could not see past the cowboy hats surrounding her. She suddenly wondered if anyone back home was a real cowboy, next to the ones she saw here. The parade lasted nearly an hour, with multiple marching bands and decked-out floats with tissue-paper flowers and streamers. Then the crowd made its way to the first of three days of rodeo competitions. Muriel could barely watch the bareback riders or bulldoggers without cringing. She did not know what bulldogging even was until the announcer explained it was steer wrestling. "What do you think?" George leaned over to ask her.

"I love it!" Muriel said with her biggest smile. Then, as the rodeo came to a close, the announcer told the crowd they had just broken an attendance record, with 8,500 people.[21] Muriel immediately exclaimed, "I don't think I've ever been in the same place with 8,500 other people!"

This day, this place, this whole experience made Muriel feel alive. In that moment, she was overwhelmed by the feeling that had been building inside her since arriving at the Peltons. She wanted to live here forever. She and Elmer had already started to build their life here. Having a baby here would only make Montana more their home. She did not need to tell Elmer now, but she would when the time was right. Maybe he was already thinking the same thing?

---

[21] Associated Press, "Bill Greenough Wins Rodeo at Red Lodge," *The Helena Independent-Record*, July 5, 1940.

THE BABY

AFTER CELEBRATING INDEPENDENCE DAY, long days of work on the ranch resumed. While Elmer returned to the alfalfa field to rake the hay he had cut two days earlier, Muriel sensed she was to be sheltered. She went to the garden to pick peas, and Forestine sent her to shell them on the front porch. She retrieved a dish towel to dry dishes, and Gladys gave her a chair to sit while she dried. One terribly hot day, when they knew Muriel needed a pick-me-up, Forestine brought Kathleen's bassinet and a few clothes into Elmer and Muriel's room, and Gladys followed with a pastel baby afghan she had knitted. Baby Sandhei was coming soon, and Muriel felt the Pelton women doing everything they could to help her prepare. They even humored her as she wondered aloud: How would she know if the baby was sick? When would the baby sleep through the night? When should she start working again? She wanted to know everything, and she intended to pull her weight again soon.

Muriel's physician, Dr. Payne in Columbus, assured Muriel she was perfectly healthy, and that the pregnancy was coming along well. His wife, Mabel, filled her in on the particulars of how to know the baby was coming. In the meantime, Muriel worked a bit less hard. She slid into her tatty brown shoes each morning and watched her ankles swell over them. She never complained.

Back home, only the parents and some of the siblings knew anything more than she and Elmer left home to get married. In her weekly letters to Josephine, Muriel kept the topics light. She described

Red Lodge, the countryside, the garden, and the Peltons in detail. She gave only brief updates on her situation, and carefully mixed them with other observations. "I'm feeling well," paired nicely with, "I'm enjoying my work on the ranch. Everyone says my mother was clearly a good teacher." Likewise, "Gladys and Forestine have helped us get settled," went well with, "We are preparing for a late July arrival."

Muriel also included news that might interest her father, hoping he might read it and soften toward her. "The men stacked hay today," she wrote. "The stack is long and at least fifteen feet high, in the middle of the field. Charley drove the team to move the hay. Elmer, George, and Robert groomed the stack. It's a beautiful sight."

On her nineteenth birthday, Muriel smiled gratefully as Elmer and the whole Pelton family sang, "Happy Birthday." Inside, she wanted no cake, no ice cream, nothing but to sit down and fan herself. It must almost be time, she silently willed. Late that night, Muriel thought she was feeling contractions, and Gladys and Forestine confirmed she was. Gladys called Dr. Payne and ordered the anxious Elmer to pull the car up in front of the house while the women packed Muriel's suitcase. Elmer went back inside to collect Muriel, and all three women were so ecstatic that he could not help but laugh as he rushed his wife to the car. "I feel like a prized heifer," Muriel joked as he guided her with extra care.

Driving as quickly as he dared over gravel in the dark, he found his way to Pike Street in Columbus, and Muriel directed him to the First National Bank building. He led her through the unlocked door and the stairs to the second floor, where Dr. Payne was waiting. Nine hours later, on July 30, 1940, Muriel gave birth to her firstborn, a ten-pound son, in the surgery room of Dr. Payne and his wife. Feeling slightly out of sorts, a tired Muriel looked up at her new, crying baby as the doctor lifted him away from her. Seeing his trace of dark brown hair and perfectly round face, she smiled in groggy relief and eagerly anticipated the moment she would hold him in her arms. Dr. Payne gently cleaned him as Mrs. Payne held him and Muriel gained her presence. Muriel eagerly asked, "Can I hold him? I want to hold him." Mrs. Payne wrapped the baby tightly in a lightweight, white blanket and softly handed him over to Muriel. Gazing at her perfect boy adoringly, with a broad smile and fast-flowing tears, she gave him the softest, "Hello, little one," and a kiss on his cheek. The moment seemed suspended in time, and all things beyond him blurred.

She did not know how long she had been staring at this miracle when the door opened, and in walked a beaming Elmer. He rushed over to kiss Muriel on the cheek and lay his eyes on his son. He embraced Muriel softly at first, wondering how much she could take after just giving birth. Her firm hold surprised him, and he returned it with his own. "This is our boy, Muriel," he whispered. "I'm so proud of you."

Left alone, the new parents were engrossed in their family of three for as long as the doctors allowed them. They handed him back and forth and noted what feature matched with each parent. After a few minutes of happy silence, Muriel asked, "Merle Elmer?" Hearing the name for the first time, Elmer smiled again and held her gaze steadily. Merle Elmer. "Perfect," he said.

But the moment did not last. Mrs. Payne returned and urged Muriel to sleep as she took Merle. A euphoric Muriel thought, "Sleep?" But Elmer assured her that rest was indeed best, and that as soon as he knew she was resting, he would drive back to the ranch and call their mothers with the happy news that they had a baby boy. The psychology worked on Muriel. "I'll be back tomorrow," Elmer said as she closed her eyes.

He walked out the door almost bursting with the news. Knowing there was nobody here to tell, he drove home wired, like electricity coursed through his veins with every heartbeat. He was running on no sleep, yet he had never felt more wide-awake.

Gladys, Forestine, and the girls enthusiastically came outside the moment they heard the car approaching. "A boy! Merle Elmer," he exclaimed as he closed the car door. "They're healthy. Muriel is doing great. She's resting now."

It was settled that Gladys and Forestine would drive into Columbus for a short visit the next morning, before Elmer went to see them in the afternoon. The girls would need to wait a few days until Muriel felt better, Gladys said to their disappointment. "It's settled. Now go on in and use the phone," she told Elmer.

Elmer called his parents and ran on adrenaline alone for the rest of the day. The coffee Forestine brought him tasted better, the sun seemed brighter, and even the cow's milk smelled sweeter. When he shared the news with the men, Charley and George patted him on the arm, shook his hand mightily, and suggested extra drinks after dinner that evening. They toasted to Elmer and his new son that night, and Elmer fell into bed knowing this was the best day of his life. He knew now that he wanted to stay in Montana. He wanted Muriel and Merle to come home, he wanted to keep working for the Peltons if they would have him, and he thought Muriel would agree.

Elmer rose before the dawn on July 31, and as he went out to milk, he could hardly wait to see Merle. Charley told him to quit at noon, eat his dinner, and take the rest of the day off. Right on schedule, the men came inside for a meal that Mim proudly finished for her mom. The phone rang, and it was Gladys calling for Elmer. Thinking he would be asked to bring along something Muriel wanted, he good-naturedly answered, "Hi, Gladys." But his expression turned to concern in an instant.

Gladys, in a tone as calm as she could muster, said, "Elmer, there's been a change in Merle. He's stable, but Muriel needs you. That's really all I know. Can you leave right away?"

Elmer rushed out of the big house to the cottage, changed into a fresh shirt, and re-emerged shaken, wishing he could pass with no eye contact. Charley and George were outside waiting for him. "We'll be praying for you and Muriel," Charley said, not knowing what else to say. Elmer nodded his appreciation. Sweet young Marilyn, holding back tears she did not even understand, had disobeyed orders to stay inside and ran to Elmer carrying a delicate bouquet of three yellow roses she had quickly plucked from the garden. He took a moment to kneel down, cup his worn ranchman's hand over Marilyn's tiny shoulder, and say, "Muriel will love these. Thank you." She returned his closed-mouth smile, and he opened the car door as she strode back to her father. The Peltons stood immobile as he drove away, raising light brown dust that lingered as it only does in the hot, still air of a sunny summer day in Montana.

Elmer barely noticed his path to Columbus that afternoon, his mind racing back and forth between Muriel and Merle. Elmer parked outside the First National Bank building, grabbed the flowers, and began running so hastily that he tripped on the curb. He caught himself and instantly realized that Muriel needed him to be steady—the exact opposite of how shaky he truly felt. He stood tall, took a deep breath, and walked upstairs to Dr. Payne's hospital.

Gladys had been watching for him. She met him at the top of the steps and reached out to his free hand, handing him a baby blue handkerchief. "I don't know anything more, but the doctors have been evaluating Merle, and they were waiting for you to arrive before giving Muriel an update. You go on in, Elmer, and if you need anything, you just call and we'll be here," she said. He wished she would tell him what to say, what to do. But Mrs. Payne was already there to usher him in for a conversation with her and Dr. Payne. As Elmer walked into Muriel's room, he locked eyes with Muriel and went to her bedside straightaway, pausing only to thank Forestine as she quietly exited.

Before Muriel could bring herself to speak, Elmer's hand came to hold hers tightly, with only the handkerchief between them. He kissed her on the forehead, and the lump grew in her throat. Neither of them cried. Neither of them said anything. And then Dr. Payne and his wife came in. Dr. Payne made no eye contact, instead bowing his head as he approached them. Mrs. Payne's face was warm and pensive, as though she came to translate her husband's doctor-speak. For the next minute, Muriel felt drowned in Dr. Payne's medical terminology. "This means that Merle has a bleeding disorder, and he has jaundice. The bleeding disorder is making the jaundice more severe than what we commonly see in babies."

"What can you do for him? Is he going to be okay?" Muriel asked.

Pausing, Mrs. Payne looked from Muriel to Elmer and back to Muriel. "We might not be able to stop the bleeding, and if we can't stop the bleeding, the jaundice will get worse," she said softly. "If that happens, he might not survive more than a few days. We are hoping that doesn't happen."

"We will do our best, but you need to prepare yourselves for the worst," Dr. Payne said toward Elmer.

In an instant, Muriel wept like she never had before, and Elmer let her. They did not even notice that the doctors left; it did not matter. "It's going to be okay, Muriel. He's going to be okay," Elmer finally said, holding her tight. They both took that statement for the made-up story it probably was, but it had to be told this way for them to make it through. A few minutes later, Mrs. Payne came in. "You will want to talk to your family and pastor," she said. "What more can I do to help you?"

"Can we see Merle?" Muriel asked.

Mrs. Payne nodded and left the room. As they waited for her to bring Merle to them, Elmer dabbed Muriel's wet cheeks with the hanky, and she noticed the yellow roses he brought with him. "From the Peltons . . . from me," he said as Mrs. Payne came to deliver Merle, indicating she would come back for him in five minutes. Muriel held him in silence as Elmer climbed in alongside her to hold them both. They said nothing. They just laid there, looking at Merle, rubbing his cheeks and forehead, admiring his wisp of hair. He did not cry.

Nine days passed. Muriel hardly knew one from the next. Under orders of bed rest, she only grew more restless. She wanted only Elmer and Merle Elmer and could not get enough of either. Sleep eluded her. Elmer drove into town as much as he could, while still being of help to Charley and George on haying and morning milking.

On the morning of August 8, Elmer walked into Muriel's room with Mrs. Payne, dressed in the suit he wore for the wedding just five months earlier. He was carrying a small suitcase. It carried the pink cotton dress Muriel had requested for herself, along with the family christening gown that Gladys had insisted upon. An hour later, Pastor Gilbertson from Immanuel Lutheran Church in Absarokee arrived, followed by Mrs. Payne, carrying a quiet Merle Elmer, dressed like an angel in flowing white satin. Merle Elmer was baptized. Muriel listened only for instructions. She stared at this boy's sweet face and stroked his tiny hands as she held him, knowing the day had come. "What a good baby you are," she whispered.

Merle Elmer died at 9:40 p.m. that night. Elmer and Muriel drove back to the Pelton ranch at midnight, knowing they could not possibly sleep. They laid in bed and waited for the sun to rise. Exhausted and devastated, they dressed and went to join the family for breakfast in the big house. Muriel let herself be served that morning and was relieved that the harvest season prevented the men from lingering at the table. Few thoughts entered her mind except the image of Merle Elmer that she already worried about forgetting. The once-vibrant nineteen-year-old did not even protest being shooed out of the kitchen as the girls did the dishes. Forestine walked her back to her bedroom, and Muriel finally felt the urge to sleep. In fact, she slept until mid-afternoon before her aching body awakened her.

Three days later, under a cloudless sky, the Sandheis and Peltons laid Merle Elmer to rest at Rosebud Cemetery on the outskirts of Absarokee. The service was brief and simple. Carried by swift west winds, the minister's words faded like the short life before them. Muriel wished she could blow away, as Dorothy did in *The Wizard of Oz*, and quickly land at home—in Fort Ransom, with her mother and Elmer. Elmer's mind returned to an afternoon so much like this one, when he stood beside his mother at his baby sister's funeral at Bucyrus. He remembered squinting into the hole in the ground, wondering about the small pine box to be placed in it. Back then, he only knew to not ask questions. Today, he knew that no answers could make him feel better.

The couple packed for their return to Fort Ransom two days later. The Peltons wanted them to stay on the ranch at least through the fall. Muriel's feeling most of July that she wanted to make a life in Montana seemed like forever ago, and she was relieved she had not mentioned it to Elmer. The pull toward home simply could not wait. They could not recover here, as nice as the Peltons were, and as lovely as Montana was. The happiness they knew for most of their days here would forever be marred by tragedy.

LIKE NOTHING HAPPENED

THE TWO-DAY DRIVE BACK to Fort Ransom was quiet. The young couple had been excited to become parents, and now they were returning to Fort Ransom without their baby. What little conversation they had focused on the wheat harvest happening outside the car windows. Muriel wondered if Elmer felt, as she did, that no words could do justice to the pain. Or perhaps the heartache was too painful for words. Muriel already knew the long silences in the car were nothing compared to the avoidance awaiting them in Fort Ransom.

People back home knew about Merle; the grandparents had shared the news of his birth when he was believed to be healthy. Merle was the first grandchild of Elise and C.A., and Muriel had no doubt that C.A. was the first to tell friends and neighbors that Elmer now had a boy to carry on the family name.

Merle had arrived too soon after the wedding, but Muriel suspected that people in Fort Ransom did the math at home and kept the discussion to a whisper in small groups. They were in on her secret now, and she assumed they would be outwardly discreet. In the case of Merle, his "early arrival" at ten pounds inhibited the conversation, and his death made him next to unmentionable.

Lost in thought as Elmer drove into North Dakota, Muriel suddenly noticed a mom, dad, and young boy with wavy, golden hair in need of a trim. Walking together into their farmhouse, the man held the door open wide while the woman coaxed the boy inside. Realizing that these were the first people she had consciously seen, she looked at Elmer and instantly knew he had admired the family too.

"My baby sister died," Elmer said.

Muriel looked at Elmer's somber face, and could not possibly have been more surprised. She did not know Elise had lost a child. She did not know Elmer had gone through this experience before.

"She was born in August 1920, before Chester and Elsa Mae. Ma had her at home, and she died the same day," said Elmer. "She didn't have a name, as far as I know. We didn't really talk about it. We just had a graveside service."

"I'm sorry. I didn't know," Muriel replied.

They grieved together through sideward glances for the next four hours. As familiar sites came into view the last few miles before arriving in Fort Ransom, a tinge of comfort actually surprised Muriel. Driving down the big hill into Fort Ransom, the mixed emotions flooded over her. Tears streamed down her cheek. The last time she was here, she was a girl, barely out of school. Five months later, she was a wife and a heartbroken new mother of a deceased baby. Yet she was expected to act like she and Elmer had simply eloped and adventured.

Elmer took her hand and softly said, "It'll be okay."

The sun had slipped past the hills by the time they drove into the Henrickson driveway. Her father and Pud were in the yard after a long day in the field; she could see that Pud had grown a few inches taller. Josephine, in her house dress, was bent over in the garden pulling squash when she heard the car approaching. Elmer came to a slow stop, and Muriel opened the car door. Without saying a word, Josephine walked up to her, put an arm lightly over her shoulders, and led her into the house. Muriel's tears flowed uncontrollably, while her mother waited sympathetically. After a couple of minutes, the calm set in, and Josephine called in the men for pork roast sandwiches and corn on the cob.

They sat down and prayed the familiar "I Jesu navn" together. Almost a lullaby to Muriel, she closed her eyes, and hoped to meet her father's when she opened them. John neither looked at Muriel nor spoke to any of them. Pud looked at her as if to beg, "Can we please end this awkwardness now?"

Josephine rescued them with an uncommonly high number of family updates. Luther was coming home soon and marrying Ida Berntson. They would move onto the farm and keep Pud; Josephine and John would move into Grandma and Grandpa Mikkelson's house in Fort Ransom. Muriel's cousins—especially Ardis—would be so happy to have her back in Fort Ransom. C.A. and Elise would sure be glad to have Elmer back, too. And wasn't the news from Europe terrible? Everyone at church was worried for their relatives in Norway. In all of the information shared, not a word was said about Merle. There were no questions about their time in Montana. They simply were to start the rest of their normal, nothing-happened lives.

Elmer stayed with Muriel in her old bedroom that night. Windows open, they heard the familiar chirp of crickets and tossed and turned as people do in a strange bed on a hot night. Each pretended to be asleep, so as not to disturb the other. Muriel's body ached to feed the living, breathing baby who was supposed to be next to her. Elmer yearned to *do* something, anything, to help the situation. Waking to the clamor of Josephine cooking breakfast, they dressed and joined the family downstairs. Muriel sensed Elmer grimacing at Josephine's runny eggs, then self-correcting. They ate like farmers eager to get to work. Elmer excused himself first, thanking Josephine and rubbing Muriel's shoulders. He was off to see his family and help his dad; he would be back after supper.

As Muriel found out later that night, there was more to his rush. Elmer needed to make plans. The time to make money in farming was now, and the place was not Fort Ransom. So, Elmer drove to his parents' place and sat down to coffee with his mother. She made excuses for his father's absence, but their open talk was evidence it was better this way. Eventually they discussed what's next. "Who do we know in Minnesota?" he asked. "I'll make more money there than here in the next few months, and I'll still be fairly close to home."

Sig Seljeseth, a neighbor from Bucyrus, farmed in Minnesota now. She had his address—New Richland, Minnesota. Elmer got on the phone and was lucky enough to reach Sig on the first try. After shooting the breeze for an anxious minute, Elmer asked if he or anyone else in the area needed a farmhand. In fact, yes, a few people might be looking. Sig invited Elmer to drive down, and said he would have a job waiting by the time Elmer arrived. "I'll be there tomorrow afternoon," Elmer promised.[22]

There was much to do that day. Elmer committed himself to supper with the family, and headed out to the field to make things right with his father and help with whatever task needed doing. Work solved most issues between C.A. and him—between C.A. and anyone, really. It was a sign of good faith, with few words required. That day, work would also give Elmer time to think of how to tell Muriel about his plan.

He returned to his in-laws' house after supper, wearing dread on his face. Muriel's body stiffened, and her heart dropped. She knew he was leaving before he said a word. "We need the money," Elmer explained.

"I know," was her soft reply.

When he left the next morning with his suitcase and two sandwiches from Josephine, Muriel willed away the tears. She hugged him, smiled, and retreated to a new place deep inside. It was where loss lived.

"It'll only be a couple of months," he said.

As Elmer would later write, he went to work for a farmer named Tom Bedney in Steele County, southeastern Minnesota, about seven hours from home.[23] "We're busy from dawn until dark every

---

[22] The average farm wage rate in Minnesota was $33.68 in 1939 and $74.30 in 1943. Louis J. Ducoff, "Wages of Agricultural Labor in the United States," Technical Bulletin No. 895, Page 85, United States Department of Agriculture, July 1945, https://naldc.nal.usda.gov/download/CAT86200887/PDF.

[23] 1940 United States Federal Census, database with images, Ancestry (https://www.ancestry.com/imageviewer/collections/2442/images/m-t0627-01962-00187?useP-UB=true&_phsrc=YpU343&_phstart=successSource&usePUBJs=true&pId=97391176: downloaded 22 October 2020), Sixteenth Census of the United States, S.D. No. 1 E.D. No. 74-9 Sheet No. 5B, Enumerated 19 April 1940, W. Carl Masche, Enumerator. The presumed connection Sig Seljeseth made between Elmer and Tom Bedney is based on the authors' best judgment of the most likely scenario, knowing about Seljeseth's move from Bucyrus to New Richland, Minnesota, from C.A. Sandhei's 1936 daybook. Seljeseth and Bedney would have lived about fifteen miles from one another, if this information is accurate. Neither the name "Sig Seljeseth" or any other resembling it was located in the 1930 or 1940 Census for either location.

day—just like home, just like Montana," he said in his first letter. "I'm earning $50 a month! Tom's wife, Bertha, feeds us well. Everything here is nice."

Muriel listened for the mail truck every day, although Elmer only wrote about once a week. Most letters were alike, talking about crops and the weather, and ending with how much time he spent thinking about her. While Elmer's letters left Muriel wanting more, she read and re-read each one. They felt like holding Elmer's hand. He was her only confidante who shared Merle. Outside of those letters, the only thing to do was get on with life. Her mother encouraged her to go to ladies' aid, and to get excited about Luther's wedding to Ida. Muriel attended, but truly, she was not ready for everyone else's happiness. About the only development that piqued her interest at all was when the language at Sunday church services consistently changed from Norwegian to English that September. Fort Ransom needed more shaking up, she thought. She hoped that the shift to English was the harbinger of some other modern ideas.[24]

The person whose presence brought the brightest light to Muriel's days was her mother-in-law. About once a week, Elise arrived with fresh buns or cake, and at the outset, she always asked Muriel how she was doing. There was a knowing glance between them—a bond. They never spoke about the babies they had lost. It was enough for Muriel to feel at ease around her mother-in-law, and to know Elise had genuine compassion.

In a letter dated October 17, Elmer started with harvest talk, as usual. But then he wrote, "I went to Hope yesterday with Tom, and we registered for the draft. Around here, people think Roosevelt will

---

[24] The shift to using English during church services was reported in the "Fort Ransom News" section as early as 1939. The first reporting of English services found in consecutive editions of the *Ransom County Gazette* came in September 1940: On September 19, 1940: "Services were held in Standing Rock church in the English language Sunday morning." On September 26, 1940: "English services were held in the Stiklestad church Sunday morning."

be re-elected in November, and almost as many think we should help England."[25]

Muriel just wanted Elmer to come home. By the time she helped her parents move and settle into their house in Fort Ransom, Elmer would be there. "Late October or early November," she repeated to herself, several times each day.

Muriel helped her mom pack crates for their move. For the first time since Merle died, she felt her purpose. Her job was to move her parents and support them in feeling like this was the natural transition. They were moving into the Mikkelson house in Fort Ransom, which Maren had deeded to Josephine in 1934, before her death in 1938. Luther was taking over work on the Henrickson farm, and John could go there anytime he wanted. There was no need for crying over spilt milk; this move was simply the logical next step.

---

[25] On September 16, 1940, Congress passed the Selective Service Training and Service Act, which President Franklin Roosevelt signed into law. The Act authorized the federal government to draft 900,000 men between 25 and 36 years of age for defensive purposes. It was the first peacetime draft in American history. In a September 19–25 Gallup poll, 52 percent of Americans favored getting involved in World War II and 44 percent opposed (with the remainder giving no opinion). Asked the same question in a Gallup poll on November 21–26, 60 percent favored involvement, to 40 percent opposed. "How did public opinion about entering the war change between 1939 and 1941?" Americans and the Holocaust, United States Holocaust Memorial Museum, accessed May 12, 2020, https://exhibitions.ushmm.org/americans-and-the-holocaust/us-public-opinion-world-war-II-1939-1941.

PROVING

MURIEL HELPED HER PARENTS MAKE a fresh start in town the only way she knew how, by attending to the details until her mother was content. This was not to say that Josephine was unreasonable; she just had high Norwegian standards. Muriel stacked everyday dishes in the few handmade cupboards, arranged the china luncheon plates and tea set in the hutch left by Grandma Mikkelson, and moved around the wooden spoons and utensils until they were in the handiest spots. She carefully placed the canned goods in perfect rows on the shelves in the cellar, following the time-honored order of fruit sauces on the top, vegetables in the middle, and pickles and relish on the bottom. Pud carried down the gunny sacks of potatoes, carrots, and onions. In the two bedrooms, Muriel fixed the bedding, decided which quilts to use and put away, and thought of Elmer's return in a few days. Keeping busy was the antidote for impatience.

Like most of the houses in Fort Ransom, this one was plain and small. Painted white as a country school, it was a one-story, perfectly square box. Each side featured three tall, skinny windows identically placed, except the front door of the same width. Its best asset was its stance past the east end of Main Street and next to the river. This was the neat house that Muriel set up for her mother, where they worked almost interchangeably. Muriel still sought her mom's approval, but here they were both wives running the house and waiting for their husbands to return. This was the home Elmer returned to on November 1, 1940.

Muriel's smile returned with Elmer. While staying with her parents was a fine temporary arrangement, she imagined getting on with life as a married couple in their very own place and was excited to talk with him about their future. To her, Fort Ransom felt right. Their families were here, their friends were here, and Elmer could farm here. But she was comfortable waiting for Elmer to settle in a bit before she pushed him on it. Elmer seemed to be on the same page, she thought. On his first two mornings back in Fort Ransom, he put on his coat moments after Muriel cleared the breakfast dishes. Was he heading to his parents' place? Probably. Was a game of pool waiting for him in the afternoon? Perhaps coffee at Elmer Anderson's house? Muriel did not know.

"I'm checking some things out," Elmer said, as though to calm her.

Rather than prod, Muriel responded, "See you at supper time," and went on doing dishes in the washtub. Her father, too, left after having his breakfast. John's new daily routine was to putz at the farm with Luther. This was apparently what farmers did, even if they lived in town. "The home place" called to them as nothing else did. There was always work to do, even if it was cleaning the barn stalls. "Our work is never done," John always said, and honestly, that seemed just how he wanted it. Farming was her father and Elmer's common ground. Muriel liked that firm ground for the mealtime conversation to stand on. Her father, slowly but surely, was warming to Elmer again. The thought also crossed her mind that John was relieved to see no evidence of their indiscretions; perhaps that too had softened John's feelings.

A week after Elmer's return, he and Muriel finally went to the Sandhei home for supper for the first time as a married couple. C.A. was cordial, and Muriel got through it with an abundance of grace from Elmer and Elise, who carefully included her on every topic. Part of her wanted to endear herself to her father-in-law with kindness and smiles, but she sensed that a reserved approach was probably wise. After all, he had not so much as glanced in her direction at church since she returned from Montana. She was sure C.A. blamed her "foolishness" for causing Merle's death. Overcompensating now might only irritate him further.

"Have you made more progress on what you'll do next?" C.A. asked, knowing full well that his good friend Carl Thompson had invited Elmer to work for him as soon as Elmer was ready, and start renting his land in the spring.

"Carl's offer is a good one. It'll do for the next year, at least," Elmer replied.

What C.A. did not know was that Elmer had his eye on Florence Olson's quarter-section, just north of Carl's place. Florence was the widow of Cedor Olson, who died the previous March. Muriel had graduated with their son Marvin, who had since left the state. Florence was still living on the farm, but the word around town was that she would not be able to hold on much longer before the bank foreclosed. In the meantime, yes, Carl's proposal was impossible to refuse. Carl lived just a mile from C.A. and a little over a mile from town. He was the closest C.A. came to having a brother nearby. They were close in age and intellect, both came from Mo I Rana, and in recent years, they sat down to Elise's coffee together almost every day. As bachelors go, Carl was as particular about his person as he was his house and barn. He treated Elmer like the son he never had. They all agreed it was an ideal arrangement.

"We'll stay with Muriel's parents for the winter. They have an open bed for us until Carl is ready for us to come live with him," Elmer said.

Muriel admired how Elmer noted her parents' spare bedroom, out of respect for his mother. All three bedrooms were taken at C.A.'s house, and Elmer did not want to relegate Chester to the couch on their account. That was how thoughtful Elmer was. Living with her parents was logical for the interim. She was in no rush to move in with Carl; she barely knew him. Sure, Carl and John were friends, but Muriel had only exchanged pleasantries with him until this newly decided arrangement came about. What she knew was that he was a bachelor; he took over the farm after his dad died, and his mother stayed with him until her own death sometime in the 1920s. Whatever else she needed to know, Elmer would have to tell her as he worked for Carl.

With their plans confirmed, the Sandheis and Henricksons settled into a comfortable winter routine. Elmer drove to Carl's place daily, John went to Luther's, and Josephine and Muriel cooked, baked, cleaned, and sewed. They attended ladies' aid activities at church—Josephine as a Zion Aid member and Muriel as a Bethania Aid member, just to have an activity to themselves. Muriel was happy to have some separation, and even happier that it was her mother's suggestion. During the second week of December, they spent three mornings making lefse. Josephine deferred to Muriel for the first time on rolling the lefse, as that was a better young woman's task. Muriel felt simultaneously honored and pressured! She had to live up to this moment, and she did. She could see it in her mother's twinkling eyes.

As they got underway the third morning, Muriel suddenly was sick. She assumed it would pass and kept working. But as the aromas of boiling potatoes and coffee combined in the tiny kitchen, she could not contain herself. She excused herself, barely made it outside before her breakfast came up, and took some deep breaths. She had felt this sensation before. She cleaned her hands in the snow, hid the evidence, and went back inside. She felt her mother's stare, but said nothing. Muriel worked through the next two queasy hours.

A week later, Muriel finally admitted what her mother already suspected: "I'm not feeling well in the mornings."

Josephine smiled and reassured Muriel the instant she saw a tear forming. "This is wonderful news," Josephine said. "You are young and married and healthy. This baby is going to be healthy too. I know it."

Muriel was not so sure. She doubted Josephine was sure either. Overpromising was just what a good mother did in this situation. Muriel tried to brush off the inference that unwed pregnancy was the reason for Merle's death. When neither woman said anything more, they changed the subject to Christmas preparations. Mildred was hosting the family on Christmas Day, and Josephine and Muriel were to bring the lefse and pies. What kind of pies should they make? They settled on pumpkin, apple, and sour cream raisin pies. They would think more about that subject after the church gift sale, for which they were sewing and embroidering a few more dishtowels. Christmas was coming; that was one of the certain aspects of life.

Over supper that night, John made his usual suggestion to play whist after the ladies finished with dishes. Muriel and Elmer paired up against her parents, and they played nearly all grand hands. In whist, grand hands signified that at least one person thought he or she had enough high-numbered cards to beat the opposing pair but could not consult with his or her partner before declaring it. They all preferred playing grand hands, so that night was true fun, with laughter and playful jabbing that suited Muriel. Cards brought out the liveliness in stoic Norwegians like nothing else. Even full-blooded Norwegians knew that for a fact; they did not need to say it out loud.

When they quit playing for the night, Elmer had no more than closed their bedroom before Muriel blurted out, "I'm having a baby!" Elmer beamed. She was relieved. They talked and laughed for almost an hour—something they had not done since their happy days in Montana. They kept their secret through Christmas and the New Year, just to be safe. But Muriel's anxiety grew during her month of silence because she felt like the pregnancy was not real until she could see and feel the baby growing inside of her, and until she had said it out loud. She did not tell Elmer how worried she was, because what good would it do? She just needed the time to pass. Fortunately, the winter did pass quickly, with Elmer gone helping Carl with his livestock chores and Muriel being a good Fort Ransom daughter and housewife. Most of the time, Muriel was able to stay busy enough with work, or occupied enough through visiting, to keep her mind from racing away with worry. Muriel and Elmer told their families about the baby in mid-February, when it was becoming obvious to everyone she was expecting. Even as a married woman, though, Muriel realized she need not mention this in public. Word gets out about such things on its own. A few women approached her, one on one, to wish her well, and she thanked them. Then they changed the topic.

As spring started to make her annual on-again-off-again appearance, Carl notified Elmer that he and Muriel could move in as soon as they were ready. "The house is finally up to a woman's standards," Carl proclaimed, which Elmer construed as containing his book collection to one room, emptying the spare bedroom, and scrubbing and re-scrubbing the stove.

March 15, 1941, dawned as a sunny, spring-like day. After the men left, Muriel and her mother opened the windows, welcoming the joyful tune of meadowlarks and a fresh breeze off the receding snowbanks. Muriel shook the winter soot out of the rugs, while her mom mixed a cake and prepared the bread dough for their baking. Fort Ransom's long hibernation ended that Saturday morning; even the most reclusive Fort Ransomites were sure to make an appearance in town that night.

But as quickly as spring appeared, she retreated. Muriel and her mom rushed to close windows as the wind picked up and huge snowflakes started falling. Even in the protected valley, the sudden change meant trouble, and Josephine hoped that John would come home from the farm soon. Within fifteen minutes, he stormed through the door, holding it tightly, with no jacket. He was cold, but just fine, he insisted. "One minute, our weather was perfect. The next, I could barely see in front of the car," he told them.

Muriel knew better than to expect Elmer; he would not leave Carl. When the valley had a blizzard, the prairies were a total white-out. They all sat down to coffee next to the hot stove, smelling the sweet cake that Josephine had just removed from the stove. They turned on the radio to WDAY out of Fargo and listened to the announcer talk about the storm being a surprise to everyone. It was widespread, he said, and showed no signs of coming and going quickly. Muriel worried about Elmer, who had left home underdressed for the radical change in weather.

She was right to be concerned. Carl and Elmer had gone in the house to grab jackets, gloves, and hats, but Elmer was several inches taller than Carl, and they scrounged to make do with what Carl had on hand. They hastily herded the cattle and horses—some about to have calves and foals—into the barn. They closed the doors to every building tightly, each taking different buildings, unable to see each other or the house. Each ran from one place to the next on feeling and memory and agreed to meet at the house when they were done. Wind-whipped with wet snow, they found the house within thirty seconds of one another, much to their relief. Red-faced and shivering, they felt the icicles melt off their lashes as they took off everything but their underclothes. This was no time for modesty. They drew their chairs near the stove to warm up, and waited for the feeling in their fingers and toes to fully return. Carl started the coffee, and Elmer asked to use the phone.

By the time the phone rang, Muriel was biting the cracked skin around her nails. He was safe. That was all she needed to know. In fact, she did not want him to even think of leaving Carl's until after the storm. He promised her he would stay put. That night and the next day were long, as Carl and Elmer trekked back outside every few hours to check the animals and shovel the snow in front of the doors to the house, barn, and chicken coop. All the animals seemed content with some feed and water. Elmer called Muriel in the morning and evening on March 16 to let her know he was alright. They all were listening to WDAY for the latest reports. "Wind gusts are estimated up to eighty-five miles per hour," the newsman said multiple times.

Finally, on March 17, the storm subsided, and Carl and Elmer shoveled paths to the barn and chicken coop to bring some relief to the weary animals. Neighbors began to touch base with each other, spreading the terrible news. Albert Jacobson and his youngest child, Albert Jr., had made a hurry-up trip to Fort Ransom before the storm started, dressed lightly, as everyone was. When the storm hit, they left for home, and the wind and snow were so ferocious that their vehicle stalled. They tried walking home and got disoriented in the whiteout. They died next to one another in the snow. Albert, Sr., was seventy-three; Albert, Jr., was only eleven.

The news on the radio told similar stories from different places, attributing the death of thirty-eight North Dakotans and twenty-eight Minnesotans to the Ides of March Blizzard. Many of those deaths came after people left their stalled cars to walk home or to the nearest farm.[26]

Muriel knew it was selfish, but thoughts of the Jacobsons led to images of her own little boy. She distracted herself by making buns for Marie Jacobson, the wife of Albert Sr. and mother of Albert Jr., who lived on a farm near C.A. and Elise with a grown daughter and three grown sons, one of whom was just months older than Muriel. Their despair must be far worse than her own. After all, Muriel was having another baby soon, she and Elmer were about to move out of her parents' house, and the next day was her first wedding anniversary. She should be happy. Muriel and Josephine brought buns to the Jacobsons and extended their sympathies. Not trusting herself to contain her emotions, Muriel let her mom do most of the talking, which they kept brief.

Then Muriel began counting the days until the snow melted and the roads dried out. That is when she and Elmer would move to Carl's place. She had trained her whole life to be a proper farm wife, and now was her time to put her training to use. She felt confident she could exceed Carl's wish for a "decent cook," as he had put it jokingly to Elmer several times in recent months. She knew all the basics, from keeping a consistent fire in the stove to making regular coffee and egg coffee. If one of the men got sick or was gone, she could milk the cows and slop the hogs. She knew tasks that many young women did not, like how to butcher a chicken and render pork lard. Even Josephine said Muriel was ready to run her own household.

---

[26] Tracy Briggs, "Ides of March Blizzard Claimed 72 Lives in the Red River Valley 78 Years Ago This Week," *Grand Forks Herald*, March 13, 2019; C.A. Sandhei, Historical Sketch of Fort Ransom Community (*Litchville Bulletin*, 1953), 17.

Driving to Carl's farm on the west prairie, tiny plumes of chimney smoke showed Muriel where every farmhouse was as far as she could see in every direction. Carl had a tidy grove of trees around the farm, but with leaves still more than a month away, she could see for miles past the barren branches. She watched as the last of the dust-topped snow melted into the north- and east-facing ditches and hillsides. She asked Elmer which fields were his, as he would start plowing soon. Renting the land from Carl, this was Elmer's opportunity to prove himself as a farmer in his own right.

Within a few days of living together, Carl shared that he had studied art, architecture, and interior decorating at the University of St. Louis. He had designed the remodeled Standing Rock Church. Muriel asked question after question, fascinated by this worldly farmer. C.A. had always told Elmer how intelligent and gifted Carl was, but Elmer too hung on Carl's every story. Musicians sought him out to make violins. He built a celestial telescope, and even ground the lens by hand. He built a pipe organ from scratch for a wealthy organist in Fargo. "That organ might be my greatest achievement," Carl said smiling, with a look that seemed a hundred miles away.

"Why, after going away to college and living in a big city, are you farming in Fort Ransom?" Muriel asked with curiosity, thinking of her own parents who had not graduated high school. "You could live anywhere, Carl. You could be crafting instruments and enjoying music and architecture."

"I love the peace and quiet of the farm," he said. "I like talking Norwegian with C.A. and the old-timers around Fort Ransom. I was born here. I'm content here. I'll die here."

Carl was endlessly fascinating to Muriel. She talked and questioned far more at Carl's house than her parents taught her was proper. Elmer chuckled as he shook his head at some of Muriel's ponderings. She was comfortable around Carl, and he seemed to like her exuberance. Living here was a happier time than Muriel could have imagined.

Muriel was most content that spring and summer in the garden. She planted and tended the vegetables Carl wanted, and in the ratio she suggested. "You should have more potatoes, Carl. You could do with fewer green beans and cabbages, and that will make space for the potatoes," she said confidently.

Her voice surprised her ears a little bit, and she smiled. Whether it was Carl's influence, the sunshine, this pregnancy, or her budding independence, Muriel was more like herself here. It was not her old self, but perhaps the next version of herself.

"You make better mashed potatoes and gravy than anyone I know," Carl replied, "so I suppose we should grow more potatoes."

Meanwhile, Muriel's belly grew larger, just like it had grown last year at this time at the Pelton's ranch. Muriel worked through it and commiserated with the only beings she could about her situation. While picking eggs first thing in the morning, she told the hens what fine eggs they were laying this spring. Noticing a mama cat feeding her new batch of four black kittens, Muriel rubbed the cat's chin and whispered what a good mother she was. Carl said nothing of her troubles; nor did the Bethania Ladies' Aid members, who hosted a baby shower in her honor. Such was the custom for all expectant mothers, who needed baby blankets, rompers, and embroidered bibs. Sitting between Josephine and Elise at the head table, Muriel oohed, aahed, and inhaled her emotions. She would exhale them later, doing her chores at the farm.

There was no one to sit Muriel down this time as her ankles swelled, though Elise liked to come by, usually with Elsa Mae, to pick produce and weed the garden. Elise had a gentle way of reassuring Muriel. She arrived at the right times, oftentimes with "extra baking," as she called it. "I was baking bread anyway," or "I just put in an extra loaf," or "I mixed up an extra-large batch of cookies," she would say.

While Elise and Elsa Mae came to see Muriel most days, Elmer and Carl saw C.A. and Chester every day. They worked together on haying and harvesting, fixing and fencing—nearly every task they had. Elmer was at the center of the whole operation. It felt natural to him, in fact. Men of Carl and C.A.'s age were on their way out. They could not physically handle the heavy work they once did, and they resisted the emerging technologies. Elmer had the ideal, easygoing personality to defer to them on points he already agreed with them on, utilize their strengths, and make them feel like they were a part of the action. But when it came to Muriel, he was prepared to drop everything and let the other men take over. He instructed Muriel that when she thought the baby was coming, she was to interrupt him no matter what he was doing.

"I'll be taking Muriel to the hospital when the time comes," he told Carl. "And I'll be waiting there until she has the baby."

"That's good, Elmer. I insist," Carl said. "I'll keep the place running while you're gone."

And so, the morning when Muriel said it was time, Elmer dropped everything and drove her to Mercy Hospital in Valley City. On July 22, Muriel gave birth to a healthy baby girl named Evelyn Louise, with barely-there light brown hair and hazel eyes. Muriel thought she was the most beautiful baby in the world, and Elmer agreed. Mother and baby stayed in the hospital for a week, and every day when Muriel woke up, Evelyn was still doing well. This time, she had a baby to take home. Elmer picked his girls up on the morning of July 29—Muriel's twentieth birthday.

Driving carefully back to Carl's farm, Elmer joked, "This is the slowest drive I've ever taken you on!"

"Just keep your eyes on the road, Elmer!" Muriel teased. It was impossible for either one of them not to stare at Evelyn, asleep and content on Muriel's lap.

The grandparents came over that night to enjoy Josephine's angel food cake, and the grandmas took turns holding the baby. Muriel was eager for the party to end, so that she could have her baby to herself again. Already thinking ahead to what should have been Merle's first birthday the following day, she was prepared to mother Evelyn to the point of perfection. Never would a baby be more loved.

Doting on Evelyn was precisely what got Muriel through Merle's first birthday. Her heavy eyes met Elmer's as they got out of bed that morning, and that glance alone spoke their grief. Every day began with the same knowing glance, and every day Muriel mothered Evelyn a little bit more. Muriel felt Merle all around the house and in everything she did. Finally, on the night of August 10, when she and Elmer walked into their bedroom with Evelyn after a day completely consumed by harvest, Elmer spoke his name: "I can't believe Merle isn't here."

The tenderness of that moment was sacred and pure to the point that it could never be mentioned again. Muriel filled her days, and still she knew she could never fill the void in her heart that was and would always be Merle. Thank God for Evelyn. What a blessing she was.

MOVING FORWARD

IF 1941 WAS ABOUT ELMER and Muriel proving they could be farmers, 1942 was to be about proving they would be farmers. They loved Carl; they even liked living with Carl for a year. His house was warm and fit all four of them perfectly well. He thanked Muriel profusely for every meal and praised Elmer for running the farm as well as he could. But Elmer and Muriel wanted a place of their own. When Elmer told Carl, he said, "I understand. You need your own space. Just don't take Evelyn too far away."

With several farms available around Fort Ransom, Elmer had his pick of any he could afford. One of the options was the Henrickson place, which Muriel's brother Luther was thinking of leaving to rent another farm nearby. Elmer preferred the open prairie to the valley, but he at least had to ask Muriel. It was her home place, and if she really wanted it, he was open to moving there. Without hesitating, Muriel said, "Definitely not. I want to move forward, not backward. But . . . Do you want it?"

Laughing, Elmer gave a relieved, "No! No offense to your father."

Really, the Olson place was the only one he wanted. It was 160 acres, less than a mile east of C.A.'s, and less than a mile north of Carl's. The setup was perfect for sharing equipment and labor. What's more, Elmer could even purchase the Olson's machinery and cattle as part of his arrangement with the Federal Farm Mortgage Corporation, which was foreclosing on the place. Now, he just had to wait for spring, when Florence Olson would vacate and Elmer would complete the paperwork.[27]

Other than farming, the main topic on people's minds that fall and winter was the war. Hitler already controlled most of Europe. A German submarine fired on an American destroyer, and now German armies were in the Soviet Union. In order to help the British, President Roosevelt switched factories over to military production and created an office to institute rationing. War seemed imminent.

To lighten the mood at night, Muriel and Carl began to play music together—she on the piano, he on the violin. "Josephine" and the "Blue Skirt Waltz" were two of their favorites. They also liked to take requests from the grandparents or whomever was visiting. Music filled Carl's house and Muriel's soul. This gave Elmer special time with Evelyn, whom he held up to dance to the music. "How ironic that you're teaching her to dance!" Muriel exclaimed. "You'll dance with Evelyn, but not with me!"

These cheerful times formed her best memories of that winter of uncertainties. As Muriel washed the Sunday dinner dishes on December 7, she went silent as news came over the radio that the Japanese had attacked Pearl Harbor. She ran out to the barn to tell Elmer and Carl. They all sat down to coffee in the kitchen and listened. Muriel's parents drove up and entered with serious faces. From that day forward, the war felt close by, even if it only came to them through the airwaves, newspapers, and draft notices. No news spread through Fort Ransom faster than which young men were being called up, and what the war meant for farmers.

As married farmers, Muriel's brothers Harold and Luther would not get called up. Their food contributions were too critical to send them off to war. Her brother Palmer, who was in the Army National Guard in Minneapolis, would likely be called to active duty. Elmer's brother Harold, a bachelor, was the first in either family to be

---

[27] According to C.A. Sandhei's 1942 daybook, Elmer and Muriel moved onto their farm on March 31, 1942. No records of the legal transaction between the Federal Farm Mortgage Corporation and Elmer Sandhei exist in Ransom County's register of deeds.

drafted, but was quickly rejected because of a heart defect. Of greatest concern were Pud and Chester, now seniors in high school. They would likely be drafted as soon as they graduated.

While no comparison to the loss of young men, Fort Ransom braced for the impacts of rationing—sugar and tires in particular. Muriel needed sugar for nearly every item she baked; later in the year she would need it to can jellies and tomatoes. The logical first step was to bake fewer sweets. Given how resourceful Josephine and Elise were from enduring the drought years, Muriel was sure they would have other ideas for getting by with less sugar; less of anything. "You'll have to eat your lefse without sugar until the war is over," Muriel joked with Carl and Elmer.

"If we can't have sugar on our lefse, I don't even want it!" Elmer exclaimed.

"If they aren't eating lefse in Norway, it's only right to not eat lefse in Fort Ransom," said Carl. "Maybe by Christmastime, the war will be over, and we'll all have lefse again."

Really, they were very fortunate to be farmers. They had their own meat, eggs, milk, butter, and lard. They grew their own vegetables and picked their own fruit. They canned, butchered, and cured. People who lived in cities purchased nearly all their food. Fort Ransom was a good place to be, they agreed.

The men foresaw flat tires becoming a problem if the war lasted more than a few months. As farmers, they had access to more gas than city-dwellers, and the U.S. had its own supplies. But with the Japanese controlling the world's source of rubber in the Dutch West Indies, there was no simple way to get more rubber.

While the war dominated conversations and altered daily life, Elmer and Muriel also had happy distractions in their upcoming move. Muriel had not seen the Olson place up close yet, but Elmer's plan to buy it was coming together, and he promised to drive her up there as soon as the bank gave the go-ahead. She only knew that it was bigger than any house either of them had ever lived in. It had six bedrooms! Thinking ahead, Muriel thought that was considerably more than they would need. Still, she hoped they might be able to fill at least three bedrooms.

In March, Muriel felt the familiar nausea again. She thought of a boy, like Merle—a farmer. She stopped herself from taking the thought any further, as a healthy baby was all she really wanted. "A winter baby," she said to herself, "a year and a half apart. That'll be just right."

She waited to tell Elmer until she could make the announcement at their new house, hopefully within a couple of weeks. When the morning came in late March, Elmer drove down the long, muddy driveway and stopped the car directly in front of the white, two-story house. It was nowhere near as grand as the Pelton's big stone house in Montana, but for Fort Ransom, it was impressive. She was instantly drawn to the two large porches—especially the screened-in porch in the southeast corner of the house. "Let's save that porch for the end," Muriel said, flashing a broad, mischievous smile and stretching her fists in the pockets of her wool coat.

Elmer grinned the way he always did when Muriel was up to something, and led her onto the adjacent open porch, squeezing her small hand in his. As the home's main entrance, there would be a lot of activity here in the years ahead, she thought, imagining little feet coming and going, and boots and overshoes parked near the door. Opening the door, they stepped into a room with a cream separator at the center, a washing machine near the wall, and empty hooks awaiting their coats. They passed through another door, which led to a large kitchen with a cook stove, an icebox, the telephone, and a pantry closet. Eyes widening, she had only seen a pantry at the Pelton's house! She would be able to store all her canning jars here, and not have to make so many trips to the cellar. Next on the tour came their bedroom and the large parlor with a duo-therm oil burner, the main source of heat for the house. "That's all yours, Elmer," she said, moving straight into her instructions for the exact spot she wanted her old piano, which Luther was to haul here.

From another room off the kitchen, they ascended the curved wooden staircase up to the second floor. A long hallway extended in both directions, with three bedrooms on one side and two more on the other. In a complete surprise, the upstairs had a *bathroom*! It had a claw-foot bathtub, a porcelain sink, and a flush toilet, with the reservoir tank high up on the wall above the commode. Beneath them was a black and white tile floor. Muriel made no effort to contain her astonishment and pleasure; she ran in place with her arms over her head! Elmer, though also impressed, had to remind her, "The house has no running water, Muriel. This bathroom has never been used."

"We'll change that," she surmised.

At the east end of the hallway was the veranda, a term Muriel doubted she had ever said aloud until then. She felt stately walking out onto it, approaching the spindled posts at the edges. "How romantic!" Muriel proclaimed.

"This is for looks," Elmer quickly said, emphasizing his words with a gentle hop on the galvanized metal covering the floor, with wintry ice still lingering in the grooves. "This floor is an accident waiting to happen. We can't let any kids out here. We probably shouldn't be out here."

The giddy pair returned to the main level, and Muriel's heart began to race. Walking into the screened-in porch, Elmer said, "Well, that's the whole house. What do you think?"

"I think I'm glad for all the bedrooms," she declared.

Elmer paused and locked eyes with Muriel. She stood on her tiptoes and nodded. "When?" he asked.

"It should be sometime in December."

Muriel and Elmer stood hand-in-hand at the screen door, looking out at what was to be their farmstead. They talked about settling Evelyn into the nearest upstairs bedroom, scrounging up furniture, and gathering chickens and livestock from C.A., Uncle Oscar, and Carl. They laughed about Muriel saving the baby news for this day. For a few precious moments, they did not think of or talk about the war. This place was going to be where they would make their life together.

A FARM FAMILY

BY THE END OF 1942, MURIEL and Elmer already knew they belonged here. On a moonlit night, they could see the buildings at C.A.'s farm a half-mile away. When the children were older, Muriel vowed to walk as a family to Grandpa and Grandma's house one night in the moonlight, no lanterns, the glistening snow showing the way. This farm was where they were meant to raise their family. At present, this was eighteen-month-old Evelyn, who was enamored with her parents' laps, and newborn Tommy, who had joined them on December 7 and hardly cried or troubled them since. Muriel was smitten with both of them.

Their first year of farming for themselves was a successful one. They had a plentiful harvest in August and September and a decent profit as well. With soldiers to feed, wartime prices for grains and livestock were good—far better than what farmers had received in years, if not two decades. Muriel and Elmer were also every bit up to the tasks involved. They had been training to farm their whole lives, and they were both hard workers in their prime. What's more, "We're a good team," Elmer regularly said to Muriel.

"We are," she agreed. "We're the Fred Astaire and Ginger Rogers of farming."

Muriel and Elmer were in love. They had a natural rhythm and mutual respect on the farm. Muriel did not manage the household so much as she owned it. She brought spirit to her work like she did her marriage and motherhood. With vigor and precision, she had a knack for making the kitchen look like it had cleaned itself while she set a gourmet meal on the table and put Evelyn in her highchair. When Elmer walked in, a calm descended on the kitchen to match the tidy surroundings. He carried himself like a man who had been farming his whole life, and he had. Elmer had an easygoing way about him; even his humor was relaxed. He and Muriel meshed like they were meant to make a life together, on this farm.

During the war years and beyond, Elmer and Muriel also had extra people around the house on an almost daily basis. Muriel's siblings had farms and families of their own to take care of, with the exception of her favorite sister Frances, who was to marry Glenn Sorby, a fellow Fort Ransom farmer. Frances and Glenn were Saturday night regulars, when the foursome would play cards and visit until midnight. Carl stopped by once or twice a week at coffee time, both to visit and bounce Evelyn or Tommy on his knee at the kitchen table. Other neighbors came for coffee about once a week as well, never on a schedule, which was just how Muriel liked it. She was always up for surprise company.

By far the most common guest at her table was Elmer's brother Chester, who became Chet as much as Chester after Evelyn took to calling him that. He came over daily to help Elmer, as Elmer did in return. The two Sandhei farms, though separate financially, operated as one in terms of shared labor, horsepower, and machinery. This had been the case since Chester's graduation from high school in May of 1942. He and Pud had gotten draft notices within days of each other. Pud failed the military physical on account of a hernia and soon moved to Minneapolis to find work. Chester failed because of his bum right leg, which he had broken two years earlier when a runaway team of horses had thrown him from the manure spreader. His injury was so severe that he delayed his senior year of school by a full year to recover.

"I've never been more thankful for Chester's broken leg than the day he got rejected by the army," his mother said after he came home.

C.A. agreed. With Harold teaching and Elmer running his own farm, C.A. expected Chester to gratefully take on the duty of farming the home place. That was the tradition in Norway, and it was an honorable one, thought C.A. Therefore, when Chester received a scholarship offer from Concordia College, C.A. had a serious talk with him about the pros and cons. Ultimately, Chester remained at home. Whether the decision to forego college and stay on the farm was Chester's or C.A.'s, Elmer did not want to speculate.

Muriel was sure C.A. was to blame. "Your brother does a good job of hiding how he feels," Muriel said wryly, "but not having a choice tends to eat at a person."

This was how three Sandhei men came to operate two farms whose land was almost next to one another. Elmer milked his ten cows, fed his two horses, and slopped the dozen hogs starting at 6:30 in the morning. He walked into the kitchen by 8:00 a.m. for breakfast with Muriel and the children. By that time, Muriel had gathered eggs from her thirty hens in the lean-to off the barn, gotten herself and the children dressed for the day, made oatmeal for Evelyn and Tommy, and made eggs and toast for the adults. As they finished eating, Chester arrived to haul hay and clean barn stalls, then the brothers did similar chores at C.A.'s place. Depending on where they were at coffee time, they came to Muriel's kitchen or Elise's kitchen. They disbursed to their own houses for dinner at noon, worked together in the afternoon, and possibly took another coffee break, when one or two neighbors might also show up to visit. Dinner was typically at home, unless Elise invited Elmer's clan over for meat and potatoes to give Muriel a break.

Around these activities, the men chopped wood, made car and machinery repairs, and endlessly fixed flat tires. Muriel washed laundry every Monday, ironed every Tuesday, and cleaned floors every Wednesday. Each Saturday and Tuesday afternoon, she prepared her cream and eggs to trade for groceries on open night. In the spring, summer, and fall, Elmer and Muriel added seasonal tasks to the routine and skipped the formal coffee breaks. Elmer worked the fields with his dad and Chester, while Muriel tended the garden, which included a heavy measure of potatoes, onions, and carrots to save on canning during the war.

Together with Elise and Elsa Mae, Muriel picked rhubarb, apples, and every berry around—both strawberries and raspberries in their own gardens and Juneberries and chokecherries from bushes dotting the prairie. Muriel memorized all the berry spots Elise showed her, knowing that someone else was now picking from the bushes in the valley, where she had filled so many pails as a girl. They canned jams and jellies together as well, pooling the extra sugar that at least one of them received for canning through the local ration board. If they were lucky, both received extra sugar; then Muriel shared with her mom or sisters who needed it, knowing they would do the same for her. Weeks passed standing at the stove, boiling sauces, and giving canning jars their hot water baths. Sweat dripped down Muriel's neck. Once her back was drenched, she felt relieved to be done with that process for the day.

The children were underfoot throughout many of Muriel's chores. She timed a few, like ironing and baking bread, around naps. Both grandmothers were eager babysitters on open nights or on short notice. Muriel washed the children's hands and faces extra well, put fresh clothes on them, and dropped them off for a few hours. Grandma Sandhei was especially popular, because the grandchildren had a vast range of places to explore on the farm.

As for Elmer, he was the most grateful, complimentary man Muriel knew. "That was delicious. Thank you," he said after every meal. Sometimes, he was more specific, like, "Carl is right. Nobody makes better mashed potatoes and gravy than you do."

After supper, he amused the children on the living room floor to give Muriel a break and get his own time with them. Elmer teased Tommy, his doppelganger, by pretending to give him spankings. He took Tommy over his knee, lightly patted him on the bottom, and Tommy belly-laughed through every second.

Elmer's favorite activity was to give "horsey rides." Sitting at the edge of the sofa, he crossed his legs, took turns putting Evelyn or Tommy on his foot, and bounced his leg up and down. As the children held on and giggled, he chanted a Norwegian verse:

> *Rida rida ranka*
> *Hesten heter Branka*
> *Hesten heter Abalgra*
> *Sit der liten guten pa*

This was the story of a horse named Abalgra who was nice to ride. For extra effect, Elmer added a neigh, like a horse, and said, "Hold on extra tight! He's feisty today!"

On nights when Muriel sewed or mended in the living room, Elmer liked to make her a character in one of his stories to amuse the children. Most of his stories involved Norway, some well-formed and likely passed down from C.A., and others completely invented in the moment. These were the warm, happy memories being made inside the home where Muriel imagined her children surpassing her height, eating her out of house and home, and getting in trouble with their cousins upstairs.

After putting the children to bed, Muriel and Elmer turned the radio on to learn the latest news from the war. Places they had never heard of—Guadalcanal, Bougainville, Tarawa, and the Marianas—were talked about for months on end. After D-Day, the optimism was high that the war would end soon. But that talk slowly faded.

Throughout the war, Muriel joined the other Standing Rock women in supporting relief efforts to Norway and needy organizations both at home and abroad. The women were almost constantly gathering clothing or money to send to Norway, which the Germans occupied. If a church event was coming up, they finished a special quilt to raffle off, with proceeds going to Norwegian Relief, which channeled supplies and funds to Norway through Sweden.[28] Charity

---

[28] Zion Ladies' Aid meeting minutes, December 11, 1941–March 8, 1945, Standing Rock Lutheran Church, Fort Ransom, North Dakota.

for the war effort was a point of pride in Fort Ransom, like it was across the country.

Making do was another badge of honor around Fort Ransom—almost a competition. At ladies' aid meetings, they had long conversations about how to be creative in the kitchen. One woman used shredded carrots to sweeten cookies in place of sugar; another tapped her box elder trees for syrup. Each had her own idea about how to stretch ground beef for the best-tasting meatloaf—one part oatmeal to one part grated potato peels, two parts oatmeal to one part chopped mushrooms, et cetera.

"We're reliving the life of our mother," Muriel said to her sister Frances one afternoon as they walked to their cars after the ladies' aid meeting. "Same place; different farms. Ma contended with nine kids and the Depression years. Surely, I can manage two kids and a war. And you aren't far behind."

"Well, we are in a different ladies' aid than Ma is," Frances joked. "See you on Sunday."

Every week in church, and at every ladies' aid meeting, Pastor Sandanger led what felt like all of Fort Ransom in prayers for their boys in danger. They all prayed for strength for these boys' families, for the farmers supporting the war effort, and for relatives in Norway. In her own prayers, Muriel asked for the heavens to watch over her sweet Merle.

Never, in all the prayers she said during the war, did she think to pray for Ethel. On June 18, 1943, Muriel stood in the doorway of the screened-in porch, enjoying her afternoon coffee while the children napped. A southeast breeze brought wafts of yellow-sweet clover through the screens and carried the swift, pillowy clouds over the grain fields. She would finish her coffee and bring the rest of the pot to Elmer in the field. But when the phone rang and Muriel heard Mildred's faint voice, she instantly began to cry. Ethel had drowned in the cistern at the Carlblom farm that afternoon. Ethel was married to Henry Carlblom; their daughter Shirley was about to turn five years old.

Muriel did not ask Mildred for more details. She dropped off Evelyn and Tommy at Elise's house, stopped to tell Elmer in the field, and drove to meet her family at the Carlblom farm ten minutes away. All she could think was, "What on earth did you do, Ethel?"

Ethel was eight years older than Muriel; their relationship was better described as "friendly" rather than "friendship." Ethel had never been social. She had seemed anxious in church, let alone a houseful of people. But while Muriel had always suspected that Ethel had nerve issues, her family had never talked about it. Nerve issues, like dead babies, were not discussed in Fort Ransom.

Following Ethel's death, the speculation around this being a suicide was rampantly *whispered* about in town chatter. Muriel confided only in Frances, and vice versa. But Josephine, like Ethel's husband, called it a "terrible accident." Ethel had stumbled and fallen. And so, that became the official family line. Here, women cried behind closed doors and moved on with their lives. It was best to get back to work and not think about the death or the gossip.

John and Josephine were not the same people after Ethel died. They were quieter, more stoic, if that was possible. John was fading. Content to listen to the radio from his easy chair in the living room, he no longer dawdled at the farm, pretending to help Luther one last year before losing the home farm at the end of 1943.[29] The farthest he walked most days was to the post office, which was in a house two blocks away, where all the town residents had boxes. Muriel wondered how much more time John had.

During every visit to her parents' house, they talked about the crops, church activities, and local young men fighting in the war. Bertram Olson, Kermit Rufsvold, Wallace Holkestad, and Ole Henrikson died in the war. Ole's father, Adolph, was John's brother; they just spelled their last name differently. Ole was a year older than Muriel, and they grew up together. Her brother Palmer was shipped to Ha-

---

[29] Ransom County, North Dakota, Document No. 86613; John H. Henrickson and Josephine Henrickson with Federal Farm Mortgage Corporation, 15 December 1943; Register of Deeds, Ransom County.

waii in early 1945, and to Leyte in the Philippine Islands that spring. In his letters to John and Josephine, Palmer wrote about his unit living in tents near the beach, waiting for the United States to invade Japan. Muriel suspected he was in harm's way, despite him saying not to worry. Meanwhile, news reports predicted the fall of Germany within days.

Throughout the waiting of wartime, through Ethel's death and her parents' decline, Muriel's rock was Elmer. Their farm was her home. As she shared with Elmer that their family was about to grow again, she felt secure this time. It was April 1945, and she had two healthy children and a good husband. He did not ask if she was worried, and she did not tell him about the moments when she was. He had lived the loss of Merle too; she did not need to speak it.

With Elmer in the field most days, Muriel sent Tommy and Evelyn to deliver lunch to him unless he happened to be in the farmyard. One sunny, eighty-degree day that summer, she walked with them. Shading herself with her hand on her damp brow, she watched, completely captivated, as they proudly ran to their dad with big smiles when he turned off the tractor. He lifted each of them up, threw them in the air, and twirled them around before they sat down to eat in the shade of the tractor wheel. As they wolfed down the lunch, Muriel admired Elmer pouring cream into his coffee cup, dwarfing it with his large hands with long fingers. He savored it like it was the best coffee he had ever tasted. He let each child take a sip. That scene stayed with Muriel, suspended in perfection to the sound of the children's hearty laughter.

BENCHMARKS

MURIEL WOULD ALWAYS REMEMBER Marjorie Ann's birth and her dad's death together. Marge came along at the happiest of times—December 21, 1945—when most of the men were home from the war, safe and sound with their families again. Fort Ransom felt whole and hopeful, with busy open nights and cars lining Main Street most days. Farming was going well. Evelyn was a good helper with her little sister, and Tommy followed Dad and Uncle Chet around most of the time, eager to start milking cows and fixing cars himself. Just as Muriel realized how nicely her life was moving along, her dad died.

It was April 22, 1946. His funeral was held in the Standing Rock Lutheran Church just weeks after Marge's baptism. At seventy years old, John had been a Standing Rock faithful for fifty-eight years. The visitation and viewing took place in his and Josephine's home, which was customary. Because everyone knew everyone else in Fort Ransom, more than a hundred people came to pay their respects and have a bite to eat. Every event, happy or sad, required abundant food, and John's wake was no different. Hot dishes, salads, sandwiches, cakes, and cookies—made by friends and relatives who had stopped by the house in advance—covered the kitchen table.

After the funeral, Muriel and her sisters helped Josephine open the cards. The men, of course, had to get back to planting. Work hours were precious. Muriel brought home leftover hot dish and ham sandwiches for Elmer late that night. She hardly remembered crawling into bed or getting up when Marge cried, and still she got up the

Elmer with his arms around daughter Evelyn, son Tom standing behind them, and Elmer's younger brother Chet at the Elmer Sandhei farm. Circa 1946. (Courtesy Tom Sandhei)

next morning, an hour before Elmer. By mid-morning, she was back at her mother's house with Mildred, Frances, and Bernice. They completed the thank-you notes, with direction from Josephine on what to "make sure to say" to those who brought food and flowers and worked in the kitchen after the funeral. Then the girls cleaned the house and divvied up the food while deciding what would become of their mother. Their decision was to change nothing, for now. Josephine was in her mid-60s, more than capable, and determined to stay in her house.

Muriel and her sisters proceeded to visit their mother more often. "I thought I'd bring you some eggs, Ma," Muriel said, and then sat down to coffee while the older children played outside and Josephine held the baby.

This kind of approach, coming with a useful purpose and staying longer than they used to, became the norm between the sisters and their mother. It went without saying that Josephine would not tolerate any obvious displays of help, care, or watchfulness. The sisters had to take turns and be coy. Muriel accepted this as a natural part of life, and so giving extra time to Josephine just became part of the family routine.

Just as Muriel would always associate her dad's death with Marge's birth, those events would also be the first after the war and the last before electricity. In the spring and summer of 1948, rural electricity came to Fort Ransom. It started with wiring homes—putting switch plates and outlets on the walls and light bulbs in the ceilings. Then came setting the electrical poles in the ground, which Chet took Evelyn and Tommy to see, and hooking up individual farms.

Finally, that June, Elmer and Muriel turned on their electricity! Of course, they already knew the conveniences of electricity from their months with the Peltons in Montana. Now the Sandheis, too, had a wall switch and corresponding ceiling light in each room of their house. They had outlets to plug in appliances. They also put a yard light between the house and the barn, and lights inside the barn.

No longer did they need to carry kerosene lanterns from room to room and out into the yard.

"I sure do wish my dad could have lived to see the farmyards all lit up," Muriel mused. "He'd have loved to see the barn from the house at night. He'd have called electricity 'quite a contraption.'"

In the months that followed, Elmer and Muriel bought a new kitchen stove that was electric on one side and wood-burning on the other. They bought a refrigerator and a new radio. Their neighbor and good friend Oscar A. Olson, who was an electrician and a farmer, converted their washing machine motor from gas to electric. These changes improved daily life. Muriel could control the temperature of her oven with the twist of a button, rather than guess based on how much heat was coming off the stove. She could store milk in the fridge in the kitchen, instead of pull it up from the well outside.

While electricity transformed home life, tractors transformed farm life. C.A. had purchased his first tractor, a Farmall F12, after he made his first decent profits from farming the Nelson place. The neighbors were rapidly transitioning from horses to tractors, and he was not one to be left behind. Elmer, who was even more caught up in mechanization, bought a used Farmall A. This meant two tractors working at a time on the two farms. Instead of a team of horses pulling the plow, disk, drag, or binder, the tractors now did that. "The tractor is faster," Elmer said plainly, "and it doesn't need to be fed."

In 1948, C.A. traded his F12 for a brand-new Farmall B, which could cultivate two rows at a time instead of one. Elmer needed a few more good farming years before he could responsibly afford to upgrade, but he knew the day would come. "It's only a matter of time before tractors replace horses altogether," Elmer supposed.

Even with help from tractors and electricity, farm life was far from idyllic every day. They still had no indoor water, although electricity would make that possible—soon, Muriel hoped. In the summer of 1948, Elmer and Muriel's well caved in about fifteen feet below ground. Elmer and Chet worked for almost a week to shore it back up with only their manpower and a few tools. In the winter, the men still chopped wood for some of the heating and cooking at both farms. They also chopped holes in the ice to give the cattle a drink from the water tank and banked snow up against the house foundations for insulation against the subzero temperatures. Elmer needed horses to haul hay through the snow and pull the sleigh to town when the 1938 Chevy could not pass through the snowdrifts. Sleighing was fun for Elmer and Muriel in December. By January, though, the novelty faded, and the cold temperatures and extra work were too harsh to enjoy, even though the children smiled in delight every time.

Muriel and Elmer sat down for coffee together after a sleigh ride to school one January morning. Marge was napping. It was an unusual morning coffee break in that they were alone—no Chet, Carl, or Oscar A. Evelyn and Tommy were not sitting on their laps, dunking cookies in their coffee. For a few moments, Muriel and Elmer sat deep in their own thoughts. "Our kids aren't going to remem-

Muriel driving son Tom (left) and daughter Evelyn (middle) in the sleigh, circa 1946. (Courtesy Tom Sandhei)

ber life without electricity and tractors, just like we don't remember life without cars," Muriel said.

"We'll always remember things as either being before electricity or after electricity," he agreed. "Evelyn started school right before we got electricity, and Tommy started right after."

"That's right," Muriel gleamed. "You'll always remember this quiet morning at the kitchen table as being after electricity. We're going to have another baby!"

PLEADING

AS ELMER AND CHET CAME in for coffee one February morning, Elmer sneezed enough times to make them all suspect that he was coming down with a cold. "I don't have time to be sick today," Elmer said. "We have a sick cow in the barn and our car to fix."

After milking that evening, though, he could no longer deny his chills. He came in sweating, winded, and ready to lay down on the sofa with an afghan. Muriel encouraged Elmer to eat some chicken soup for supper, as her mother had often done when John or someone else in the house was sick. Elmer had little interest and no appetite.

Muriel phoned Elmer's mother for advice and added cold cloths to the treatment. When his fever spiked the next morning, February 13, Muriel begged him to let her drive him to Valley City. He refused. Muriel suggested calling the doctor in Lisbon to the house. Again, the response was no. Within an hour, he started experiencing moments of delirium. The children witnessed nearly all the chaos; there simply was nothing she could do to prevent that. Knowing cool cloths could do little more for him in this state, Muriel had no choice but to call the doctor in Lisbon, who said he would be out in about three hours. Concerned about the doctor getting through the snow in the yard, Muriel called Chet to clear a path to the house. Chet hurried outside to a car that did not start, and instantly elected to trudge through the snow to Elmer's place.

The doctor arrived and found Elmer in bed, barely alert. One lung was congested, he said, but he was cautiously optimistic that a sturdy man such as Elmer would recover at home. The doctor returned to Lisbon with orders for Muriel to keep Elmer in bed and comfortable until the fever passed, and to call again if symptoms worsened. Muriel stayed by Elmer's side other than to call her sister Frances to ask for help the next day, and Chet stuck around long enough to occupy the uneasy children until their bedtime, then sat in the silent living room while Muriel helped them change into their pajamas and tucked them into bed. When she reappeared in the living room, she thanked Chet and offered to make a fresh pot of coffee. She knew she would get no sleep that night. She felt haggard after days of endless caretaking, while trying to keep the children away from their father. She had not taken Josephine or Elise up on their repeated offers to help. She had barely slept. She had accepted food from Frances, who had not taken "no" for an answer, so that the children were well fed without Muriel having to cook. She and Chet said very little over coffee. "I'll walk home tonight and be back to do chores in the morning," he finally said, as Muriel stood up to go check on Elmer again. "I want to leave Elmer's car here in case of emergency."

Their goodbyes were hardly audible as Chet opened the door and a frigid draft blew in. At sunrise, Muriel knew a car would do her no good. Elmer was unconscious when she called for an ambulance from Valley City, which had the best hospital nearby without going to Fargo. She would not consider the doctor from Lisbon ever again for any reason. Chet arrived just after she called the ambulance, which was nearly an hour away. Frances arrived to find a frantic Muriel and ordered her to stay with Chet while she roused the children and brought them back to her house before they heard the siren of the ambulance. Chet called his parents with orders to get dressed and find a ride to the hospital while he did chores and made sure Muriel was not alone. "I'm not sure he's gonna make it, Ma," Chet said in a broken voice. A North Dakota farmer, durable Norwegian, and resonant tenor in the choir, Chet had never sounded lower. Muriel overheard him and shivered, feeling suddenly as though she was hovering above herself, no longer in her body. She willed the unfolding story beneath her to blow away in the wind biting at the windows.

The wait for the ambulance was agonizing. Muriel did not really know what was happening. For her, there was no wondering who would feed the children or the cattle that morning. Laundry, which she did every Monday like clockwork, never came to mind. Nor did the last time she combed her hair. She restrained her emotions to reassure the children that they would see their father that night, after their aunt Frances helped them to school that day and Mom helped Dad feel better. She managed a smile as Frances ushered them quickly out the door. Unconsciously, she donned a fresh gray top and sweater and navy wool pants to be ready for the ambulance. Not even then did she think of the life inside her. The door slammed. "Chet," she reminded herself, not going to check, but rather holding Elmer's hand as she rubbed it with her free hand. Elmer's breathing was labored; he gasped at times after not taking in a breath for several seconds. Shook to the core, she ran a cool washcloth gently over his face to try calm his tremors. "It's okay, Elmer," she said softly. "Help is coming. Just a little bit longer. I'll stay with you. You're going to be okay."

Elmer's eyes were closed, and he gave no indication he could hear her, yet there was no calming him. The sirens announced the ambulance. Chet held the door open for the two men, who rushed in with a stretcher. Muriel moved to the far corner of the bedroom to make room for them. One was about her age, and barely taller or heavier than her; the other was around fifty and burly. Keeping her eyes on Elmer, she almost looked through them. The older of the two asked, "Mrs. Sandhei, what can you tell us?"

"He's been unconscious since 7:15 this morning, just a few minutes after he asked me for water. He couldn't say anything else," she said with such a dry mouth that suddenly she began to cough. Recovering after a few seconds, she started again as the men checked Elmer's breathing and pulse. "The doctor from Lisbon was here yesterday. One lung was congested. He thought Elmer would be better today."

Chet appeared in the doorway, holding a glass of water and staring listlessly at Muriel. As she walked toward him, the older man said with a kind voice, "We'll be ready to move him in a moment, Mrs. Sandhei. You are welcome to ride along with us." She drank as much as her body could stand, which was not half the glass, and went to put on her coat and shoes. Chet went to the kitchen with the glass, and as Muriel buttoned her coat and grabbed her purse, he asked, "Okay if I come with you?"

"Of course," she said without a pause, and they walked toward the bedroom together just as Elmer was transferred to the stretcher. Muriel swallowed hard and blinked rapidly to hold in the emotions. Chet went to open the door. Before she had another thought, she was inside the ambulance and did not know how she had gotten there. She was in the back beside Elmer, with the older stranger who gave his name without her catching it. Chet was in the front passenger seat. They started moving, with no sign of any change in Elmer, other than the light of day revealing how pale and damp his face was. His breaths were arduous and erratic.

As they turned out of the driveway, the driver turned on the siren, and Muriel spotted a glimpse of C.A., Elise, Harold, and Elsa Mae crammed into a car driven by their neighbor Art Highness. He must have been waiting for the ambulance at the end of the driveway and would follow them to Valley City. Muriel gazed at Elmer's face, ran her fingers over his clammy hand, and said nothing aloud. With her entire being, she pleaded to God to not take this precious man away from her. She implored Elmer to stay and reviewed, one by one, what each child loved most about him, and how they all needed him.

By the time the vehicle stopped at Mercy Hospital, Elmer's breathing seemed worse, but Muriel was not sure if that was real or if she had worried herself into believing that. The men from the ambulance wheeled him inside, Elmer was moved behind closed doors, and Muriel and Chet were urged toward the reception area. She approached the middle-aged woman dressed in all red behind the desk, decorated with tissue paper hearts. "It's Valentine's Day," Muriel thought to herself. Last week she had helped the children write on Valentine cards for their classmates, yet now she was not sure if the children had even taken their cards with them that morning. "May I have your name, please?" Muriel was transported back into the moment and felt a shallow echo inside as she answered that and a dozen more questions. Was this happening?

The woman told Muriel she could take a seat in the waiting area until the doctor had an update for her. She walked over to Chet and the rest of the Sandhei family. "What can you tell us, Muriel?" asked Elise.

Assuming Chet had shared everything significant about the day thus far, she shared the only news she had: "The doctor will come talk to us as soon as he's examined Elmer." She sat down in an uncomfortable wooden chair alongside the others and closed her eyes for just a moment. She felt utterly vacant. The family sat in silence for the next thirty minutes, save C.A. telling Chet, "We'll ride home with Art later today so you can take care of the cattle chores, and make sure Elmer's car starts."

Muriel was too exhausted, too focused on Elmer to pay any mind to her father-in-law's priorities that day. Then the doctor appeared and asked to have a word with Mrs. Sandhei. Muriel rose immediately, as did C.A. and Elise. Muriel nodded at nobody in particular, but in general consent. They followed the doctor down the hall for privacy and made their introductions. "I've admitted Elmer to the hospital," the doctor began. "He has the flu and pneumonia in both lungs. I've given him penicillin and will do everything I can to help him. But Elmer's case is severe. It's advanced. His chance of survival . . . is low . . . I'm so sorry to have to tell you this."

"What is low?" enquired Muriel, her eyes filling but holding.

"Possible, but low," he said. "I suggest you say all that you want to him now."

Muriel looked down to her shoes. Her countenance fell. For a few seconds, she stood perfectly still. She did not look to Elmer's parents for any response. They did not reach out to one another. Muriel fixed on the doctor's face, and he motioned for her to follow him. Soon the entire family was behind her and the doctor. When the doctor stopped at the door to Elmer's room and asked for no more than one or two visitors at a time, Muriel held firm in her position at the front, and felt herself exhale in relief when no one joined her.

She walked in to meet Elmer, clinging to life in a hospital bed, and the gravity set in. Approaching him slowly, she spoke to herself calmly. "Okay, Muriel. You can do this. You have to do this."

Muriel took her time with Elmer, pleading with him to recover. When she exited, Elise and C.A. went into the room, while Elmer's siblings awaited their turn. Muriel excused herself to call Frances about keeping the children and giving them no specifics, besides telling them their dad was still sick and their ma was helping him. Then, suddenly and silently, Muriel and Elise were alone with Elmer. They took turns resting their eyes and sitting beside him until the sun rose on February 15. Pastor Sandanger and C.A. came to the hospital that day, and Muriel softly urged Elise to go home with them and get a full night of sleep. C.A. agreed with her for once, and Elise relented.

Muriel savored the next few hours. She studied Elmer's kind face and yearned to see his eyes. She talked softly to him about her dreams for their children. "I will make sure they learn to be good helpers and grow up around their grandparents. I'll make sure they study and do well in school. They will go to college, Elmer."

After she spoke all her words, she dozed for a bit at his bedside, until his convulsing body woke her. She ran out to alert the nurse, who instantly went into Elmer's room and asked Muriel to wait in the hall. Reemerging a few minutes later, the nurse sympathetically told Muriel the end was near. At 1:30 am on February 16, Muriel made her final call to Elmer's parents. They came, and they stayed.

Elmer died at 2:30 p.m. on February 17. Muriel had lost all track of the days. The date had not mattered to her until she sat down to write his obituary. That date would be eternally etched in her mind. She was twenty-seven years old, she had three little ones to feed, and she was expecting. In the home pasture, there were ten cows to milk, and they would be calving in a few weeks. There were thirty chickens, fifteen pigs, and two horses. There were also snow-covered fields expecting Elmer to seed them in a couple of months. And by far the worst reality: Three perfect children were waiting for their dad to come home and play horsey. How could this have happened?

Everyone who came to see Muriel looked like they were terrified for her. Make no mistake—she was petrified. She needed no help realizing she had no source of income. She felt like an emotional wreck while she faked being a pillar of strength. This was the only way she could get through the wake and funeral and the endless comings and goings of a community devastated by Elmer's death. They meant well.

The next few days resembled the days following her father's death, but ten times worse. The wake was held the next Tuesday at the farm, which scared the children and made Muriel's pain even harder to bear. "That's how it's done," said Reverend Sandanger; far be it for a grieving widow to change *that*.

Andrew B. Olson, the snowplow operator in Fort Ransom, came to do extra clearing up to the farmstead, so that folks could come pay their respects. Elmer was a vital person with a beautiful young family, a successful farm, and "so much life ahead of him." That was what everybody said. Muriel remembered almost no specifics, except her brother Palmer putting his arm around her as they stood near the casket in front of the oil burner in the living room. He put his arm around her shoulders, and moments later the door was opened to friends and neighbors who she had known her entire life. That day they seemed almost translucent to her, like there was a light behind them drawing her in.

The funeral was held at Standing Rock the next afternoon. The narthex was filled with men's wet overshoes, and the pews were packed with every able-bodied person from the Fort Ransom community. She left the children with an older cousin, as a funeral was no place for them. Muriel's and Elmer's siblings were in attendance other than her brother Pud from Minneapolis and his sister Alfhild from Omaha. Traveling to North Dakota in February was not a minor trip.

Muriel proceeded with her mom to the front pew as the organist played "A Mighty Fortress Is Our God." She stared ahead, focusing on her grip around her mother's arm as they walked, and settling the weight of her world into the hard, oak pew in front of the pulpit. Pastor Sandanger's words passed by Muriel for the next forty minutes, none really reaching her, but still bringing quiet tears. Some fell slowly into her handkerchief; others she held in for so long that her temples throbbed. She staved off the pain until she returned home three hours later, after the handshakes and obligatory lunch that she could not remember eating.

BOLDNESS

THREE DAYS AFTER ELMER'S FUNERAL, Muriel awoke with a start. She could not lay in bed and cry. She could not wait to be rescued. She noticed her barely perceptible belly as she dressed and walked into her kitchen to start the coffee. The children were still asleep, exhausted from a lack of routine and the heightened activity at all hours of the day. As their mom, exhaustion was not an option. As Elmer's widow, she could not allow his work and dreams to be in vain. She had decisions to make.

First, she knew that staying in this house and on this farm was not feasible. She could not afford it, and she could not keep up with the work. More importantly, thinking of the happy memories she and Elmer had made here would only bring her pain. How could she ever shake the image of Elmer playing horsey with the children on the sofa? Or taking his first sip of morning coffee at the kitchen table and smiling, in delight, that she had made egg coffee? She had to move, and there was only one logical place to go: her mother's house in Fort Ransom.

With her decision made, Muriel took on the business of how to leave the farm. She enlisted Frances's husband Glenn to help her. He was both level-headed and on her side. He was a Fort Ransom farmer, but not a Sandhei. For all those reasons, Muriel believed Glenn was the ideal person to have at her side. Together, they spoke with Andrew Jacobson, a neighbor who was just one month older than Elmer, about renting the house and the land. Andrew, his wife

Lettie, and their daughter Georgia Lee would move onto the farm after the school year ended. In the meantime, Oscar Hans and Chet would continue to do the livestock chores until the animals were sold at the auction sale on March 28. Evelyn and Tommy were at school that day; Muriel stayed in the house with Marge and Frances, who kept her company while they made lefse.

Muriel with Tom (left) and Evelyn (right) next to their farmhouse, circa 1947. (Courtesy Tom Sandhei)

"I want to be home, but I don't want to hear people clamor over Elmer's belongings," she told Glenn. "You're here to represent me. If you need anything from me, I'm close by."

Glenn agreed, and at the end of the sale, he came inside to join the women for fresh lefse and report the outcomes. Elmer's best cow had brought $230; the best horse, $62; the Farmall A, $400; and his tan 1938 Chevy, $250. "You made $4,000 today, Muriel," he told her. "That's very good! That is your money to use as you need."

Muriel knew that $4,000 was a lot of money and that she would need every penny. Without a car, she would also need to rely on the kindness of others. The good news was that seemingly everyone in Fort Ransom was ready to help her in any way they could. She had offers of rides, movers, and babysitters from people she only knew in passing, and some she had never known to be overly generous. There were times when the mere thought of people's generosity toward her brought her to tears. That was true on April 27, when about twenty neighbors on tractors converged on Elmer's 160 acres, where they completed the plowing, discing, harrowing, and seeding in one day.

"People are so good," she said to herself. "Everyone in Fort Ransom is watching out for me."

As the school year came to an end and the grass was just tall enough to wave in the prairie winds, Chet, Frances, and Glenn moved Muriel and the children in with Grandma Henrickson. They brought clothes, canned goods, and little else. Muriel left the furnishings at the farm for the Jacobsons and cleaned her and Elmer's house for the last time with help from Elsa Mae. Muriel walked out the door that day with a pit in her stomach. She had washed Elmer's fingerprints off the switch plates and doorknobs. Although the house was hers according to the mortgage, the new memories made here would belong to someone else.

Josephine's house was nowhere near big enough for five—and soon, six—people. Having experienced four adults living there for a few months, Muriel knew that her three children and a baby would push the limits of two bedrooms, a small living room, and a kitch-

1949

Mch. 25 Clearing off and thawing
enough to be sloppy.
Sign up meeting at Ft. R.
I spent the day there.
Chester took me down, and
also took Elsa Mae to Ludvig
Olson. She and Dorothy went
to a tears meeting in Lisbo.
I rode home with Martin
Libak.
Chester took the cornpicker
home.
Dance at Ft. R. in the evening.

Mch. 26 Foggy weather.
Not much doing except chores.
Young folks went to basketball
game in the evening.

Mch. 27 Sunday. Above 30. Snowing
some. Clearing off in the
afternoon.
Young folks went to show.

Mch. 28 Fair & muddy.
The sale at Elmers place was
held today. It must have
brought $4000.ºº. One cow
brought $235.ºº. 20 head.—
large and small averaged
about $130.ºº.
One horse $62.ºº
Tractor $400.ºº, car $250.ºº

C.A.'s daybook
entry for March
28, 1949, details
the day of
Muriel's auction
sale. (Courtesy
Tom Sandhei)

en with a table for four. But they would make do. Marge slept with Grandma Henrickson, while Muriel and Evelyn slept in the other bedroom. Each bedroom had a bed and a small cabinet for clothes, no closet. Tommy slept on the living room sofa. The children were adaptable, and Muriel had them well trained on compliance.

In the summertime, the children made the tight quarters more bearable by spending nearly every daylight hour outdoors. They played ante-I-over the woodshed, explored Fort Ransom on bike, and tended to explore too close to the river for their mother and grandmother's liking—especially Tommy. For that reason, Tommy stayed with Grandma and Grandpa Sandhei and slept with Uncle Chet much of the summer. In fact, he would stay with them most weekends and every chance he could year-round. Muriel knew that time apart would save Josephine's sanity and would help keep her own relationship with her mother solid. They had always gotten along well, and Muriel did not want her children to jeopardize that—especially when she could not cope without her mom's help.

Muriel's only other coping mechanism was to work hard. Of course, this included gardening. The large lot where Josephine's tiny house stood provided ample space for a garden, and the rich soil along the river was perfect for raising vegetables. With five mouths to feed, Josephine and Muriel planted plentifully that spring. Josephine was sixty-seven years old, and Muriel was in her third trimester of pregnancy, but by no means did that inhibit their work. Not until the first lettuce and radishes were ripe that June did Muriel even look pregnant.

Yet she thought about this baby and Elmer constantly. In the daytime, while she worked, Muriel's rational mind told her this baby would be perfectly healthy. When she crawled into bed, though, Muriel's mind raced. She thought God might still be punishing her for having to get married. First, she had lost Merle. Then Elmer. Would something be wrong with this baby? If only she could talk to Elmer. Bedtime had been their opportunity to catch up on each other's days and thoughts for nine years. Now Muriel dreaded this time. Instead of talking and drifting off to sleep, she was trying to turn off the worries and not cry beside Evelyn. She was lonesome for Elmer.

Perhaps the hardest moments came as the hollyhocks made their annual appearance in yellow, soft pink, and fuchsia. The baby should arrive any day. Elsa Mae's wedding was coming up on August 14. Regardless of which one came first, "I should be happy!" Muriel said to herself.

Instead, when the wedding day arrived, she felt immense and anxious in the cream and blue floral wrap dress she had sewn for herself. She sat up front with her in-laws; the children were at home with her mother. Surrounded by family and people she had known forever, she felt completely alone as "The Wedding March" resounded through the pews of Standing Rock. "Elmer should be here," Muriel thought, squeezing the baby blue handkerchief he had given her after Merle's birth. "But here I am. I'm going to have to do this."

Muriel did not even know what "this" was. Life in general, she supposed. She reminded herself to focus on the present and reserve her thoughts of Elmer for later, just for herself. This day, she was to share in Elsa Mae's happiness. Muriel was to visit with her brother-in-law Harold and sister-in-law Alfhild, and with everyone she had not spoken to at the ice cream social two nights previous. She was to throw rice as the couple exited the church. And that was precisely what she did, with all the grace she could muster in her floral maternity dress.

After the wedding day passed, Muriel focused on the next moment, which was walking around, trying to nudge this healthy baby into making an entrance. On August 18, the wait finally ended. Sweet Elizabeth, whose instant, robust cry brought such relief to Muriel, was born at Mercy Hospital in Valley City, the very place Elmer had died. Muriel stretched her arms to take in Elmer's final creation, and silently but fervently she thanked God. She searched this angel's face for familiar features, and immediately found Elmer's nose. Liz was a beauty.

Back home in Fort Ransom, Muriel lived the "cleanliness is next to Godliness" adage religiously. Anytime the family appeared in public, she scrubbed and polished the children to the nth degree. She also focused on raising four polite, helpful, studious children. Fortunately, Grandma Henrickson and the whole community supported her on that front. Muriel was grateful for all the parents, grandparents and teachers who watched out for her children around town, when they wandered too far from home. She was thankful for her mother, who reinforced their saying "please" and "thank you," setting the table properly, and picking only the ripe vegetables.

Having help from others enabled Muriel to find a job that fall. She almost obsessed over earning money and saving money. Until now, money had been her father's worry or Elmer's worry. But now, she alone was in charge of supporting the family. She talked her plans over with Glenn, who confirmed they were achievable. With his moral support and her mother's help with the children, Muriel began working part-time at George Anderson's new grocery business on Main Street. George owned one of the three stores in Fort Ransom at the time. Olson's was a general store, Bud Hendricks' store offered fresh meat from his locker plant in back, and George's store was a traditional grocery. Muriel cashiered, stocked shelves, and was as popular with customers as she was with George.

"You're a hard worker, Muriel," George assured her. "You could take my place in a heartbeat."

While Muriel had no such intention, she realized that she really was good with customers, and she loved the social aspect of her job. It gave her a break from the rest of her life, which she did not know how badly she needed until she had it. She was happier on account of this job. She was a more patient, more playful mom because of it.

When Muriel worked at the store, Grandma Henrickson babysat Marge and Liz and watched Evelyn and Tommy after school. Josephine was soft-spoken with them and enforced the rules that every child born in Fort Ransom was intrinsically supposed to know:

1) Respect your elders.
2) Do not interrupt adults when they are talking. (This rule might overlap with rule number one, but its importance cannot be overstated.)

3) Play outside.

4) Clean your plate.

5) Show good manners, which almost always begin
with silence.

Muriel appreciated that her mother's teachings were giving her
children the structure that she alone struggled to provide and giving
Muriel herself the mental space to carry through the boldest act of
her life so far. Only Josephine, Frances and Glenn knew about it until
after Muriel had officially done it. She wondered if it was possible
until then.

On November 14, 1949—nine months after losing Elmer,
and three months after having his last child—Muriel paid off the
farm mortgage. She would always remember the remaining balance:
$2,214.02.[30] Riding home with Glenn from Lisbon that day, she had
to pinch herself while the reality set in. She had used some funds
from the auction sale plus Andrew Jacobson's rent payment for the
year to be free and clear of any debt. Moving forward, she would use
Andrew's payments and her earnings from George's store to buy groceries and help her mom pay the electricity bill.

"I'm officially a grownup," Muriel joked to Glenn. "You've
helped me become a grownup."

"I don't know about that, Muriel," Glenn said. "I'm just helping
the best I can."

"Ten years ago, I thought I was an adult," Muriel continued.
"But I wasn't. Now I am. Thank you."

"You're welcome, but I didn't do much," he insisted.

Muriel felt lighter and more capable than she had since Elmer
had been alive and well. She smiled and nodded yes to her mother
when she walked into the kitchen. Josephine returned the expression,

---

[30] Ransom County, North Dakota, Document No. 94034; Muriel Sandhei with Federal
Farm Mortgage Corporation, 14 November 1949; Register of Deeds, Ransom County.
The balance of $2,214.02 remaining on the mortgage would have been below the market
value of the farm and reflects a presumed arrangement dating back to March 1942 and
previous payments from Elmer Sandhei to the mortgage company.

her heart obviously swelling with pride. "You're just in time for dinner," she said. "Marge helped me set the table."

Just like that, Muriel's family took a big leap forward. Muriel washed the dishes while her mother dried, then sat down on the living room floor to play "Tommeltott" with her two young daughters. Muriel had no better understanding of its real meaning now than she did as a child herself, but still she pinched the girls' fingers one by one, chanting:

> Tommeltott
> Slikkepott
> Langemann
> Gullebran
> Lille petter spellermann.

UNCLE CHET

WHEN MURIEL PASSED THE ONE-YEAR anniversary of Elmer's death, she believed she had done the best that she could with the situation she had been given. She did not miss Elmer any less, but her year of firsts was over and done. Not anticipating the next first was a bit of relief. And while Josephine's house was overcrowded, the inhabitants were still getting along without complaint. With responsibilities at work, ladies' aid, and choir practice, Muriel was getting out of the house enough to keep her good humor.

But she had no sooner passed the one-year milestone than her mother informed her that she was going to live with Pud and his wife, Betty, in Minneapolis for the next year. Muriel did not ask why. Initially, she panicked that her mother's departure would present a childcare dilemma. But after sleeping on it for a couple of nights, Muriel realized this would give her and the children some extra space. Besides, she had gotten through tougher predicaments than this one.

Muriel quickly decided to not give up her job or activities. Without her mother at home, she would need time with adults more than ever in order to stay coherent while raising four children. So, Muriel talked with Frances about possible ideas. She also considered, but decided against, approaching her mother-in-law. Elise already helped raise Tommy half the time; Muriel appreciated her too much to ask for more. Before school let out in the spring of 1950, the perfect solution presented herself: Darlene Sorby. She was Glenn and Frances's sixteen-year-old niece, and her parents were willing to let her live with Muriel during her junior year of high school. It was an example of what Muriel did not take for granted about Fort Ransom. People genuinely wanted to help her, and she was humble enough to accept it when it came to her children.

Darlene was beautiful and warm. The children were immediately taken with her, like she was the older sister they had always wanted. On weekdays, Darlene, Evelyn, and Tommy walked to school together down Main Street in a scene worthy of a Norman Rockwell painting. On evenings and weekends, she helped care for Marge and Liz.

Darlene also supervised sledding with Tommy and Evelyn on moonlit nights, when the siblings trudged up the Fort Ransom hill, pulling their steel runner sleigh behind them. The cars had packed down the snow until it was ice. When cars struggled to make it to the top of the hill, the conditions were perfect for sledding. Sometimes Evelyn and Tommy gained enough speed to coast all the way down Main Street before coming to a stop near Grandma Henrickson's house. Then they turned around and climbed back up the hill. Whether sledding or ice skating on the river, Muriel did not worry about the children with Darlene close by.

This was a time when Muriel felt some degree of freedom, even while she relied on others to get anywhere out of town. She still had not replaced the car she had sold at the auction, nor did she intend to do so anytime soon. Her mother had never driven, and as such had no car either. But Muriel had two favorite chauffeurs, and they were happy to help her. First was Peder Bang (pronounced "Bung") Larson, who had the contract for the Star Mail Route. His job was to drive to Lisbon every day except Sunday, pick up the Fort Ransom mail, and deliver it back to the post office in Fort Ransom. Because he was driving to Lisbon anyway, he shuttled Fort Ransomites like Muriel who needed to go to the bank, hardware store, or pharmacy. He would even wait outside the dentist or doctor's office.

The children loved Muriel's stories from her car rides with the friendly, gregarious Pete. Muriel might have one or two new stories, but typically, she told the same ones over and over again, and the children hung on every word, like she was telling them a fairytale. Most of these stories began with, "When Pete was a young boy in Norway," or "When Pete lived in Alaska..." The adventures of Peder Bang were sure to please, every time.

Muriel's second chauffeur was Chet. He was still living with his parents, which was exactly how C.A. liked it. Muriel liked it too, because he was Tommy's closest connection to his father. Sending Tommy to Grandma Sandhei's house was giving him an education in farming from Uncle Chet, which was second only to learning from Elmer. Aside from running into Chet on open nights or waving at him as he picked up or dropped off Tommy, Muriel mainly saw him at family birthdays and on mixed chorus nights. Chet picked her up for their weekly choir practices at Standing Rock and for their performances in neighboring communities from Lisbon to Kathryn. Nobody thought anything of it, including Muriel, at first.

Two years his senior, Muriel had only ever thought of Chet as Pud's friend and Elmer's brother. He was different from Elmer—more social, sarcastic, and studious. He read as much as C.A. or Carl and had the intellect to match them. Unlike Elmer, Chet liked to disagree with his father on everything from political issues to farming methods. Full of rhetoric, Chet said things like, "If he had one more wit, he'd be a half-wit."

His wry sense of humor was not for everyone, but still he was one of the most popular guys around town. Muriel could see why. He was smart, yet common. He was nice-looking, but still blended into the crowd. At six foot three inches, Chet was an inch shorter and not as broad as Elmer. His chin and nose were pointed; Elmer's were square. He was light-complected; Elmer, by Norwegian standards, was medium. Chet wished to have even half of his brother's hair. In short, Muriel did not see much of Elmer in Chet, for which she was thankful.

Even in the tiny community of Fort Ransom, Chet found different activities than those preferred by his older brother. In addition to singing tenor in the mixed choir and the Nokken men's choir, Chet was a highly regarded first baseman for the local baseball team. Locals gathered in the Sons of Norway Park every Sunday afternoon during the summer to watch the friendly competition between Fort Ransom and neighboring teams.

Every summer night except Sunday, Chet and other local men frequented the horseshoe court next to Collette's Tavern on the north side of Main Street. The competition was usually friendly, and more about the beer and comradery than the game itself. Chet, however, was committed to the practice that horseshoes required. He talked the talk and walked the walk and was prepared to argue the benefits of his technique with any man who would debate him.

"You start with the open part of the shoe pointed to the right," he told Muriel, as though she would have the occasion to play sometime soon. "Then you throw it with just enough twist so that the shoe makes three-quarters of a turn to be 'open' when it hits the stake."

Chet did not talk a lot about farming, at least not to Muriel. He seldom mentioned Elmer or C.A. Likewise, she did not confide in him about missing Elmer or raising the children alone. That was not the nature of their friendship. Instead, they shared the talk of the town, the choir, and Tommy. Chet told her what he was reading and kept her up to date on current affairs, which he had more time for than she did. And Muriel was not scared to challenge him on a point or share her opinions. "I'll do my best to get your goat every time," she promised.

And so, Chet picked Muriel up, dropped her off, and nothing else. When Josephine returned home after school let out in 1951, little appeared to have changed in her household. Darlene was living at home again with her parents, until she was to get married that fall. Tommy was spending most of the summer at Grandma Sandhei's house. And Muriel was still working for George and singing in the mixed chorus. Josephine moved right back in with her girls and assumed her role as grandmother/babysitter.

RETURN TO THE FARM

ALL TOLD, MURIEL AND HER children spent five years living in her mother's house in Fort Ransom. As a thirty-three-year-old widow, the mother of four children ages five to thirteen, the breadwinner in her family, and outright owner of 160 acres of farmland, Muriel was not the average woman in town. How she came to be that woman was a blur. Occasionally as she awakened, she even thought for a split second that she was living her good, ordinary life with Elmer back at the farm. It beckoned to her like morning coffee.

Muriel's final year of living with her mother was much like those before. Liz was still at home with her and Josephine, the other children were in school, and Muriel's slate of work and activities was full. Unplanned and without fanfare, though, Chet's pick-ups evolved into coffee at the kitchen table before taking Tommy to the farm. His drop-offs after choir practice became later at night, following a few hands of cards with Frances and Glenn. After Josephine gave her silent approval, Muriel knew Evelyn and Tommy would soon sense the relationship if they had not already. Indeed, they said nothing and acted as though it was perfectly natural. The whole community caught on within the month, in fact. This topic fell into the broad category of realities that spoke for themselves. People in Fort Ransom treated Chet and Muriel like they had been a couple all along.

No one was surprised, then, when Chet and Muriel shared the news in March 1954 that they were engaged. After the children got out of school and Chet put in the crop, they would get married

Muriel and her children lived in Fort Ransom with her mother for five years after Elmer died. Back, left to right: Evelyn and Tom beside Grandma Henrickson (Josephine). Front, left to right: Liz and Marge beside Muriel. **Circa 1953.** (Courtesy Tom Sandhei)

and move back to the farm. Muriel first told this to Frances, who with raised eyebrows said, "You're planning to move to the house you shared with Elmer?"

"I own it," Muriel replied. "It's the logical thing to do."

Muriel assumed that the rest of the family thought exactly as Frances did. So did she; the farm was inextricably tied to Elmer. How could she return to the same farm, the same house, the same bedroom with his brother? How could Chet take Elmer's place? But the reality was that nothing made more sense than bringing her children back to their father's farm, the farm to which she had the title. If Chet was going to farm, and he was, then this was the right decision. She and Chet must silently bear the difficulty until, in time, the place felt like theirs.

Before word started to spread in the community, Chet and Muriel drove out to deliver the news to Andrew Jacobson. Muriel had not been down this driveway in five years. Fidgeting her fingers in her lap and rubbing her muddy black shoes against the floor of Chet's '41 Chevy, her eyes took in every familiar detail. She could still see Elmer hoisting Evelyn up to open the mailbox, and Elmer opening the barn door with Tommy at his side. She put each memory in the box she kept tucked safely in her heart. Neither she nor Chet spoke until Andrew greeted them as they exited the car. Andrew was understanding, even good-natured, and promised to find another place.

With that, Chet began to prepare to operate his father's farm and this one. At age seventy-four, C.A. worked longer and harder at his Remington typewriter than he did on the farm. He was editor of *Nord Norge*, a Norwegian-American newspaper with nationwide circulation, and he had preferred that to farming since Elmer's death. That left Chet to do the bulk of the work, with more and more help from Tommy as he got older. The two of them would be able to handle the combined 320 acres, but only with a second tractor. So, Chet wasted no time in purchasing a used Farmall H, which could pull a three-bottom plow. C.A.'s old Farmall B could pull a two-bottom plow, which was perfect for Tommy to operate. "Can I get out of school early to help plow and plant?" Tommy asked one night when Chet came to pick up Muriel.

"May I," Muriel interjected. "The question is, 'May I get out of school early?' The answer is a firm no."

"Listen to your mom," Chet said plainly. "You'll get the same answer from me."

The anticipation of that spring was far greater than the normal eagerness for the first rhubarb from the garden or the fields to turn from black to green. Muriel was excited to make her children part of a farm family again. She promised them big bedrooms to themselves and kittens in the barn. For herself, Muriel yearned for her own space, even as she wondered how it would feel to be in Elmer's realm. She wanted to work for herself again and be truly in charge. She wanted to be married.

Before the wedding came, Muriel thanked her mother one more time for all she had done, packed up her and the children's belongings, and resettled them back at the farm. Her intent was to get the five of them into their own routine and new rooms before Chet joined them. She put her clothes back in dark-to-light order in the closet, starting with dresses, then skirts, then pants, then shirts. She left Chet the amount of room she knew he would need. In the entryway, she left the first two hooks open for his coat and overalls, and a spot next to the hooks for his boots. She arranged her pantry exactly as it had been, as though she had never left. Busying herself to the extreme, Muriel worked and mothered until bedtime. She held off on going to bed until she felt tired beyond the shadow of a doubt.

On June 12, 1954, Muriel stood on her porch, coffee in hand, watching the sun rise over the dewy grass and grains, a sea of brilliant green waving gently toward the valley. She had eggs to pick, breakfast to make, and children to bathe earlier than usual. She wanted to give herself extra time to primp her hair and apply lipstick and a hint of rouge for the occasion. But for a few minutes, she wanted to stand still, right here, and think of Elmer. She had only herself to talk to about marrying her late husband's brother, who was to raise his nieces and nephew on the same farm.

"Am I doing the right thing, Elmer?" she asked. "I want our kids to have a good life. I think this is what you would want."

That afternoon, Pastor Sandanger married Chet and Muriel at the parsonage in Fort Ransom. Glenn and Frances were witnesses. No one else attended. Muriel shared few opinions in common with Pastor Sandanger, but not bringing young children to a wedding was one of them. In fact, the newlyweds picked up Liz from a birthday party on their way from the parsonage to Josephine's house for the reception. While everyone still looked immaculate, Frances lined up the new family for a photo in the yard—Muriel in the belted taupe dress suit of her own making, Chet squirming in his only suit, Tommy in slacks and a starched white shirt, and the girls in new pink dresses with crinoline underneath. Marge picked lilies of the valley from Grandma Henrickson's flower bed and tucked the sprigs behind her and Liz's ears. "Okay, you may go play," Muriel said to her antsy children as they bolted to play tag with their cousins.

Meanwhile, Josephine rushed around, refilling the buns, sliced ham, and pickles for the thirty-or-so guests. Mildred cut and served the white cake with Muriel's favorite seven-minute frosting. Two hours later, the newlyweds changed into comfortable clothes and headed for the 1941 Chevy amidst the sprinkling of rice and cheers. Chet's friends had soaped the windows and hung a sign on his car reading, "Hot springs tonight, Deadwood tomorrow!" As Chet pulled away from the waving crowd, a string of tin cans clinked behind the car, and the couple got sustained whiffs of Limburger cheese melting on the manifold as it burned off! Of course, their friends knew that Chet and Muriel were good-humored enough to laugh at the smell of sweaty feet.

Muriel looked back laughing and knew that marrying Chet was the right thing to do. Chet was the only father figure that Liz and Marge had known. While Evelyn and Tommy had good memories of Elmer, they were comfortable around Chet and never questioned their mother about the new arrangement. Soon they would be settled into the farm, surrounded by people who wanted the best for them all. This was everything Muriel could want.

By the time thirty-three-year-old Muriel and thirty-one-year-old Chet returned ten days later from their honeymoon to Mt. Rushmore and the Black Hills of South Dakota, the butter lettuce and radishes were ready to pick, and the first alfalfa was ready to cut. The couple was ready to get to work, and Muriel, more than anything, wanted to make life normal for the children.

But the very next night, an hour after Muriel announced, "Bedtime!" the steady honking of car horns awakened the whole family. She and Chet laughed and quickly got their bearings. She ran upstairs to let all four children know they were safe and should get dressed. "Get up! It'll be fun," she assured them. "It's called a charivari."

Charivaris were a popular tradition in Fort Ransom. Organized by the newlyweds' friends and executed shortly after they were confident the couple was asleep, they formed a line of cars and drove slowly down the driveway, honking their horns and flashing their headlights until the newlyweds came outside. Nearly twenty cars paraded into the Sandheis' farmyard that night, and everyone brought an ample supply of adult beverages. Grain Belt beer was the top choice, with whiskey a distant second. Usually this was an adults-only party, because the newly married couple would not have children yet. However, in this case, the friends who had children brought them along, so that Muriel's four children could have fun too. The party lasted until 2:00 a.m., with the children running around the yard the whole time, playing at an uncommonly high volume to match the noise of their parents.

"What did you think?" Muriel asked her children as their guests departed.

"It was great!" was the general consensus. Red-cheeked and sweaty, the children crawled into bed for a second time that night while Chet and Muriel finished their drinks in the kitchen to wind down.

And the partying continued. That Saturday night, they heard cars approaching again with horns beeping at 11:00 p.m. Most of the original group recruited a few extras. Muriel did not know of any other couple in Fort Ransom who had been celebrated with two charivaris.

"We're pretty popular," Chet said, in his typical jest.

"I don't know about that," she said, getting dressed. "I think people just know we like a good party!"

As the second charivari arrived, the children came flying down the stairs without hesitation. "Life is good," Muriel thought. "This is home."

FARM FAMILY

*I*N THE YEARS THAT FOLLOWED the Sandhei family's return to the farm, Muriel embraced farm life as a mother. She intended to raise her children exactly as she and Elmer would have, only with Chet standing in for his brother. And so, while Chet schooled Tommy in field work and livestock chores, Muriel took charge of leading the girls' upbringing and teaching life's lessons to all four children. Being a mother was her most important job, and she performed it as only she knew how—one part Josephine and one part school of hard knocks. She had experienced her fill of knocks. And without her even noticing, her mind had transformed those experiences to protective instincts.

What Muriel had absorbed from her own mother was to teach by example. In other words, *show* the children how to do the work properly and expect them to follow suit when their time came. That was the Norwegian way, the Fort Ransom way. It involved more action and assumption than discussion. With Josephine, the time for her children to perform what she had taught them had been almost immediate. Muriel had known how to set a proper table before she knew how to spell. She had been a part of canning and lefse-making as far back as she could remember. Thirty years later, however, Muriel's expectations of her own children were different. Yes, they were to watch and learn. But she had them tearing lettuce, peeling carrots, and mixing salad dressing while she stood over the hot stove boiling potatoes or pulling bread out of the oven. She had them husking corn while she and Frances canned it with the pressure cooker. Muriel demonstrated every task, and certainly showed her children how to work hard. She had no patience for dawdling. And still, she kept the riskier work for herself. "Your time will come soon enough," she promised.

To the extent she could, Muriel also made work fun. Laughter was as much a part of her life now as it had been when she was a girl herself, and her mother had given her a sideward glance that spoke, "Oh, Muriel. Whose child are you?"

The demonstrating of work and fun played out as Evelyn, Marge, and Liz picked and shelled peas from the garden. First, Muriel reiterated her mother's teaching to only pick the pods that were plump with peas. She showed the girls a handful of examples; that was their one lesson. Then, she reminded them: "A few peas are for dinner. The rest are for canning."

Muriel walked away to fill pails at the well, only to see Marge putting a whole pod in her mouth as she returned. Admitting that she could not resist fresh peas either, Muriel smirked and shelled a few of her own to eat on the spot. She had not said not to eat any peas. The girls giggled and followed her lead. Here they stood in the hot July sun, doing the same chores that Fort Ransom farm girls had been doing for three generations. The reality that some things had not changed comforted Muriel.

If eating peas in the garden was a simple pleasure, making ice cream was a thoroughly worthwhile one. When Marge turned nine in December, she requested ice cream instead of cake, and Muriel happily accommodated. Making ice cream was a family affair, beginning with Tommy bringing in the pail of milk that morning. Muriel put it in the separator in the entryway to separate the milk from the cream. In the afternoon, Muriel had the girls measure three cups of cream into a kettle with egg yolks and sugar. They took turns stirring it as it cooked into a thick custard on the stovetop. They poured that mixture into a bowl to cool, then they repeated the process, but with one cup of cream this time. Over the course of years, the children developed a belief that their mom's ice cream was better than any other because of this fourth cup of cream, added separately. Then came the churning. The children, including Tommy now, took turns churning. Nearly an hour into it, as they worked harder and harder to crank the churn, they asked their mom if it was done.

"It ain't done," Tommy interjected, trying to get a rise out of his mother.

"Isn't," Muriel corrected him. "Tommy is right about the ice cream, though. It isn't ready quite yet. Keep churning."

They kept asking until, upon testing it herself, Muriel finally confirmed, "Yes! It's ready!"

Grins of eager delight came across their faces, and they bantered about whose turn it was to lick the beater until Muriel settled the matter. "Marge is the birthday girl. She gets the beater today," she said, laughing along.

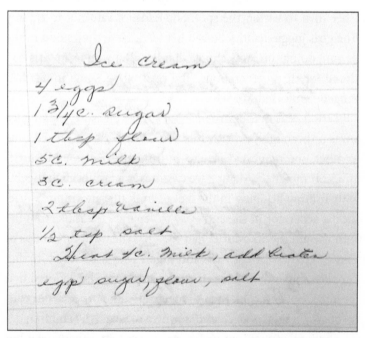

Muriel's recipe for ice cream, written in her own hand in the 1990s. (Courtesy Tom Sandhei)

Not surprisingly, Muriel wanted her own children to play and laugh even more than she had as a young girl. "The whole farm is your playground," she said. "Jump in the hay. Look for kittens in the barn. Climb trees. Just don't leave the yard without telling me."

Marge and Liz made mud pies in the driveway, just as Tom and Evelyn had done years earlier when Elmer was farming. They passed hours a day "baking pies" in cast-off tins in the discarded cook stove, which stood next to the clump of lilac bushes on the edge of the farmyard.

While his younger sisters "baked," Tommy lobbied for a puppy. Oren Tommeraus, a farmer on the east prairie, had collies for sale, and Tommy showed Muriel the five dollars he had been saving to buy something special. "Okay, you can get a puppy," she approved. "You'll need to feed it and brush it. Are you prepared to do that?"

Tommy assured her that he would take good care of the dog, and the matter was settled. The next day, he brought home Mickey, who looked like Lassie from the TV show, only whiter and smaller. Mickey was as devoted to Tommy as Tommy was to her, following each other around the farm like best friends during recess. One day when given too much spare time, Tom decided it would be fun for Mickey to pull a cart. So, he built a cart out of old tricycle parts and harnessed Mickey to it. The dog dutifully pulled it, and it was great fun for the children to give her odds and ends to haul around the yard. After the novelty of hauling objects wore off, Tom put an eager Liz in the cart. He walked beside Mickey to the end of the driveway, ordered the dog (and Liz) to stay, and walked back to the farmyard. "Come, Mickey!" he yelled.

Liz got the ride of her life as Mickey raced for home. Seeing the antics through the window, Muriel ran out of the house, ready to yell at Tommy. Instead, she began to laugh. "Tommy!" she said, trying to cover her amusement. "That will be the last time that Mickey takes your sister—or anyone—for a joy ride."

Not one to be deterred, Tommy sometimes rode the tamest cow back to the barn when he gathered the cows for milking each morning and night. The cow ambled along, and Muriel had no problem with it. But one day, while his mom was gone on an errand, Tommy decided to ride one of the calves. Wearing his brand-new blue jeans, which were intended for the upcoming school year, Tommy caught his pants on a nail sticking out of a post in the calf pen. The tear went from the top of the right leg, down nearly the whole length of the seam. Muriel got home, saw his torn jeans, and gave him a look that could have frosted a window that August afternoon. "I better sew that up for you," she said dryly.

Muriel's lesson to him was in the repair, as she took her time with it, and he only had one other pair of everyday pants. When she was good and ready, she sewed the torn leg tighter than the other one. This was an instance of the natural consequences that Muriel regularly taught her children. Having sufficiently taught the lesson, Muriel moved on.

On long winter nights, after the girls helped Muriel clear the table and do the supper dishes, the family played cards. Muriel and Chet taught Evelyn and Tom to play whist, the game of choice in Fort Ransom. Muriel and Chet always played as partners against Evelyn and Tom, who became worthy competitors within the span of a month. The foursome sat around the kitchen table, silently engrossed during each hand of cards. In between hands, they gave spirited complaints or praise about which cards they were dealt in the previous hand. Marge and Liz watched from their stools, completely bored! Sometimes Muriel started out the night of card-playing with go fish, so that the younger girls could play before bedtime.

As the years passed on the farm, with Muriel setting a good example for her children at work and at play, she increasingly embraced that her most important job was to raise her children to be modern versions of who she had once dreamed of becoming. Muriel would not trade being a wife and a mother for anything. But she had not gone to college. She had gotten pregnant and married in the wrong order. When Elmer died, she had been caught unprepared to support herself. And so, she must raise her children not only to be hard-working, happy, polite, and well-spoken, but also to be well-educated and self-supporting. What's more, she desired to show her father-in-law that her children would equal or exceed his level of education, which he had never allowed of Elmer or Chet. All four of her children would go to college. She would help them make something of themselves, like her own self-worth depended on it.

LOSING GROUND

WHEN MURIEL MOVED BACK TO the farm with Chet and the children, she did so with the confidence that she owned the farm outright, that Chet was an experienced farmer, and that Tommy was already competent at many of the tasks of farming. As a farmwife, she was more than capable at every domestic chore, not to mention milking when she was needed. She had every reason to believe that life on the farm would be prosperous, as it had been under Elmer. In fact, she had no concerns aside from a selfish one: everywhere she looked on the farm, she was reminded of Elmer. She just needed to keep that to herself and wait for new memories to replace the old ones.

As the children went back to school and the end of harvest was in sight in 1954, Chet and Elsa Mae's husband Marvin were helping each other combine. Each had his own combine, and after filling the grain wagon, each took his turn hauling the oats to the granary until Tommy joined them after school. On the night of September 1, Chet came home coughing. "Oat dust," he insisted, citing a common farmer's complaint.

But the next day, Chet's cough was far worse. In a few bouts, he coughed so hard that he could not catch his breath. "I don't think I can combine today," Chet said.

Muriel called their close friend Jimmy Collette, even while Chet objected. She had a way of recruiting people to her point of view with little effort, and ten minutes later, Jimmy was at the door, insisting along with Muriel that Chet get to a doctor. Chet refused to go anywhere but Lisbon, despite Muriel's reservations. Allowing Chet that one concession in the interest of time, Muriel stayed home with Liz while the two men got on the road.

Two hours later, Jimmy called with an update: "Chet has pneumonia, Muriel. He's being admitted to the hospital. They're giving him antibiotics. That should take care of the problem."

Frantic at the word "pneumonia," Muriel's heart instantly raced five years backward. She had heard of doctors using antibiotics to treat pneumonia patients now, but she had no experience of her own and had difficulty not fearing the worst. Nonetheless, she maintained a calm and steady tone when she told the children about Chet after they got home from school. She perceived Evelyn and Tommy's concern, but they kept quiet for the sake of their younger sisters. Muriel put Evelyn in charge, stopped to pick up C.A. and Elise, and went to see Chet.

Jimmy had been right. Chet was still very sick, but he was getting better. The next day, he was even better. After spending three days in the hospital, Chet came home with antibiotics and orders to continue resting. Tom and Marvin filled in for Chet on the farm, with milking help from Muriel. "We'll get through this just fine," Muriel told her mom and Frances.

But just as Chet was ready to get back to work, the dominoes fell at the Sandhei farm. On October 13, Tom came down with the mumps. Two days later, Chet relapsed and landed back in the hospital in Lisbon, where he stayed overnight before going home to more sick children. One by one, the girls succumbed to the mumps that Tom and many of their schoolmates had. Then, on October 18, Chet had such severe pain that he finally agreed with Muriel: He needed big-city doctors. Mildred's husband, Loubert, drove him to St. Luke's Hospital in Fargo. Chet was hospitalized for four days with kidney stones.

Muriel felt physically and emotionally exhausted. Never one to complain, she found herself alone in her bedroom several times a day, composing herself before going back to the kitchen or the children's sick beds. Each day seemed longer and harder than the one before, with no relief in sight. She did not leave home for fear of spreading the mumps, which she had never had, or one of the children getting sicker while she was gone.

Neighbors helped finish the Sandheis' combining, and on October 26, eight neighbors arrived with their tractors and plows to complete the fall's work in one day, in spite of the light covering of snow on the ground. Finally, just as Chet and the children started to improve, Muriel came down with the mumps the first week of November. Mumps in adults were usually much more severe than in children, and Muriel was no exception. She became very ill, swelling to the point that her neck was nearly as wide as her shoulders. In her misery, she slept as much as she could, and in her waking hours, she reflected on her adult life. She could not help but wonder, "Has all of this really happened? What next?"

After a week of bed rest and care, mainly from Evelyn and Elise, Muriel began to recover. A couple weeks later, she got back to her usual routine. She knew she would need to work extra hard and be extremely frugal to keep the household afloat.

That first year back on the farm could not have gone much worse in terms of money. With Chet's hospital bills consuming most of their income, year two would need to be much more lucrative. If this had happened to Elmer, he would have known what to do to make up for the losses. He was as good a farmer and manager as he was a husband and father. Of Chet, she was not sure yet.

Farmers around them seemed to be getting bigger or getting out. Muriel heard the men's conversations and the farm report on the radio: In order to succeed, farmers needed to take on more acres. "Too risky," chimed Chet when Muriel brought up the subject.

The next spring, and regularly from then on, a banker from Lisbon stopped by the farm. Livestock, machinery, and grain seed cost money. "We'll pay it all back when the crop comes in," Chet always said.

For the next couple of years, they managed to pay just enough of their bills to get by. Muriel saw right before her eyes that Chet did not have the same knack for farming that Elmer did. And so, the family worked even harder and longer. When their well caved in, like it had a decade earlier, Chet spent a week fixing it himself while Tom picked up his slack around the farm. Muriel sewed, patched and mended to keep them all in clothes. Evelyn babysat Jimmy and Rosie Collette's four children for spending money. And indoor plumbing and TV remained far down on the wish list. Occasionally, their neighbors Art and Ragna Anderson invited them over to watch *The Lawrence Welk Show*.

Most importantly, the Sandheis virtually fed themselves. Muriel often butchered a chicken for Sunday dinner. Chet butchered a cow or a pig every few months as their meat supply dwindled. With no deep freeze at home, the only expense was keeping their supply at the locker plant in Fort Ransom. They consumed their own eggs, cream, and milk. With the proceeds of their egg and cream sales at George Anderson's store each Tuesday and Saturday night, they bought butter, flour, and sugar. Everything else, they grew in the garden or picked wild. They wasted nothing and heartily ate whatever was put on the table. In fact, homemade bread slathered in cream and chokecherry syrup was one of their favorite meals.

Muriel allowed only a couple of indulgences for her and Chet. When she sold eggs and cream at open night each Tuesday and Saturday, Chet went to Collette's Tavern, which his friend Jimmy operated. Sometimes he also hit Knutson's Tavern, which was fifty steps farther west at the end of Main Street. Knutson's and Collette's taverns were beer joints—no liquor—and Chet enjoyed a few drinks while commiserating with the other farmers. On Friday nights, he and Muriel regularly attended the dances in Fort Ransom, Kathryn, or Nome. Chet socialized outside with the other beer drinkers, while friends and acquaintances sought Muriel out to visit and dance.

This was the great dichotomy of Muriel's life: To the outside world, she was carefree. She had a twinkle in her eyes as she talked, and when she laughed, her whole body followed. Any room was livelier with her in it. She and her children appeared and talked with polish every time they left home. But privately, she felt as though she was patching her life like a worn-out pair of overalls. If she patched herself well enough, her siblings and the rest of Fort Ransom would never have to know the truth.

At the end of 1956, when they had managed to barely pay the bills for the third straight year, it became clear that hope was not a strategy for surviving 1957. The first change, which came to them more as a blessing, was C.A. and Elise's move to a house in Fort Ransom that fall. C.A. was seventy-seven years old and had only been waiting for Elise to turn sixty-five so that they could exit the farming business and live off their Social Security income. That took the burden off of Chet and Tom to run two farms.

Next, Chet applied for a road construction job to build Interstate-94 between Valley City and Jamestown. He would be gone for full weeks at a time starting in the spring, and his steady paycheck would help pay the bills while Tom and Muriel kept the farm going.

So began the execution of their plan in which fourteen-year-old Tom was to do the field work, while he and Muriel shared milking and livestock chores. Muriel took on her additional duties with the lighthearted attitude she brought to most everything. Like his mother, Tom aimed to bring fun to even the most tedious jobs. While milking, for instance, he liked to aim the milk at the nearby farm cats, who were hungrily awaiting their treat. "Tom, the milk is supposed to go into the pail," Muriel said with mild reproach and a soft chuckle.

Muriel and Tom, whose resemblance to his father was unmistakable, made a good team outside. The girls pulled extra weight inside, keeping the house clean. Teamwork really was not a choice if they wanted to stay on the farm, which Muriel was adamant about. She thought it all went quite smoothly with the five of them at home and all on the same page about what needed to be done.

ASHES AND DUST

ON MAY 23, 1958, THE WHOLE family dressed up to attend Law-rence Jorgenson and Verney Strander's wedding dance in Fort Ransom. Muriel lined up the children for a photo on the front porch steps before rushing Marge and Liz into the 1949 Chevy sedan. Tom and Evelyn followed in the 1948 Plymouth, knowing they would want to stay at the dance later than their parents. Chet sped out of the drive-way, sending Tom the message that it was okay to leave the farm-stead in the dust. Muriel usually frowned upon that, but school was out, the evening air was warm, and tonight they were going to have some fun. This felt like the first evening of summer, and the party beckoned them.

Virtually everyone from Fort Ransom was at the Sons of Nor-way Hall that night—a few hundred people, nearly all of them fam-ily, friends, or acquaintances. In Fort Ransom, a wedding dance was practically a civic event, hosted by the father of the bride. The invita-tion to the dance was neither published nor mailed, but understood.

Muriel danced with the same men she had had as dance part-ners since she was a teenager, and with every bit as much fervor as twenty years earlier. When she noticed Liz slowing down, Muriel sat down to visit with friends until Liz fell asleep on her lap; then she pulled Marge off the dance floor and found Chet outside the hall. This was where the men who were not dancing drank their beer, as alcohol was prohibited inside. A lot of the men kept a stash of small bottles in the glove compartment or beer cans under the seat. As soon as Chet saw Muriel and the girls, he set his can on the ground. He knew it was time to get the younger girls to bed.

Tom and Evelyn had both been confirmed, which was still the prerequisite for dancing in Fort Ransom. Like Muriel at her age, Evelyn's dance card was full. Tom and most of the older teen boys were visiting outside, training to be men. But right after his mom and Chet left, the rain poured down, and everyone ran inside. The band drowned out the thunder and lightning, and the dance floor was fuller than it had been all night. People had their last bit of fun as the party started to wind down.

Shortly after midnight, the storm passed, and Evelyn and Tom headed for home. Tom fought to keep the wheels on the grass above the muddy ruts cutting into their driveway. The two of them walked into the sleeping house, careful not to let the screen door slam behind them and leaving their muddy dress shoes in the entryway. Their mother would have them clean and shine their shoes the next day, but tonight, they were tired enough not to think about that. They quietly climbed the stairs, both skipping the creaky third and final steps, and went to bed.

What happened a couple of hours later, the entire family would remember forever. Evelyn was not sure afterward whether she saw the bright light outside her bedroom window or heard the crackling first, but a fire on the porch roof woke her. "Tom! Fire! Tom!" was her first scream at the top of her lungs.

The two of them threw on their everyday clothes and rushed into Marge and Liz's bedrooms. Liz's room was already in flames by the time the four children ran down the stairs, screaming frantically to wake their parents.

"Run outside and stay outside," Tom said, with every bit of calm firmness he could muster. "I'll be right there with Mom and Chet."

Rushing toward the main-level bedroom, Tom yelled, "Fire! Mom . . . Chet . . . Wake up! Fire!"

Muriel and Chet were already grabbing the nearest clothes. The three of them darted out of the house and spotted the girls in the yard. "Back up!" Chet yelled. "Get away from the house! Get out in the driveway!"

Muriel herded the girls backward and tried to shield them with her arms and assurances.

"We need to disconnect the fuel oil barrel!" Chet exclaimed with wild eyes, looking at Tom and running toward the west side of the house. "Grab a wrench," he ordered Tom, who blindly found one in the woodshed and raced back to the fuel oil barrel. The two of them disconnected the line and rolled the tank away.

As they rolled the tank to the garden and ran toward the house, Muriel held her breath, hearing Chet tell Tom where the important legal documents were. In what seemed like forever but was likely less than a minute, they re-emerged, carrying the chest of drawers from their bedroom. Her deed to the farm was in one of those drawers. Only later did she learn that as they carried the chest through the living room, the ceiling was already engulfed in flames.

They entered the house one last time to grab everyone's coats, which were hanging at the base of the stairs. As Chet and Tom came out with their arms full, Muriel could see from the flames that the main floor was nearly totally engulfed.

"That's enough! Please don't go back in there," she begged.

The power line dropped off the house, draping itself across the Plymouth. Moving the car had been next on Chet and Tom's list. Knowing it was too late to do anything more, they moved Muriel and the girls farther back, and the whole family stood watching the flames consume their home.

Soon neighbors began to drive into the yard, beginning with Oscar A. As he arrived in his pickup truck, he lunged out and asked how he could help. Chet stared at the Plymouth, and Oscar got back in his truck. Parking a short distance behind the car, Oscar grabbed the log chain from the truck box, attached it to the front of his truck, and carefully laid the chain on the ground leading up to the back bumper of the car. He then tapped the rear bumper of the car with the chain. Chet watched, motionless; Muriel closed her eyes. She shielded Marge and Liz, facing them in the opposite direction.

"It's grounded," Oscar A. yelled, as though there had been no doubt.

He hooked the chain to the car and pulled it backwards, and the power line fell lifelessly to the ground. Muriel let out a sigh of relief and rubbed Liz's arm in reassurance. As they all stood watching the house burn to the ground, the fire department arrived from Lisbon.

"What happened? Lightning?" the fire chief asked Chet.

"Most likely," he said, his tone shifting from urgency to dejection. "We think the fire started outside one of the upstairs bedrooms, where the phone line came into the house."

The men surmised that lightning had struck the telephone line at the pole about halfway between the house and barn. The lightning then overheated the line, which entered the house under the cedar shingles on the porch roof outside Evelyn's bedroom. When Tom and Evelyn arrived home after the storm, the fire was likely already smoldering under the shingles.

As the dawn of May 24 appeared on the horizon, Chet, Muriel, and the children slowly departed the farm, wheels rolling through the dewy grass above the muddy ruts, made worse by all the traffic that night. Muriel caught Chet's exhausted glance as she looked back into the beautiful faces of her and Elmer's children. Evelyn's quick reaction had saved their lives. Muriel was so proud of her and so relieved that they were all okay. Still, every worry crossed Muriel's mind in the next few minutes. They had almost no clothes or shoes. They had no food and nothing at all from the kitchen. All her precious photos were gone.

The pain of the moment hit Muriel like the previous night's lightning. Tears rolled down her face, yet she did not make a sound. They simply escaped. As the family approached Glenn and Frances's farm on the other side of the valley, Muriel composed herself and said gently, "It's time to wake up for just a minute, kids."

Muriel was unaware of the dried tears, some outlined in black, others smudged, which held Frances's sympathetic gaze as she led Muriel and the children from the car to the house. Muriel and Frances put the children to bed for a nap and got busy in the kitchen. Side by side, the sisters fried eggs and bacon, made toast, and gathered everyone for a big breakfast the way that their mother had taught them. The conversation slowly picked up, and the coffee and calories elevated everyone's spirits a bit.

"Well, Tom," said Chet as he took his last sip of coffee, "The cows need milking."

The tall, lanky pair wordlessly headed outside. As they drove into their farmyard, smoke was rising from the embers. Most of the wood frame of the house was gone, but the original log house at the center of the structure was still smoldering. The iron beds, stoves, and fridge parts lay tangled in the ashes, a dismal—almost numbing— sight. Chet and Tom forced themselves not to stare at it. The cows needed milking, and the hogs and chickens needed feeding.

Tom walked out in the pasture and herded the cows into the barn. He sat down on an upside-down pail between his legs and pulled on the teats in rhythm until the last drop was drained from the udder. Meanwhile, Chet balanced on his one-legged stool that Tom had always marveled at, but never asked about. Muscle memory did the milking that morning.

Suddenly, Luther appeared in the doorway of the barn. "What's been going on here?" he asked accusingly.

Overtired and lost in their own thoughts, Chet and Tom were in no mood for Luther's abrupt comment. "We had a fire," Chet said, ending the conversation and urging Luther out the door.

Muriel could not bring herself to return to the farm that day. She had to get Liz and Marge temporarily situated with Mildred, the rest of them with Frances, and a longer-term plan for them all. What she knew was that their life on Elmer's farm was over. They would never rebuild; never live on the farm again. They had been hanging on by a thread *before* the fire. At only thirty-six years old, Muriel felt the pang of loss from her heart to her stomach. But she never spoke aloud of it, not even to Frances. Muriel tucked away the fire into her box of heartaches. The rest of the world would only see her grace under pressure.

RESILIENCE

*I*N JUNE 1958, MURIEL AND CHET moved the family into a rental house in the northwest corner of Fort Ransom. They had practically no familiar belongings. Most of what they possessed had been donated to them at the church's benefit. Some of the clothing was ill-fitting. Everything in the house was mismatched, from plates and silverware to a sofa and end tables. Enough money came from the freewill offering to buy mattresses and groceries. With so little to call her own, Muriel felt an aversion to the material things around her, right down to the house itself. Fort Ransom in general was starting to feel like a bad association. Yet this place was all that she knew. Her support system was here, and she had certainly leaned on it. "Be grateful," she kept telling herself.

Chet and Tom drove to the farm each morning and night to milk the cows. They also needed to grow and harvest that year's crops, which they had planted before the fire. Knowing that he was needed at home, Chet stayed put rather than return to road construction. He and Muriel hayed and harvested, while Tom worked as the farmhand of Elmer's good friend Emil Pederson. Evelyn did her part by working as the hello girl at Telephone Central in Fort Ransom. Muriel, Evelyn, and Tom also picked and bagged potatoes for a local farmer for two weeks in September, as Chet took a short-term job constructing rural phone lines north of Valley City. Collectively, the Sandheis made all the money they could to survive 1958.

The most valuable possession that Muriel had was her land. Chet could sell the milk cows and farm implements, but he knew better than to suggest selling the farm. For Muriel, not keeping it would be disloyal to Elmer. The farm had been their dream. So, after she and Chet harvested the 1958 crop, Muriel was contemplating potential renters when a story on the radio caught her attention.

She had heard about the Soil Bank Program before; Congress had enacted it in 1956 in response to grain surpluses and farm income declines. But not until now had the concept registered with Muriel. Essentially, the Soil Bank Program paid farmers to remove land from crop production. Muriel completed her application in Lisbon the next week, and her land was accepted into the program beginning in 1959. All she had to do was keep her land out of production for ten years, seed it with natural grasses, and keep it relatively weed free. The initial annual payment was $3,000—a lot of money to the Sandheis! Such reliable income, which involved minimal effort, brought sheer relief to Muriel.

Not only did the family need to endure the short term; they needed funds to send four children to college, starting with Evelyn in the fall of 1959 and Tom in 1960. Chet, Muriel, Evelyn, and Tom would all need to work to make that happen. As soon as the spring weather allowed, Chet returned to road construction, which took him away from home for a week at a time building I-94 overpasses every six miles across North Dakota. He came home on Saturday nights and left again on Sunday nights. Muriel, meanwhile, saw an opportunity for both herself and the children right here in Fort Ransom. The town's only restaurant had recently closed. George Anderson had also closed the grocery store where she had worked for five years and opened a larger store down the street. Like Muriel had done when she bought the farm, she made a bold move.

She approached longtime friend Walter Johnson, who owned the building. Walter had been a grandfather figure in her and her children's lives since her days of working at the grocery store. "I'm thinking of opening a café," she said directly. "I'd like to open it in your building, if you'll rent me the space."

Walter raised his eyebrows and smiled with pride. "You know the building has no running water, right?" he asked. "The closest well is behind Grothe's Garage on the other side of the street."

"I know!" she responded. "The only time I had running water in my house was when I worked in Montana twenty years ago. It's hard to miss something that I'm not accustomed to having."

"A café is a great plan, Muriel. The town needs a café. The building is yours," he said, and the friends easily came to a rental arrangement.

Despite the support of Walter, whose wife was the postmistress, Fort Ransom in general viewed bold moves as unbecoming a married woman. Muriel knew that some people would gossip about her working while she had four children to raise and a husband on the road making a decent living. She would be asked, "So, how does Chet feel about you owning the café?" Neither consideration impacted Muriel's decision in the slightest. She could do as she wished and *would* do what was best for her family. If her food was good and the prices were reasonable, the chatter would fade. Besides, her children's college education was worth any amount of gossip.

On May 8, 1959, Muriel's Café opened on the south side of Main Street, in the same building where she had once worked at George's store. The building was white with a false front and one large picture window facing the street. The space fit only about twenty customers—ten on stools at the counter and another ten seated at the four tables. Those seats were nearly always full at mealtime, and the counter stayed steady with coffee customers at all times of the day. Muriel unlocked the door at 6:00 a.m. daily, stayed open until 6:00 p.m. five days a week, and extended her hours until 2:00 a.m. on Tuesday and Saturday. That was when the men congregated at Knutson's and Collette's taverns to play cards or pool while their wives sold cream and visited in their cars. After the beer joints closed for the night, their customers inevitably wandered into Muriel's Café.

Her menu was simple, consisting of hamburgers, potato chips, soft drinks, ice cream, vanilla or chocolate milk shakes, a rotating pie and cookie selection, and brownies. Muriel's brownies had a moist texture and chocolate icing and were her most sought-after baked goods. Asked regularly what made her brownies so delicious, her hazel eyes lit up behind her cat eye glasses as she answered, "They're brownies! I don't know if they're any better than anyone else's brownies."

Muriel's engaging personality was a big reason for her business success. She was the café's mainstay, doing literally every job the business entailed at every hour of the day in her "uniform," which was a button-up day dress with short sleeves, a full skirt, collar, and matching fabric belt. She made several versions from the same pattern in different fabrics and wore one of a drawer-full of aprons over the top. She greeted every customer by name with a big smile and hearty hello and struck up a conversation with each one as long as she had enough

Muriel working at her café in Fort Ransom, circa 1960. She owned and operated the café for three years, with the help of her children and her mother-in-law. (Courtesy Tom Sandhei)

helpers to keep up with the workload. Visiting was important, and Muriel was naturally good at it.

As planned, Evelyn, Tom, and Marge were her biggest helpers. Ten-year-old Liz was a bit too young. Tom preferred to work in the kitchen, flipping burgers and washing dishes. Evelyn and Marge liked working the lunch counter and waiting tables. Muriel's mother-in-law, Elise, frequently worked in the kitchen during the day, while the children were in school or at another job or activity. But whenever they were not occupied elsewhere, the implicit expectation was for them to be at the café.

Within a couple of months, the café had regulars and required as much work as the family could handle. It was a bright spot in the community and a place where Muriel and her children shined together. Muriel had her preferred customers, of course. She loved watching all four of her children lined up on stools at the counter—talking, laughing, and devouring supper. She had a rapport with all well-behaved children, in fact, especially the ones who liked to chat. Four-year-old Ronnie Olson was at the top of her list. Walking into the café ahead of his parents one afternoon, he sat down on a stool and said, "I'll have a cup of coffee and a molasses cookie, goddamnit," to which Muriel burst out laughing.

Another favorite was Ralph Hansen, the Ransom County Sheriff, who was five years older than Muriel and a bachelor. He was 6' 2" tall, with big shoulders and a coifed wave of dark brown hair with a strong right-side part. His nature was too pleasant for a lawman, she thought, but that is likely what gave him his appeal. While Fort Ransom had virtually no crime, he made at least one trip a week to the tiny village, always at coffee hour, and usually on a day when Muriel baked brownies. Sheriff Hansen sauntered in like he belonged there and ordered a cup of coffee. After half an hour of exchanging stories with Muriel, he headed back to Lisbon with a dozen brownies to share with the county courthouse staff.

Brothers Alan and Russell Larsen were popular with both Muriel and her children. They were bachelors with a large farming operation between Lisbon and Fort Ransom, and they sponsored the annual Fourth of July rodeo. Alan, the elder brother, was several years younger than Muriel. In the summer, he introduced the Sandheis to small-town rodeos; in the winter, he taught them to ice skate. Russell, who was several years older than Evelyn, had a crush on her. With a ruggedly handsome face and dark brown hair that curled up at the ends under his cowboy hat, Russell should have asked her on a date. Instead, he spent his free time studying history and writing and directing local plays, and he never got around to dating. Wherever Alan and Russell went, they brought along two high school cowboys, Howard Hoff and Tim Berg. Marge and Liz took a liking to Howard. He was the blonde version of Rowdy Yates, Clint Eastwood's character on *Rawhide*. Tim, a wiry cowboy with sandy hair that seldom saw the light of day, called Muriel "Mom."

This foursome became known as "the rodeo crowd" at Muriel's Café. They stayed past closing time to visit, and as the Fourth of July drew closer, Muriel saw the rodeo crowd more often. They stopped by the café each day after their work converting the ballpark into a rodeo arena and preparing for a couple thousand people. Given how quiet this hundred-person village typically was, the rodeo was a huge event. It also created the biggest money-making opportunity of the year for Muriel's Café. With help from her children, their friends, and the rodeo crowd, Muriel set up lunch stands near the rodeo grounds. She sold hamburgers for a quarter, soda pop for a dime, and vanilla ice cream cones for a nickel.

After closing down the lunch stands and café on her first Fourth of July in business, Muriel counted $1,000 in lunch-stand sales. "That's great!" Muriel told her children and the rodeo crowd, all seated at the counter, exhausted from a busy day on their feet. "Now that we know what we're doing, the goal for next year is to exceed $1,000."

Chet's income covered their rent, cars, gas, and other essentials. Every bit of money the café earned went toward the children's clothes, spending money, and—most importantly—their college funds. Evelyn was the first to need those funds, when she enrolled at Valley City State College in September 1959.

Dropping Evelyn off at college was a proud moment for Muriel, maybe the proudest in her entire adult life. Muriel had raised a smart, dedicated young woman, the salutatorian of her high school class, who was ready to step into independence. Evelyn was the first verifiable proof that Muriel and her children would become something. As Muriel drove away from Evelyn that afternoon, she smiled and waved. Her pride swelled as she passed under a canopy of green leaves, some turning to gold. Elmer would be so happy, Muriel thought. His girls were working hard and doing well.

With several months of steady business under her belt, Muriel settled into her café routines and poured herself into the work. She was almost constantly in motion or in conversation with a customer. Any cleaning that she did not get done during the day, she did early the next morning while brownies baked in the oven. If Muriel needed extra help with the baking, she asked Elise, or Elise volunteered before she was even asked. Muriel filled out her food orders and supply lists after the children went to bed.

No matter what, Muriel refused to miss any of her children's plays or concerts. If they stayed up late playing cards or visiting with friends, she stayed up with them and had as much fun as they did— arguably more.

At Christmas that year, a new favorite activity entered the Sandheis' routine. After years of hearing the children say, "Everybody else has a TV," Muriel bought the family's first television set as a present for the whole family. It was the only Christmas gift that mattered. Finally, they learned firsthand why *Rawhide* was all the rage.

Muriel was happy. The hard physical work and long hours took their toll on her back and feet, yet she returned for more the next day with equal vigor. As Tom joined Evelyn at Valley City State in the fall of 1960, Chet went through a series of construction jobs, and the family moved to a new rental house about once a year, the café remained a constant in Muriel's life. She knew it like a comfortable old shoe. Her black flats needed a regular buff-and-polish, yet they were the only pair she wanted when she was on her feet all day. Sure, she could buy new black flats, but would they fit her as well as her current pair?

In early May 1962, Sheriff Hansen came in for his usual morning coffee, conversation, and a dozen brownies to go. "You're a glutton, Muriel," he said as she walked out of the kitchen to greet him with her back arched, like she had been standing in one place, hunched over, for too long.

"Just had to get moving, Ralph," she said with a smile, pouring his coffee.

Muriel set down the coffee pot and leaned against the back counter. He asked about each of her children, and Muriel asked about his dad and brother, both of whom Ralph enjoyed hanging out with. As a few more customers filed in and joined the chat, Muriel boxed Sheriff Hansen's brownies and settled his tab.

"See you next week, Sheriff Hansen!" Muriel said as he got up from his stool and she returned to the kitchen.

The next Saturday afternoon, Muriel was washing dishes after the dinner crowd left and listening to WDAY Radio. It was opening day of the fishing season, the radio news host reported. "A tragic story out of Lisbon, North Dakota, today," he said. "Ransom County Sheriff Ralph Hansen dove into the cold Sheyenne River to try to save a boy from drowning near the dam in Lisbon. Thirteen-year-old Eugene Foyt was brought to shore and resuscitated, but the strong currents pulled Sheriff Hansen underwater. Bystanders were unable to rescue him. His body was recovered an hour later. Stay tuned for updates as more details become available. A true American hero."[31]

Muriel's sudsy hands gripped the sides of the wash tub. As she stared into the still dishwater below her, she felt nothing but her heart, beating harder and harder. Elmer passed in front of her, then Ralph. She noticed her white knuckles and inhaled a deep breath.

---

[31] "Sheriff Drowns in Atmosphere of Heroic Acts," *Ransom County* [North Dakota] *Gazette*, 10 May 1962.

Muriel had another funeral to attend. She would go alone; the children would be in school, and Chet would be at work. She would ask Elise to run the café for a few hours. Although she had never met Ralph's father or siblings, she considered them friends, because Ralph was her friend.

Hearing the pastor's sermon about Ralph's legacy of generosity toward friends, neighbors, and complete strangers, Muriel already missed the idea of Ralph popping into the café to visit with whomever was at the lunch counter. Elmer would have liked having coffee with Ralph and swapping stories.

Soon came Syttende Mai—May 17—Norway's Constitution Day. "Happy Syttende Mai," each new customer said to Muriel, who smiled widely and returned the greeting. What she thought and did not say was: "Today is Elmer's fiftieth birthday."

Muriel baked two pans of brownies that morning. She spooned the black batter into the pans, put the brownies in the oven, and took off her apron. She was restless and distracted. Grabbing that week's *Ransom County Gazette* off the lunch counter, she sat down in Ralph's spot and began skimming the headlines. Her agitation grew as she read about the Ransom County Sheriff candidates and scanned the "Fort Ransom News" section for who visited whom last week. Feeling the increasing urge to crawl out of her skin, Muriel swiveled around on her stool and looked through her picture window at Main Street. There were no cars, no people. Instead, there was the spot where she had her first real conversation with Elmer in 1938, right in front of what would become her café.

Muriel shot up from her stool. She had been considering a big change long enough. The time had come to move away from Fort Ransom. She wanted to feel happiness somewhere else.

EVERYDAY PLACES

MURIEL'S LIFE HAD CHANGED A number of times in an instant. Things had happened to her. That Syttende Mai inside her café, she made something happen. To her, this was bigger than buying the farm or opening the restaurant. Those decisions were ambitious, but they tethered her to the past. This one—the decision to leave Fort Ransom—was reaching for her future.

She was sure that Valley City was the right place. With a population of nearly 8,000, it was big enough to have a variety of job opportunities for her to choose from. Located along I-94, it was also a convenient home base for Chet as he drove to construction jobs. She had her children in mind as well because Tom could save money by living with them for his last two years of college, and Marge and Liz could live at home when it came time for them to go to college. Most importantly, almost nobody knew her there. Muriel longed for a feeling of some unfamiliarity.

For a few days, Muriel planned and kept her thoughts to herself. "I have an appointment in Valley City on Monday," she told Tom and Elise, who knew how to run the café without her.

After Chet left for work and Marge and Liz left for school, Muriel dressed in a teal floral skirt, matching button-up blouse, and sensible black flats. She had made no appointments; she simply intended to scope out available houses and job openings in Valley City. She started near the college campus, where students had recently finished the spring quarter. Many of them had left for the summer, as evidenced by the "For Rent" signs on a number of front lawns. At one of these unremarkable, white two-stories, a tidy, middle-aged man dressed in a white t-shirt and blue jeans was mowing the lawn. Muriel parked the green 1953 Oldsmobile on the street and approached him with a hello and a smile. He showed her around the house, which had three bedrooms, a bathroom, and a kitchen sink with running water. She gave no indication that she was impressed, but she was thrilled about the prospect of indoor plumbing.

"It'll be available as of June 1," the man told her, "after I give the main level a fresh coat of paint."

"I only just started my search," Muriel responded, "but I'll think about it and get back to you. Thank you for showing it to me."

Her heart raced as she got back into the car. She did not need to see any other houses. She wrote down the phone number on the sign and continued her drive. She then stopped at several restaurants and two grocery stores to enquire about mid-level positions. Muriel was too ambitious to settle for a waitress or clerk position, but she did not want the headaches associated with owning another business of her own.

Eating a sandwich at Foss Drug's lunch counter, Muriel gathered her thoughts. She was certain she would find a job in Valley City if she kept looking and remained patient. The best plan was probably to make the move first and look in earnest after getting settled. Feeling confident about her approach, Muriel paid her bill and decided to make one more stop before heading back to Fort Ransom.

She returned to the house she had toured that morning and parked in front. The owner was gone, so Muriel spent a minute gazing at the house and running it through her mental checklist of priorities. She then walked to Old Main on the college campus, about two blocks away, to check on potential food service openings.

Seeing a stout older woman taking stock of the cafeteria kitchen, Muriel gave a friendly, "Hello!" in a slightly raised voice, and the woman looked up, seemingly surprised to see anyone.

The woman happened to be the director of food services, Mrs. Ruhland, who struck Muriel as bland, but not unfriendly. Her starched white apron and buffed, well-worn Oxfords spoke of care and hard work, a combination that Muriel gravitated toward.

"I'm here to enquire about a position," Muriel said, sensing that Mrs. Ruhland was the sort to skip pleasantries.

"In fact, I'm about to start looking for a pastry chef," Mrs. Ruhland said plainly. "Would that job interest you?"

Muriel considered for a moment if being a pastry chef *would* interest her. She had never thought of such a job before. She indeed baked for a crowd every day at the café, and she *was good* at it. "Yes, I think I'd like that," Muriel replied. "I'd at least like to learn more about the position."

"Do you have time to talk now?" Mrs. Ruhland asked, seeming to surprise herself.

The two women sat across from each other at a table in the cafeteria, and before Muriel knew what was happening, she was in a job interview. Muriel was talking about her café; her lifetime of experience in baking pies, cakes, and lefse; and her recipe for pie crust, which she recited as easily the alphabet. Her qualifications were impressive enough so that Mrs. Ruhland told Muriel about the job duties and the early-morning expectations. Finally, she asked Muriel about her experience in training young people how to cook or bake. Again, Muriel more than delivered, describing the café as a family business that was putting her four children through college.

"We've gone out of order today," Mrs. Ruhland said, "but if you're interested in the position, I'll give you an application to fill out before you leave. I could check on more of the details this week and let you know where things stand by Friday."

"That sounds perfect," Muriel said enthusiastically as she shook Mrs. Ruhland's hand. "Thank you so much."

Muriel had cautious excitement as she walked back to her car. Could the move really be as simple as saying yes to the first house she saw and being offered the first job for which she interviewed? Of course, she might not be offered the job, or maybe the wage would be too low. There was no need to get ahead of herself. Still, she was hopeful. Driving back to Fort Ransom, Muriel cranked up "Crazy" on the radio and sang with Patsy Cline. She hoped to sing out all of her anticipation during her forty-minute drive, so that when she arrived back home, the children would think everything was normal. For now, she had to wait. She had to make sure the move was real before telling anyone.

The next several days passed too slowly for Muriel at the café. Each day, she wished for and did not receive a call from the college. Finally, after the dinner crowd cleared out and Muriel was alone on Friday afternoon, the phone rang. She listened calmly as Mrs. Ruhland offered her the pastry chef job. "May I have until Monday to let you know? . . . Okay. Thank you. I will call you on Monday."

Muriel did not need to consider the offer; she would earn nearly as much money without the responsibilities of owning a business. She really only needed to tell her family. She assumed Chet would be happy to shed time off his work commute by living in Valley City, so she was eager to talk to him after he came home that night. Evelyn, who was completing her first year of teaching in Oakes, North Dakota, had no intention of returning to Fort Ransom or Valley City. Tom was living with Grandma and Grandpa Sandhei for the summer while building local power lines, and he could live with Muriel and Chet during his junior and senior years at Valley City State College, so he had no reason to oppose the move. Marge felt excluded in Fort Ransom, so she might be happy about the prospect of more friends in her senior year of high school. Thirteen-year-old Liz, though, would likely be terrified to change schools.

As Muriel informed Chet and the children, their reactions were as she predicted. When she told her mother after church on Sunday, Josephine remarked, "It's so far away from home."

"Valley City is only forty-five minutes away, Ma. You'll still see me," Muriel said, trying to focus on the positives. "Besides, you'll still have Mildred and Frances nearby. And a fresh start is exactly what I need."

On Monday morning, Muriel's first order of business after doing the breakfast dishes was to call her soon-to-be-boss to accept the job at Valley City State. That afternoon, she began informing customers that the café would close its doors on Sunday, June 3. "I'm done! I'm worn out!" she said with a smile in a joking tone, even though it was the truth. The never-ending work and the long hours had taken their toll on her feet and back, and she yearned for a Monday to Friday job that she could leave at a sane hour.

In the final two weeks of operating the café, Muriel heard two common sentiments: "We sure will miss your brownies" and "We'll be sad to lose the café." She most appreciated the few brave friends who said, "We'll miss you, Muriel." That level of emotion was too direct for most of the locals, but Muriel heard it from the rodeo crowd. They even offered to help her and Chet move to Valley City.

After Muriel locked the doors of the café for the last time, she walked home with Tom and Marge and relived memories of Chet tossing an unruly customer into the snowbank and laughing with the rodeo crowd into the wee hours of the morning. She was glad for the happy conversation on a day that otherwise felt like an ending. After forty-one years in Fort Ransom, save five precious months in Montana, she was on the brink of leaving her hometown for good.

Muriel had one week to prepare for the move and have the "last visits" with her family and friends. On Saturday night, she and Chet played whist with Glenn and Frances and laughed until 1:00 a.m. about a lifetime of Fort Ransom antics. The next Monday afternoon, Mildred insisted on hosting a farewell coffee party for Muriel. About a dozen women attended, lunching on Muriel's favorite white layer cake with lemon filling and seven-minute frosting. Of course, no self-respecting Fort Ransom woman served anything but made-from-scratch cake. "Who's buying those boxed cake mixes?" they wondered aloud at Muriel's party. "And has anyone tried the frozen meals called 'TV dinners'?"

Catching up on the latest town news and sharing her own, Muriel observed how familiar this "party" felt, and how much she yearned for something totally different. She would always be *from* Fort Ransom, but she would be relieved to be a resident of Valley City. Not everyone would know her full life story. She would not know every nook and cranny of her surroundings. She would not see Elmer everywhere she went. As Muriel said her goodbyes at the end of the coffee party, she flashed her big, signature smile and reminded them, "Stop for coffee when you come to Valley City!"

Three days later—June 12, 1962—Muriel gave her house a last scan and walked out the front door, carrying the kitchen garbage can. This house had been one of four rentals in four years that she had felt no attachment to. There was nothing to be emotional about because the memories had never had time to accumulate inside any of these houses. Their possessions had no family history. Her only sentimentality was tied to the farm and to Fort Ransom itself—the whole collective place.

"You ready to go, then?" asked Chet, who was leaning against the grill on the front of Grandpa Sandhei's 1941 Ford pickup.

He required no answer besides her opening the passenger door of the pickup and stepping inside. They backed out of the driveway and drove out of town in silence. Not a soul was outdoors to wave at them or smile at C.A.'s pickup, hand-painted with a brush in barn red, left over from a past project. A light dust hung in the air behind them, and the long Fort Ransom hill rose ahead. Carrying a heavier-than-usual load, the climb seemed to last an eternity. Muriel felt a lump forming in her throat and tears gathering in her eyes. Never again would this be her home. Her eyes would no longer loiter at the spot on Main Street where she and Elmer had their first long conversation. In all the years Elmer had been gone, she had gazed into the distance at his fields whenever she passed by. After today, she would seldom drive by their farm. With Chet next to her, oblivious, she willed her tears not to fall. Not once in their thirteen years without Elmer had the two of them talked seriously about losing his brother or her husband. The lump in her throat grew.

Muriel sat in her sorrow until they descended the big hill into Valley City. She breathed in her new Sheyenne Valley home, and the rush of adrenaline hit her so quickly that she started out of the truck the second Chet shut off the engine in front of the white house she had wanted at first sight. Howard and Tim from the rodeo crowd were already there, with most of the family's largest possessions in their own truck. "Okay, boys," she said, relieved and ready to assemble her new life.

After instructing the men where to place the furniture, Muriel spent the afternoon unpacking boxes. Chet organized the garage and generally stayed out of the way. She went to Red Owl for groceries and made a late evening supper of sandwiches and creamed cucumbers for the two of them. She filled a small pitcher of water at the sink, smiling as the water streamed from the faucet.

"It's our eighth wedding anniversary today," Muriel observed as she set the plates in front of them and sat down.

"It is. Yes. Happy anniversary," Chet said, giving her a nod and a closed-lip smile.

Sleep that night came easily; Muriel's body ached just as it had after long days at the café. As her brain awakened at the usual 5:00 a.m. the next morning, she thought it was time to get dressed and walk to the café. But when she got her bearings, she realized she could stay in bed a few minutes longer. Chet was still asleep, and she did not start her job until August. Yet sunrise came a few minutes later, prompting her to find her summer housedress, which hung from a nail on the closet door. She walked into her new kitchen to make coffee and oatmeal for Chet. He hurriedly ate, walked out the door with his Thermos full of coffee, and went to his job building rural power lines. Quickly cleaning up the dishes, Muriel again reminded herself to slow down.

When had she last relaxed? She did not really know; it had been years, certainly. She poured herself a second cup of coffee and sat down at her Formica table. Hearing the kitchen clock tick . . . tick . . . tick . . . she stared out the window and let her mind wander toward

Elmer. In all the years he had been gone, she had told herself not to think about him, only to see his image in front of her a moment later, in a place familiar to the two of them. Fort Ransom was one big, painful reminder.

Here in Valley City, her and Elmer's farm was far out of sight. She still owned it and intended to always keep it. It was the only earthly possession she had of Elmer. But the everyday places where Elmer had been were no longer Muriel's everyday places. Here, she would bring Elmer up in her memories when and where she allowed. This morning, Muriel let Elmer pass over her for a long while, like the puffy white clouds traversing the sky outside. She saw the excitement on his face coming home from shearing sheep in Montana. She felt his hand in hers as they walked through their farmhouse for the first time. She heard their children's laughter as he playfully chanted, "Rida rida ranka . . ." She thought of how proud he would be of the children going to college. She even thought how happy he would be that Chet had helped raise them.

As she finished her last sip of coffee, Muriel rose from her chair with a start. She dusted off her apron out of habit. Arousing no flour or dust, she smiled. "Life is good," she told herself.

AFTERWORD

MURIEL NEVER SLOWED DOWN WHEN it came to hard work. During her twenty-four-year career at Valley City State College, she made as many as fifty or sixty pies per day, Monday through Friday, from 4:00 a.m. to 1:00 p.m. She loved her job and was a favorite of

Muriel and Chet at home in Valley City, circa 1963. (Courtesy Tom Sandhei)

Mrs. Ruhland, her co-workers, and the students she mentored in part-time food service jobs. She continued to have little to no patience for anyone who did not work as hard as she expected. "Kids nowadays just don't know how to work," she commented to her own children, who knew her expectations to a T.

Muriel enjoyed more time to herself in Valley City than she had in all her years in Fort Ransom, and her amount of free time only increased as Marge and Liz left the nest and all four children moved away, onto adult lives of their own. After work, she enjoyed watching *As the World Turns*, meeting friends for coffee uptown at Foss Drug, and doing crossword puzzles. At night, her go-to hobbies were playing cards and reading romance novels, except on Fridays, when she and Chet were regulars at the Valley City Eagles Club, and Sundays, when *Bonanza* aired. She preferred whist in the company of four people, or cribbage when only two or three could play. She was known to stay up past midnight playing games and still get up at 3:00 a.m. to get ready for work. If she was tired or had aches or pains, she never hinted at anything of the sort to her children.

One by one, the Sandhei children attended Valley City State College and moved into successful adult lives. Evelyn received her two-year teaching certificate and taught two years in Oakes, North Dakota, before marrying and finishing her degree a few years later. Her income helped pay for Tom's college tuition and expenses. Tom completed college in 1964, got his initial teaching job in West Fargo, North Dakota, and helped cover Marge's college costs. Marge graduated from Valley City High School in 1963 with more friends than she had ever had in Fort Ransom, and then graduated from Valley City State in 1966. By the time Liz graduated from high school in 1967, Muriel and Chet had enough savings built up to help her complete college without funds from her older siblings. In 1970, Liz accomplished Muriel's dream of all four children graduating from college.

C.A. and Elise continued living in their small Fort Ransom home until C.A. died in 1969. Elise stayed put until the last few years

Tom received his teaching degree from Valley City State College in 1964. His mother and Chet (back) and Sandhei grandparents (front, with Tom in between) were on hand to celebrate his achievement.
(Courtesy Tom Sandhei)

of her life; she died at age ninety-five in 1985 while living at Parkside Lutheran Home in Lisbon. Josephine lived with Muriel's sister Mildred near Fort Ransom during the last several years of her life. When Stiklestad burned to the ground in 1968, Muriel could not help but laugh when her mother called it divine intervention. The Sorlendings had to attend Standing Rock with the Nordlendings full-time if they wanted to go to church in Fort Ransom. By the time Josephine died at age ninety-five in 1977, the once-clear division between Standing Rock and Stiklestad members had virtually disappeared.

Chet worked various construction jobs from April to November and drew unemployment in the winter until 1965, when he became a lineman for the Rural Electrical Association. Dual year-round incomes enabled Chet and Muriel to buy a small home in northeast Valley City that same year. When the couple retired in 1986, they sold their home and moved into a nearby apartment. Chet died at Mercy Hospital in Valley City in 1994.

Around that time, Muriel made a point of passing on some of her signature recipes, including those for krina lefse, brownies, and ice cream. Potato lefse and Hardanger lefse required no written recipes in her opinion; they were made based on "feel." Finally, now that her children were fully capable adults, she also shared her lefse-making methods with them that she learned as a child from her own mother.

Muriel's brownie recipe gave no instructions on baking temperature or times, simply, "Do not overbake." As for her ice cream, which her children believed was superior because of the fourth cup of cream added later than the first three, Muriel indicated her method was nothing special at all. "That was the size of my kettle," she said nonchalantly.

Muriel and Elmer's farmstead remained vacant, never to be a residence again following the fire in 1958. After the barn fell into disrepair, Chet burned the remaining buildings on the farm in the 1980s. The crop land remained in the Soil Bank Program and its successor, the Conservation Reserve Program. In the late 1990s, Muriel put the 160-acre farm into a life estate, which essentially deeded the land to her four children upon her death.

Muriel was highly autonomous and capable for her entire lifetime. After moving to Valley City, she rarely returned to Fort Ransom and never spoke of Elmer. Her children understood not to ask about him. In adulthood, Liz once asked Muriel if Elmer knew about her before his death. Muriel warmly, but tersely, said, "Yes, he was excited about you."

Around her eightieth birthday, Muriel was diagnosed with colon cancer. After a two-year battle, she died on March 6, 2004, surrounded by family. Muriel's children are forever grateful for her determination to send them to college and nurture their work ethic. They admire her courage, humor, and quest for happiness.

Muriel's Brownies

½ C shortening
1 C sugar
2 eggs
¼ C milk
1 C flour
4 TBSP cocoa powder

Add dash of nuts, salt and vanilla.
Mix. Pour in greased 9 x 13 pan. Do not overbake.*

* *Many of Muriel's early recipes did not provide an oven temperature, because she baked in a wood stove. For today's bakers, the brownies bake best at 350 degrees for about 30 minutes.*

ACKNOWLEDGMENTS

Thank you to Tom's sisters—Evelyn Dawson, Marjorie Herr, and Elizabeth Lamb—for providing their memories and supporting us in sharing this story with an audience beyond Muriel's family.

Many thanks to Tricia's mentor and friend Dr. Thomas D. Isern, mother Arlene Velure, and friend Ann Slanga for reviewing drafts of the manuscript and providing feedback that made this book possible.

The research required by this project was extensive, and we greatly appreciate the people and organizations who assisted us: Pastor Bradley Edin and the parish of Standing Rock Lutheran Church, Harlan Enerson of Bucyrus, Tricia's mentor and friend Dr. Lori Lahlum, Barnes County Historical Society and Director Wes Anderson, Ransom County Historical Society, the Ransom County Gazette, and the State Historical Society of North Dakota. The chapters of this book that are set in Montana would have been impossible to write without the assistance of Pelton family descendants Bill Pelton and Ed Hamilton, who were very generous with their time and insights, as well as Joan Brownell and Wally and Michelle Keith.

Other colleagues, friends, and family members offered invaluable support, encouragement, and advice as we collaborated on this project over the course of more than two years. We want to acknowledge a few of them by name: Kristi (Blom) Anderson; Curt Granlund; Al Grothe; Ann Jonell; Karen Overn; Melford Rufsvold; Scott Schmidt; Jerry Sorby; Marilyn Sorby; Todd Velure; Melinda Voss; Melinda's late husband, Jack Coffman; and Solveig Zempel. Dr. Suzzanne Kelley, Mike Jacobs, and the people of NDSU Press believed in us as first-time authors, for which we will be eternally grateful.

BIBLIOGRAPHY

Published Sources

"A Brief History of the Zion Ladies' Aid for 75th Anniversary." *Favorite Recipes of Members of the Zion Ladies' Aid*. Fort Ransom, ND: Zion Ladies' Aid, 1959.

Associated Press. "Bill Greenough Wins Rodeo at Red Lodge." *The Helena Independent-Record*, July 5, 1940.

Briggs, Tracy. "Ides of March Blizzard Claimed 72 Lives in the Red River Valley 78 Years Ago This Week." *Grand Forks Herald*, March 13, 2019.

"Fort Ransom News." *Ransom County Gazette*, September 19, 1940, and September 26, 1940.

Fort Ransom 125th Anniversary Book Committee, ed. *Fort Ransom Community History, 1878–2003*. Fort Ransom, ND: Fort Ransom 125th Anniversary Book Committee, 2003.

Sandhei, C.A. "Historical Sketch of Fort Ransom Community." *Litchville* [North Dakota] *Bulletin*, 1953.

"Sheriff Drowns in Atmosphere of Heroic Acts." *Ransom County* [North Dakota] *Gazette*, 10 May 1962.

Thorfinnson, Snorri. *Fort Ransom Area History, 1878–1978*. Fort Ransom, ND: Fort Ransom Community Club, 1978.

Unpublished Sources

Brownell, Joan L. "Pelton House," *National Register of Historic Places Registration Form*. Washington, DC: U.S. Department of the Interior, National Park Service, 2016.

Henrickson, Gary. Interview by author Tom Sandhei. Personal interview by phone. October 18, 2020.

Henrickson, Josie. Interview by Larry Sprunk. Personal interview at Henrickson's home in rural Fort Ransom. North Dakota Oral History

Project Records, Collection 10157. State Historical Society of North Dakota, Bismarck. October 3, 1974.

Pelton, Bill. Interview by author Tricia Velure. Personal interview by phone. October 16, 2020.

Ransom County, North Dakota. Land Records. Register of Deeds Office, 1899, 1910.

Ransom County, North Dakota. Mortgage Records. Register of Deeds Office, 1943, 1949.

Rufsvold, Melford. Interview by author Tom Sandhei. Personal interview by phone. February 18, 2020.

Sandhei, C.A. Daybook entries, 1936–1969. In the possession of author Tom Sandhei.

United States, Bureau of the Census. Sixteenth Census of the United States. Washington, D.C., 1940.

Zion Ladies' Aid. Meeting minutes, December 11, 1941–March 8, 1945. Standing Rock Lutheran Church, Fort Ransom, North Dakota.

Online Sources

Ducoff, Louis J. "Wages of Agricultural Labor in the United States." Technical Bulletin No. 895. Washington, D.C.: United States Department of Agriculture, July 1945. https://naldc.nal.usda.gov/download/CAT86200887/PDF.

State Historical Society of North Dakota. "North Dakota Studies Unit 5: Set 4. The Spanish Flu in North Dakota—Introduction." Accessed November 10, 2020. https://www.history.nd.gov/textbook/unit5_4_intro_flu.html.

United States Department of Agriculture. "Census of Agriculture Historical Archive—Montana." Accessed May 12, 2020. http://usda.mannlib.cornell.edu/usda/AgCensusImages/1940/01/38/1266/Table-03.pdf.

United States Department of Agriculture. "Crop Production Historical Track Records." Accessed December 28, 2020. https://www.nass.usda.gov/Publications/Todays_Reports/reports/croptr18.pdf.

United States Holocaust Memorial Museum. "How did public opinion about entering the war change between 1939 and 1941?" Accessed May 12, 2020. https://exhibitions.ushmm.org/americans-and-the-holocaust/us-public-opinion-world-war-II-1939-1941.

INDEX

Some of the Henrickson family dropped the use of the "c" in their name. Adolph, Gregor, Lars, and Peder spelled their last name as Henrikson. Their names have been left in the index as Henrickson to avoid confusion.

Page numbers in **bold** type indicate photographs or illustrations.

19th Amendment to the US Constitution, 29

A

Absarokee, MT, 99, 117
Adams County, ND, x, 68, 72, 75
Arctic Circle, 7
Anderson, Andy, 34
Anderson, Art, 73, 193
Anderson, Elmer, 61, 73–77, 126
Anderson, George, 170–71, 176, 193, 202, 203
Anderson, Mildred, 73, 74
Anderson, Ole, 37
Anderson, Ragna, 193

B

Barnes County (ND) Historical Society, xii
Beartooth Mountains, 109
Bedney, Tom, 122, 123
Berg, Tim, 206, 216
Bethania Ladies' Aid, 134, 147, 173
Billings, MT, 94, 99, 100
Bismarck, ND, viii, 34, 96
Black Hills, 182
Bucyrus, ND, x, 67–**69**, 71, 72, 79, 88, 117, 121

C

Carlblom, Ethel Henrickson, **ix**, 3–5, 21, 25, 27, 34–35, 46, 58, 147–49
Carlblom, Henry, 147–48
Carlblom, Shirley, 147
Catholic, 92
Church of Norway, xi, 36
Collette, Jimmy, 190–91, 193
Collette, Rosie, 193
Collette's Café, 73, 74, 92
Collette's Tavern, 92, 176, 193, 203
Columbus, MT, 99, 111, 112, 114, 115
Concordia College, 40, 144
Conservation Reserve Program, 222
  See also Soil Bank Program
Coolidge, President Calvin, 30

D

Dakota Territory, viii, x, 7, 8
Dickinson, ND, 96

E

Eastern Montana Normal School, 100
Englevale, ND, 18, 34, 86
English language, 14–15, 42, 59, 68, 123
Europe, 91, 107, 121, 138

F

Fargo, ND, viii, 30, 34, 58, 92, 130, 133, 157, 191
farming
  harvest, 3, 5–6, 17, 26, 48, 60, 69, 71, 117, 119, 123, 136, 142, 190, 201
  lambing, 105–108
  shearing, 106–108
Federal Farm Mortgage Corporation, 137
Fishtail, MT, 94, 100, **101**
Fort Ransom, ND, x–xii, 7, 9, 10, **11**, 12, 13, **14**, 15, 31, 34, 36, **38**, 39, 41, 50, 55, 62, 67–68, 71–72, 74, 75, 77, 79–81, **87**, 89, 90, 92, 95, 98, 99–100, 103, 110, 117–118, 119–121, 123, 124, 125–126, 129, 131, 137, 138–139, 140, 147, 148, 150, 162, 164, 168, 169, 170, 174, 175–176, 177, **178**, 181, 184, 188, 194, 201, 202, 203, 205, 206, 209, 210, 211, 213–217, 220, 221, 222
  booze runners, 30
  charity, 146–47, 166, 174, 192, 201
  charivaris, 182–83
  dam, viii
  dances, 52–53, 60–61, 75–78, 86, 193, 195–96
  east prairie above, 9, 13, 18
  electricity installation, 152
  farmer, x, 133, 143, 164
  flour and feed mill, viii
  Fourth of July rodeo, 206
  general store, 15, 170
  geography, viii
  Grothe's Garage, 203
  hill, 174
  history of, vii–x
  incorporation, ix
  "Little Norway," 8
  locker plant, 193
  Main Street, 30, 52, 57, 58, 88, 125, 150, 170, 174, 176, 193, 203, 209, 215
  military post, viii
  Muriel's Café, 202–209, **204**, 210, 212–14
  population, ix–x, 95, 130, 174
  Lutheran, 28, 36–40, 52
  Norwegian, xi–xii, 28, 31, 37
  Sons of Norway Hall, 195

Sons of Norway Park, 176
Telephone Central, 201
west prairie above, 10, 18, 68
Fort Ransom School, 46, 50, 57–58, 68, 80, 139
Fort Ransom Township, ND, ix, x
France, 29
Frazier, Governor Lynn, 32

G

Glendive, MT, 96, **97**, 99
Great Crash, 44–45
Great Depression, xi, xii, 49, 61, 88, 103, 147
Great Plains, 8
Great War. *See* World War I
Gronvold, Dr., 3–5, 20–21, 29

H

Hansen, Ralph, 205, 208–209
Harding, President Warren G., 29, 30
Hauge Synod, xi, 37
Hendricks, Bud, 170
Henrickson, Adolph, 7, 148
Henrickson, Andor "Pud," **ix**, 20–22, 26–27, 33, 80, 88, 89, 90, 95, 120, 121, 125, 139, 143, 163, 173, 175
Henrickson, Bernice, **ix**, 5, 21, 23, 26, 46, 55, 58, 85, 94, 152
Henrickson, Betty, 173
Henrickson, Borghil, 55
Henrickson, Gregor, 7
Henrickson, Harold, **ix**, 3, 19, 27, 30, 32–33, 55, 57, 63, 138
Henrickson, Ida Bernston, 121, 123
Henrickson, Johannes "John," vii–viii, **ix**, xi, **11**, 15, 24, 80, 93–94, 148–149, 156
  Andor "Pud," birth of, 20–22
  card playing, 46, 129
  church, role of, 36, 39–40, 53–54
  death of, 150–152
  Ethel, death of, 148–149
  family, **ix**
  farming, viii, 14–19, 24, 90, 126, 128
  fatherhood, 14, 20–22
  financial hardship, xii, 44–45, 48, 49, 63, 90–91, 104, 148
  Josephine
    farmstead, 13–**14**
    introduction to, 7, 12
    marriage to, **11**, 12, 13
  modernization, 30–31
  move to Mikkelson home, 121, 124
  Muriel, birth of, 3–6, 14, 32
  politics, 29–33, 58
  upbringing, 7–9, 13, 20
Henrickson, Josephine Nelson, vii–viii, **ix**, xi, 7, 32, 46, 80–81, 93–94, 95–96, 120–22, 128, 130, 132, 148–49, 156, 157, 163, 164–68, **178**

birth of, 9–10
birth of Andor "Pud," 20–22
church, role of, 10, 12, 36, 39–40, 53–55
death of, 221
Ethel, death of, 148–49
family, **ix**
farm life, 15–19, 23–27, 33, 88, 90
financial hardship, xii, 44–45, 48, 49, 63, 90–91
grandmother, 170–71, 176
John
  death of, 150, 152
  farmstead, 13–**14**
  introduction to, 7, 12
  marriage to, **11**, 12, 13
lefse-making, 50–51
motherhood, 14, 23, 29
move to Mikkelson home, 121, 124, 125, Muriel
Muriel
  birth of, 3–6, 14, 30
  living with, 164–172, 173, 177
  supporting, 93–94
politics, 29–34
upbringing, 10–12, 28
Henrickson, Lars, 7
Henrickson, Luther, **ix**, 3, 19, 21, 27, 32–35, 63, 88–91, 93, 121, 123, 124, 126, 137, 138, 140, 148, 199
Henrickson, Palmer, **ix**, 3, 19, 33, 34–35, 58, 63, 138, 148–49, 162
Henrickson, Peder, 7
Henrikson, Ole, 7, 8–9, 148
Hettinger, ND, 68, 77
Highness, Art, 159–60
Hoboken, NJ, 29
Hoff, Howard, 206, 216
Hold the Fort flour mill, ix
Holkestad, Wallace, 148
Homestead Act of 1862, 8
Hope, MN, 123

I

Ides of March Blizzard, 132
Independent Voter's Association (IVA), 32
Interstate 94, 194, 202, 210

J

Jacobson, Albert Jr., 131–32
Jacobson, Albert Sr., 131–32
Jacobson, Andrew, 164, 171, 179
Jacobson, Georgia Lee, 165
Jacobson, Lettie, 165
Jacobson, Marie, 132
Jamestown, ND, 96, 194
Johnson, Walter, 202–203
Jorgenson, Lawrence, 195

K

Kathryn, ND, 39, 52, 86, 175, 193
Knutson's Tavern, 193, 203

L

Larsen, Alan, 205–206
Larsen, Russell, 205–206
Larson, Peder Bang, 174, 175
lefse, 50–51, 96, 99, 128–29, 139, 165, 166, 184, 212
   Hardanger, 51, 222
   krina, 51, 222
   potato, 50, 222
Libak, Elsa Mae Sandhei, 79, **81**, 120, 134, 145, 159, 166, 169, 190
Libak, Marvin, 190, 191
Lisbon, ND, 8, 10, 12, 30–31, 35, 57, 89, 92, 156–158, 171, 174, 175, 191, 192, 198, 202, 205, 206, 208, 221
Lutheran, vii, 90, 92
   church, 36–40
   confirmation, 52–56
   missionary, 10
   philosophy, 37, 52
   practices, 36–40, 54
   reading for the minister, 36, 53–54
   See also Standing Rock Lutheran Church; Stiklestad Lutheran Church

M

Madagascar, 10
making do, 44–45, 49, 50, 131, 147, 168
Massachusetts, 29
McClusky, ND, viii
Medora, ND, 99
Mercy Hospital, 135, 159, 169, 222
Mikkelson, Jacob, 10, 12, 28, 121, 124
Mikkelson, Maren, 10, 12, 28, 121, 124, 125
Minneapolis, MN, 58, 85, 94, 138, 143, 163, 173
Minnesota, viii, 70, 121, 122
Missouri, 100
modern technology, 30–31, 89, 103
   electricity, 103–104, 152–53, 155
   farming, 135, 153
   running water, 103–104, 141, 153, 193, 203, 211
   TV, 187, 193, 207
Mo I Rana, Norway, xi, 7, 8, 12, 41, 67, 68, 127
Montana, xii, 94–96, 98, 103, 106, 107, 110, 114, 115, 118, 121, 123, 127, 129, 140, 152, 203, 214, 217
   south central, 94, 99
Moorhead, MN, 40
Mt. Rushmore, 182

N

Nelson, Andor, 28–29
Nelson, Axel, 14
Nelson, Christ, 28–29
Nelson, Christine, 8, 10
Nelson, Dagmar, 70
Nelson, Hilmer, 61, 70
Nelson, Lizzie, 3, 47, 48
Nelson, Peder, 8, 10
Nestos, Governor Ragnvald, 32
New Jersey, 29
New Richland, MN, 121
Nokken, 39–40
Nokken men's choir, 39, 176
Nome, ND, 52, 86, 193
Nonpartisan League (NPL), viii, 31–32
Nordlendings, 36, 221
Nord Rana, Norway, xi
North Dakota, vii, viii, xi, xii, 17, 96, 102, 105, 106, 119, 132, 157, 163, 202
   central, viii
   eastern, 71
   economy, 45
   harvest season, 5
   House of Representatives, viii, 32, 34
   Legislature, 44
   politics, 29–32
   progress for women, 29
   prohibition, 30
   soldiers, 28
   South Dakota border, 67
   southwest, x, 67
   State Historical Society of, xii
   State Mill and Elevator, 32
   western, 71, 72, 81
North Dakota Mill and Elevator Association, 31
Northern Pacific Railroad, viii
Norway, vii, x–xi, 7–9, 13, 14, 19, 20, 31, 36–37, 54, 67, 107, 121, 139, 144, 146–147, 175
   Constitution Day, 209
   northern, xi–xii, 36
   southern, xi–xii, 37, 51
Norwegian(s), vii, 37, 53, 95, 129, 157, 184
   American, vii, viii, xii, 23, 179
   farmer, 17
   folklore, 39–40
   immigrant(s), viii, x, 8, 10, 31
   language, 37, 40, 42, 48, 53, 123, 133
   northern, xi–xii
   population in Fort Ransom, xi, 28, 58
   prayer, 39
   southern, xi–xii
   standards, 89, 125, 175
   verse, 146
Norwegian Relief, 146

O

Oakes, ND, 213, 220
Olson, Andrew B., 162
Olson, Barbara, 7–9, 12
Olson, Bertram, 148
Olson, Cedor, 127
Olson, Florence, 127, 138
Olson, Hans, 68, 71, 74, 75, 79, 165
Olson, Henrik, 7–9
Olson, Marvin, 127
Olson, Ole, 73
Olson, Oscar, 68, 72, 74, 77–78, 95, 141, 165
Olson, Oscar A., 153, 154, 197, 198
Olson, Petrine, 68, 71, 74, 75, 76, 79
Olson, Ronnie, 205
Omaha, NE, 163

P

Payne, Dr., 111–12, 115–16
Payne, Mabel, 111–13, 115–17
Paynesville, MN, 9
Pederson, Emil, 73, 201
Pelton, Art, 103
Pelton, Charles "Charley," 94, 99–110, **101**, 112, 114–118, 134, 140, 152
Pelton, Forestine, 100–104, 107–109, 111–115, 117
Pelton, George, 100–103, 106–110, 112, 114, 116
Pelton, Gladys, 94, 96, 99–110, **101**, 111–118, 134, 140, 152
Pelton, Kathleen, 100, 102, 103
Pelton, Lois "Marjorie," 100
Pelton, Marilyn, 100, 114
Pelton, Miriam "Mim," 100, 105, 114
Pelton, Robert, 100, 110, 112
pregnancy out of wedlock, xii, 92–98, 119
prohibition, 30

R

Ransom County, ND, x
    Sheriff, 205, 208–209
Ransom County Gazette, 209
Red Lodge, MT, 109, 112
Red River, viii
Roosevelt, President Franklin D., 123, 138
Rufsvold, Anna, **11**, 12
Rufsvold, Ardis, 43, 86, **87**, 88, 121
Rufsvold, Christine, 9, 12
Rufsvold, Clarice, 42, 46, 86, 88
Rufsvold, Cornelius, 7, 9, 12, 13
Rufsvold, Henry, **11**, 12
Rufsvold, Kermit, 148
Rufsvold, Loubert, 88, 191
Rufsvold, Mildred Henrickson, **ix**, 3–6, 20–21, 23, 25, 27, 35, 41–43, 46, 49, 50, 51, 57, 61, 63, 88, 129, 147–148, 152, 181, 191, 199, 213, 214, 221

Ruhland, Mrs., 211–13, 219–20
Rural Electrical Association, 222

S

Sandanger, Gustav, 30, 37, 40, 53–56, 80, 88. 147, 161–163, 181
Sandhei, Alfhild, 68, **81**, 163, 169
Sandhei, Chester "Chet," 79, **81**, 88–90, 94–95, 109, 120, 127, 134, 139, **151**, 152, 154, 166, 168, 188–189, 195, 203, 209, **219**, 220, **221**
    construction work, 194, 201, 202, 207, 210, 222
    Elmer, death of, 156–63
    illness, 190–94
    Muriel
        courtship, 177–80
        farmstead, 179–80
            farming, 186, 190, 192–93, 201–202
            fire, 196–200
            marriage to, 181–84, 206, 216–17
        move to
            Fort Ransom, 201–02
            Valley City, 213–17
        friendship, 173, 175–76
    nickname, 143
    working at Elmer and Muriel's farm, 143–45, 150, 153, 156, 165
Sandhei, Christian "C.A.," x–xi, xii–xiii, 68, 70, 73, 77, 79–**81**, 95, 119, 121, 122, 126–27, 132–35, 137, 141, 142, 144, 146, 153, **167**, 175, 176, 179, 191, 194, 215, **221**
    daybook, xii, **167**
    death of, 220
    Elmer, death of, 159–61
Sandhei, Elise Olson, x–xi, 67, 68, 79–**81**, 95, 119–21, 123, 126, 127, 132, 134, 139, 144–45, 148, 173, 191, 192, 194, 205, 207, 209, 210, 220, **221**
    death of, 221
    Elmer, death of, 156, 157, 159–61
Sandhei, Elizabeth "Liz," 169, 170, 174, 177, **178**, 181, 185, 187, 188, 191, 195, 198, 199, 205, 206, 210, 213, 220, 222
    birth of, 169
Sandhei, Elmer, xi, 68, **69**, **81**, 148, **151**
    death of, 161–63
    departure from Bucyrus, 68–70
    draft, 123
    farming, 72–73, 77–78, 142–43, 150, 156
        in Minnesota, 121–23
        with Carl Anderson, 126–28, 132–35, 137
    fatherhood, 138, 145–46, 149
        Evelyn, birth of, 135–36
        Merle Elmer, 112–14
            birth of, 111–14
            death of, 114–18, 119, 149
    financial hardship, 69–70

Fort Ransom, 67–68
  farmstead purchase, 137–41
  return to, 70–73, 77, 119
  illness, 156–61
  move to
    Carl Anderson farm, 132–34
    Montana, 94–98, 99
  Muriel
    courtship, 86–91
    farm life, 142–45, 150, 153–55
    introduction to, 61–63, 75–76, 77, 80
    marriage, 96–98, **97**, 99, 142–43
    pregnancy, 92–98, 111
  pastimes
    card playing, 73, 129, 143
    dancing, 74–77
    pool playing, 73, 77
    violin playing, 138
  Pelton ranch, 99–110
    arrival, 99–105
    duties, 105–110
Sandhei, Evelyn Louise, 137, 138, 141, 142–44,
  146, 148, 149, 150, **151**, 152, **154**, 155, 165,
  168, 169, 170, 174, 177, **178**, 179, 181, 185,
  187, 188, 191–93, 195–96, 198, 201, 202,
  205–207, 213, 220
  birth of, 135–36
Sandhei, Harold, 68, **81**, 144, 159, 169
Sandhei, Marjorie Ann "Marge," 150, 154, 165,
  168, 170, 172, 174, **178**, 181, 185–89, 195,
  196, 198, 199, 205, 206, 210, 213, 214, 220
  birth of, 150
Sandhei, Merle Elmer, 113–18, 119, 121, 123,
  124, 127, 128, 135–36, 140, 147, 149, 168,
  169
Sandhei, Muriel L. Henrickson, vii, xii, xiii, **ix**,
  47, **87**, **154**, **165**, **178**, **204**, **219**
  birth of, 3–6, 14, 28, 30, 32
  brownies, 204, 205, 207, 208, 209, 214,
    222
    recipe, 223
  Chester "Chet"
    courtship, 177–80
    friendship, 173, 175–76
    marriage to, 180–83, 216–17
  college
    Muriel's aspirations, 60–61, 63,
      85–86, 88, 90, 188
    Muriel's children, 161, 189, 202, 203,
      206–207, 210, 212, 217, 220, **221**,
      223
  confirmation, 53–56
  death of, 223
  grade school, 41–43, 46
  high school, 46, 57–63, 85–88
  Elmer
    courtship, 86–91
    death of, 161–63, 188

  farm life, 142–45, 153–55, 199
  illness, 156–61
  introduction to, 61–63, 75–76, 77, 80
  marriage to, 96–98, **97**, 99, 103, 105,
    142–43
  remembering, 164, 168–69, 173, 177,
    179–81, 190, 192–93, 198, 202,
    207, 208–09, 215, 217, 222
  farmstead, **165**, 202, 217, 222
    auction, 166, **167**
    financial hardship, 192–94
    fire, 196–200
    leaving, 164–65
    purchase, 137–41
    return to, 177–179, 184
  farmwife, vii, xii, 128, 129, 132, 134,
    142–46, 184–89, 190, 192–94
  Fort Ransom
    return to, 119
    leaving, 210, 213–17
  ice cream recipe, **186**
  independence, 134, 170–72, 177, 222
    decision-making, 164–65, 173–74,
      179, 203, 210–13
    financial, 171, 179, 201–202
    running the farm, 192–94
    Muriel's Café, 202–209, **204**, 210,
      212–14
    working outside the home, 170,
      202–209, 211, 213, 219–20
  Josephine, living with, 166–68, 170–71,
    177, **178**
  ladies' aid, 146–47, 173
  motherhood, vii, 142, 145, 146, 149,
    161–62, 164, 169–71, 177, 184–89, 207
    Elizabeth "Liz," birth of, 169
    Evelyn Louise, birth of 135–36
    illness, 190–92
    Marjorie Ann, birth of, 150
    Merle Elmer
      birth of, 112–14, 136
      death of, 114–18, 119, 124, 127,
        128, 135, 149, 168–69
    pregnancy, **101**, 103, 105, 128–29,
      134–135, 140, 141, 149, 155, 162,
      168–69
    out of wedlock, xii, 92–98, 119,
      128
    Tommy, birth of, 142
    training, 21–22, 26–27
  move to
    Carl Anderson farm, 132–34
    Fort Ransom, 201
    Montana, 94–98, 99
    Valley City, 210–213
  pastimes
    card playing, 129, 143, 177, 188, 207,
      214, 220

dancing, 56, 60–62, 63, 86, 88–89, 193, 195–96
gardening, 48, 90, 134, 168
lefse making, 50–51, 128, 165, 184, 212, 222
piano playing, 45–46, 138, 140
sewing, 48–49, 55
skiing, 86, **87**
swimming, 46–48, **47**
pastry chef at Valley City State College cafeteria, 212, 219–20
Pelton ranch, 99–110
arrival at, 99–105
duties, 103–104, 105, 107–108
reading for the minister, 53
upbringing, 50
childhood, 28, 32, 33–35
church, role of, 39–40, 52–56
farm chores, 23–27
financial hardship, xii, 44–45, 60, 61, 90–91
womanhood, vii, 48–49, 59, 85–91
Sandhei, Tom "Tommy," 142–46, 148, 149, 150, **151**, 152, **154**, 155, **165**, 168, 170, 173–76, 177, **178**, 181, 187–88, 190, 191, 193, 195–99, 207, 210, 213, 214, **221**
birth of, 142
farmhand, 179–80, 184–86, 190, 191, 193–94, 199, 201, 202, 205
Seljeseth, Sig, 121–22
Sheyenne River, viii, 8, 13, 15, **47**, 58, 168, 208
Sheyenne River Valley, 18, 43, 71, 216
Skonnard, Mr., 59–60, 85–86, 88
Skonseng, Bernard, 14
Social Security, 194
Soil Bank Program, 202, 222
See also Conservation Reserve Program
Sorby, Darlene, 173–74, 176
Sorby, Frances Henrickson, **ix**, 5, 21, 27, 30, 33, 35, 43, 45, 46, 48, 53, 54, 55, 56, 58–60, 85, 90, 143, 147, 148, 152, 157–58, 161, 164, 165, 166, 171, 173, 177, 179, 181, 184, 191, 198–200, 213, 214
Sorby, Glenn, 143, 164, 166, 170–71, 173, 177, 181, 198, 214
Sorlendings, 37, 221
South Dakota, 67, 182
Spanish Flu pandemic, 28–29
Springer School No. 2, 27, 33, 41–42, 44, 46, 57, 59
Springer Township, ND, 9, 13, **14**
Standing Rock Lutheran Church, xi, 10, 36–39, **38**, 52–55, 57, 74, 79, 134, 146, 150, 162, 169, 175, 221
Bethania Ladies' Aid, 134, 147, 173
Zion Ladies' Aid, 10, 37, 40, 123, 128

Steele County, MN, 122
Stiklestad Lutheran Church, xi, 37–39, 52–54, 58, 90, 221
Stillwater County, MT, 99
St. Luke's Hospital, 191
Stock Market Crash of 1929, 44–45
Strander, Verney, 195

T
temperance, 28, 30
Thompson, Carl, 73, 127–35, 137–39, 141, 143, 145, 154, 175
Tommeraus, Oren, 187

U
United Norwegian Lutheran Church (UNLC) of America, xi, 36, 37
United States, 8, 29, 107, 139, 149
Army National Guard, 138
Census, ix–x
Congress, 202

V
Valley City, ND, 27, 33, 60, 63, 135, 156, 157, 159, 169, 194, 201, 210–217, **219**, 222
Eagles Club, 220
Foss Drug, 211, 220
High School, 220
Old Main, 211
Red Owl, 216
Valley City State College, 207, 219, **221**
Valley City Teachers' College, 33, 85

W
Walker's Mill, 15, 18
West Fargo, ND, 220
Wisconsin, 70
woman
Christian, vii, 96
farm, vii
voting rights, 29, 32
World War I, 28–29
World War II, 91, 103, 107, 138–39, 146–47, 150
D-Day, 146
draft, 138–39, 143
Pearl Harbor attack, 138
rationing, 139, 145
wartime, 142, 148–49

Y
Yellowstone National Park, 109
Young People's Hall, 63

Z
Zion Ladies' Aid, 10, 37, 40, 123, 128

ABOUT THE AUTHORS

Tricia Velure is a personal historian who helps elders share their life stories with their families. Known for being easy to talk to and interested in life's everyday details, Tricia has been talking with elders about "the old days" since she was a young girl dunking cookies in her grandma's coffee. She grew up on her family's cattle and small grains farm near Kathryn, North Dakota, where she was her father's official parts runner and helped her mom cook every meal from scratch. After graduating from Litchville High School in 1991, Tricia earned degrees in English and history from Valley City State University and a master's degree in history from North Dakota State University. Her subsequent twenty-year career in public relations further developed her love of researching, interviewing, writing, and archiving. In 2019, she started her own business, Storyography, to interview elders and preserve those stories for their kids and grandkids. Tricia lives in suburban Saint Paul, Minnesota, and is a fitness enthusiast, avid traveler, and research buff. She loves to return to the farm, which four generations of her family have operated since 1904.

Tom Sandhei is a retired school administrator who grew up on his parents' and grandparents' farms near Fort Ransom, North Dakota, in the 1940s and 1950s. From an early age, he milked cows and cared for livestock. He operated tractors from a standing position until he was tall enough to reach the clutch pedal while seated. Thanks to the influence of his strong mother, he recognized that education was the way to a good life of his making. Following his graduation from Fort Ransom High School, Tom received a Bachelor of Science degree from Valley City State College, which qualified him for a teaching license. He taught upper elementary students his first few years, during which he became interested in school administration. He then earned a Master of Science degree in elementary school administration from North Dakota State University. Tom's career in education spanned almost forty years, including more than thirty as an elementary school principal in Colorado and Minnesota. Tom married Linda Edwards in 1965, and the couple raised three children before she passed in 2015. Tom lives in suburban Saint Paul, Minnesota, where he is active in his church, enjoys spending time with his children and five grandchildren, and has a love of golf and travel.

ABOUT THE PRESS

North Dakota State University Press (NDSU Press) exists to stimulate and coordinate interdisciplinary regional scholarship. These regions include the Red River Valley, the state of North Dakota, the plains of North America (comprising both the Great Plains of the United States and the prairies of Canada), and comparable regions of other continents. We publish peer reviewed regional scholarship shaped by national and international events and comparative studies.

Neither topic nor discipline limits the scope of NDSU Press publications. We consider manuscripts in any field of learning. We define our scope, however, by a regional focus in accord with the press's mission. Generally, works published by NDSU Press address regional life directly, as the subject of study. Such works contribute to scholarly knowledge of region (that is, discovery of new knowledge) or to public consciousness of region (that is, dissemination of information or interpretation of regional experience). Where regions abroad are treated, either for comparison or because of ties to those North American regions of primary concern to the press, the linkages are made plain. For nearly three-quarters of a century, NDSU Press has published substantial trade books, but the line of publications is not limited to that genre. We also publish textbooks (at any level), reference books, anthologies, reprints, papers, proceedings, and monographs. The press also considers works of poetry or fiction, provided they are established regional classics or they promise to assume landmark or reference status for the region. We select biographical or autobiographical works carefully for their prospective contribution to regional knowledge and culture. All publications, in whatever genre, are of such quality and substance as to embellish the imprint of NDSU Press.

Our name changed to North Dakota State University Press in January 2016. Prior to that, and since 1950, we published as the North Dakota Institute for Regional Studies Press. We continue to operate under the umbrella of the North Dakota Institute for Regional Studies, located at North Dakota State University.